Of Chastity and Power

Of Chastity and Power

Elizabethan Literature and the Unmarried Queen

Philippa Berry

Routledge
London and New York

First published 1989
by Routledge
2 Park Square, Milton Park, Abingdon, Oxon, OX14 4RN

First published in paperback 1994
by Routledge

Simultaneously published in the USA and Canada
by Routledge
270 Madison Ave, New York NY 10016

Transferred to Digital Printing 2006

© 1989, 1994 Philippa Berry
Set in 10/12 Times Linotron 202
Data conversion by Columns of Reading

British Library Cataloguing in Publication Data
Berry, Philippa
  Of chastity and power: Elizabethan literature and the unmarried
  queen.
  1. English literature, 1558–1625 – Critical studies
  I. Title
  820.9'003

Library of Congress Cataloging in Publication Data
Berry, Philippa
    Of chastity and power: Elizabethan literature and the unmarried
  queen / Philippa Berry.
    p.   cm.
    Bibliography: p.
    Includes index.
  1. English literature – Early modern, 1500–1700 – History and
  criticism.   2. Elizabeth I, Queen of England, 1533–1603, in fiction,
  drama, poetry, etc.   3. Feminism and literature – Great Britain –
  History – 16th century.   4. Women and literature – Great Britain –
  History – 16th century.   5. Power (Social sciences) in literature.
  6. Kings and rulers in literature.   7. Single women in literature.
  8. Sex role in literature.   9. Chastity in literature.   10. Queens in
  literature.   I. Title.
  PR428.E43B47   1989
  820'.9'351 – dc19   88–30479

ISBN 0–415–05672–1 (pbk)

Publisher's Note
The publisher has gone to great lengths to ensure the quality of this reprint
but points out that some imperfections in the original may be apparent

Printed and bound by CPI Antony Rowe, Eastbourne

For my mother and father, who shared with me their love of history.

Man hath weav'd out a net, and this net throwne
Upon the Heavens, and now they are his owne.

John Donne, *The First Anniversary*

La verité s'y avère complexe par essence, humble en ses offices et
étrangère à la réalité, insoumise au choix du sexe, parente de la mort
et, à tout prendre, plutôt inhumaine, Diane peut-être . . .

Jacques Lacan, *Ecrits*

Contents

List of plates

Acknowledgements

My work on different versions of this book has spanned nearly ten years; during that period I have been advised and supported by many friends, teachers and colleagues, as well as by members of my family. My decision to undertake a critical project in the field of the Renaissance was first motivated by the gifted tuition of Jean Wilson and Peter Holland. The initial formulation of this text, as doctoral dissertation, was guided by the scholarship and critical insights of J.B. Trapp, Margaret MacGowan, and Alan Sinfield. The book's feminist perspective derives from the inspiration provided by many women, some of whom I know only through their writings. The works of Luce Irigaray, Julia Kristeva, and Marina Warner have especially challenged and encouraged me. Between 1977 and 1979 Christine Berg, Cora Kaplan, Jennifer Stone, and other members of the Marxist-Feminist Literature Collective helped me to develop my understanding of Marxist and feminist theory, and to begin to think about the relations between gender and political power. The conversion of thesis into book owes an especial debt to the wise guidance of my editors, Merrilyn Julian and Jane Armstrong; also to the combination of sisterly encouragement with constructive academic advice provided by my readers, Lisa Jardine and Catherine Belsey. Several former colleagues have stimulated and inspired me by their shared enthusiasm for the Renaissance; most notably David Aers, Tony Gash, Zara Bruzzi, Tony Bromham, and Susie Hamilton. Helen McNeil, Margaret Clayton, Elizabeth McGrath, and Gavin D'Costa offered helpful and perceptive comments on individual chapters. Margaret MacGowan generously advised me in the preparation of the French translations. Paul Berry and Jan Parker gave me the confidence to think more deeply about the theme of sexual ambiguity inscribed in the mythology of Diana. Teresa Brennan gave valuable last-minute advice about the introduction. Tom and Celia Berry were there whenever I needed them, which was quite often! And I owe an especial debt to the spirited and loving support of Bernard, Teresa, Paul, and Joan. Any errors of fact or judgement which may remain after so much generous assistance are of course my responsibility alone.

The author and publishers are grateful for permission to quote from the following: Pietro Bembo, *Gli Asolani*, trans. Rudolph B. Gottfried, by permission of Indiana University Press. Chrétien de Troyes, *Yvain*, trans. Ruth Harwood Kline, © 1975 the University of Georgia Press, by permission of the University of Georgia Press. Giordano Bruno, *Cena de le Ceneri*, trans. Frances Yates in *Astraea: the Imperial Theme in the Sixteenth Century*, by permission of Routledge & Kegan Paul. *Giordano Bruno's The Heroic Frenzies*, trans. Paul Eugene Memmo Jr, by permission of the University of North Carolina Press. *Dante's Divine Comedy*, trans. John D. Sinclair, by permission of Bodley Head. Marsilio Ficino, *Commentary on Plato's Symposium*, trans. Sears Jayne, by permission of Spring Publications. *The Letters of Marsilio Ficino*, trans. the London School of Economics, by permission of Shepheard-Walwyn Ltd. Hildegarde of Bingen, *Liber divinum operum*, trans. Kent Kraft, reprinted in *Medieval Women Writers*, ed. Katharina M. Wilson, © 1984 the University of Georgia Press; reprinted by permission of the University of Georgia Press. Pico della Mirandola, 'Commento sopra una canzona di amore', trans. in Edgar Wind, *Pagan Mysteries in the Renaissance*, by permission of Faber & Faber Ltd and W.W. Norton & Co. Inc. *Petrarch's Lyric Poems*, trans. Robert M. Durling, © 1976 by Robert M. Durling, by permission of Harvard University Press. Philo, *Quod Deterius Potiori insidiari soleat*, trans. John Dillon, *The Middle Platonists*, by permission of Duckworth & Co. Peire Vidal, 'Ab l'alen tir vas me l'aire', trans. Anthony Bonner in *Songs of the Troubadours*, by permission of Allen & Unwin and Shocken Books. Virgil, 'Eclogue iv', trans. by H. Rushton Fairclough in *Virgil: Works*, by permission of Loeb Classical Library.

The author and publishers are also grateful for permission to reproduce the illustrations in the plate section. All sources are gratefully acknowledged (see the list of plates) with the exception of those institutions which specifically requested to remain anonymous.

Introduction

What is the genealogy of western ideas of love? And what can a feminist interpretation of a specific instance in this complex chain of represent-ations reveal? In undertaking this literary critical project, which is also an essay in cultural history, my aim is to clarify the contradictory relations of gender inscribed in the discourses of idealized love which influenced so much Renaissance literature: Petrarchism and Neoplatonism. What, I ask, are the implications of the paradox that is central to both Petrarchism and Renaissance Neoplatonism, whereby the elaboration of new concepts of masculine subjectivity was dependent upon an image of woman? And why does woman function in these systems as the privileged signifier of a sacred or supernatural dimension?

These issues are thrown into vivid relief by a consideration of the curious interrelationship between the love discourses and the literary 'cult' of a female Renaissance ruler – Elizabeth I of England. In the literary texts which the book considers, issues of sexual authority are often closely intertwined with a contest for political as well as imaginative power. I explore the implications of the fact that in sixteenth-century France as well as England, idealized attitudes to love were appropriated by the ideology of absolutist monarchy, and helped to shape the aesthetic representation of ideas of kingship. My argument is that with its assimilation of Petrarchism and Neoplatonism, Renaissance absolutism adopted a potentially unorthodox model of gender relations, whose inner contradictions became especially apparent in literary representations of an unmarried queen as an object of sublimated desire. Most importantly, the idea of feminine chastity which was emphasized by Petrarch and the Renaissance Neoplatonists acquired a new and unexpected significance when associated with a woman who was possessed of both political and spiritual authority.

Attitudes to love derived from Petrarchan love poetry and Florentine Neoplatonic philosophy were widely disseminated among western courtly societies during the European Renaissance. Although, as I shall show, these discourses differed in several respects, both systems combined a

1

curiously paradoxical conception of a beloved woman with emphasis upon the search of a male lover for a new identity. The female beloved was declared by poets and writers to be the true object of the processes of emotional enquiry delineated in their discourses of love, and was accorded an exaggerated emotional and imaginative authority. Yet her function in the love discourses was strictly codified (at least, when she did not happen also to be a queen). This figure was usually little more than an instrument in an elaborate game of *masculine* 'speculation' and self-determination, for the philosophical enterprise common to both Petrarchism and Renaissance Neoplatonism used woman as a 'speculum' or mirror of masculine narcissism.[1] The hypothesis that a chaste woman could serve as a bridge between the material world and an invisible spiritual dimension enabled Petrarchan poet and Neoplatonic philosopher to elaborate a new concept of masculine wholeness and self-sufficiency through or across her idealized figure. By this means, they affirmed Renaissance man's conviction that he could achieve a godlike control, not just over his own nature, but over his environment as well. So, paradoxically, this idea of woman as the sign of a supernatural or spiritual domain might be said to have enabled man gradually to reject the claims of an outer religious or spiritual authority.

It seems that in Renaissance literary texts which were influenced by concepts of idealized love, we may be able to trace an important preliminary stage in the definition of the extremely powerful (because rational) and implicitly *masculine* subject who was to provide the secular new philosophy of the late Renaissance with its first principle. The distinctive character of the rational subject of late sixteenth- and early seventeenth-century philosophy and science was indeed crucially indebted to a revolutionary shift in western epistemology which had been initiated by humanism. One result of this change was that the interior and spiritually oriented contemplative life privileged by medieval Christianity declined in philosophical status, and a secular and rational life of action gradually came to be accorded more value and importance.[2] Yet if we read the Renaissance discourses of love as orchestrating one of its earliest appearances, it seems that this new secular, rational, and active subject owed some debt to the very intellectual systems it ultimately dethroned: namely, to the Platonic and Neoplatonic traditions, as well as early Christian thought, all of which had defined subjectivity in contemplative, indeed spiritual terms. As we shall see, both Renaissance Neoplatonism and Petrarchism articulated a quite complex and contradictory relationship to the contemporary debate around the relative merits of the *vita contemplativa* and the *vita activa*, and these contradictions left their trace on representations, not only of the male lover, but also of his female object of desire.

An emphasis upon the sublimation of sexual desire in order to obtain (self-)knowledge was central to Plato's *The Symposium*, reintroduced into western culture at the end of the fifteenth century through the translation of Marsilio Ficino. This text provided a vital impetus to the new version of Neoplatonic love philosophy which Ficino and members of his 'Platonic Academy' began to expound. In contrast, Petrarch and his poetic predecessors (the Italian *stilnovisti* and Dante in particular) had no direct access to Plato's love doctrines; they had assimilated a Platonic conception of love indirectly, via the work of Christian writers influenced by Platonism and early Neoplatonism, such as St Augustine and pseudo-Dionysius. But Renaissance discourses of love combined Platonic with other motifs (derived from medieval courtly love, from Aristotelianism, and from other, esoteric sources usually referred to as Hermetic philosophy). The systems which resulted challenged both Platonic and Christian conceptions of love in several important respects. The transcendent and spiritual subject privileged by both Platonism and Christianity (which they asserted could be forged by sublimating earthly desires in the contemplation of deity), was always by implication subordinate to God. In these Renaissance systems, however, claims for man's spiritual or godlike attributes were not so obviously subordinated to a higher spiritual authority. Yet the most curious and most significant of the modifications made by these systems to the Platonic and Christian paradigms (both of which were distinctly misogynistic) was undoubtedly their focus upon a female, rather than male, object of sublimated desire. In fact, they accorded woman *qua* woman a significance she had not previously enjoyed within the context of western philosophy.

Ironically, the intellectual revolution within which Renaissance attitudes to love were implicated did not ultimately challenge the long tradition of western philosophical dualism, whereby the category of spirit was seen as being in fundamental opposition to that of matter. Instead, it merely reversed the pre-eminence which medieval thought had accorded a spiritual dimension over both the material world and its chief inhabitant, man.[3] Inevitably, the category of spirit became progressively less significant in a philosophy committed to the search for empirical proofs upon which to found its hypotheses.[4] But in Renaissance literature influenced by Petrarchism and Neoplatonism, this philosophical transition was still in process. And while she is typically constructed merely as the passive instrument of man's struggle for power over himself, over nature, and over an immaterial, 'other' world, the chaste beloved is occasionally seen as actually reconciling the opposition of spirit and matter within her person. The Renaissance discourses of love certainly attempted to deny the materiality of the 'chaste' woman they idealized: to exclude the female body, and feminine sexuality, from their idea of a chaste woman as exclusively spiritual (and as thereby inspiring a conviction in man's own godlike powers). But the mysterious bodily presence of woman haunts these systems, insisting upon a paradoxical conjunction of nature and spirit under the sign of woman.

My study begins by tracing the genealogy of this contradictory figure of a chaste female beloved within early western culture. Chapter 1 commences with a discussion of what appears to have been a primary theological/ philosophical source of western representations of woman as the object of an idealized desire: the biblical figure of a female Wisdom (otherwise known as Sophia or Sapientia). The Wisdom figure seems to have been a key influence upon the Renaissance use of a chaste woman as a mediatrix between heaven and earth. As such she throws an interesting light upon a perplexing parallel which is occasionally hinted at in the love discourses, between the female beloved as the site of a mystical union between spirit and matter, and the incarnate male saviour of Christian doctrine. Both figures, albeit in different ways, are the bearers of meaning, of *logos*. At the same time, the figure of Wisdom affords a vital precedent for the interrelationship of concepts of love and politics in the French and English Renaissance texts which I explore in later chapters. This first chapter then proceeds to investigate the various metamorphoses of the figure of an idealized beloved within a range of late medieval and early Renaissance representations, from medieval courtly love and Dante's *Divina Commedia* to those texts which codified Renaissance (as opposed to medieval) attitudes to love: Petrarch's *Rime Sparse*, and the philosophical writings of the Florentine Neoplatonists. Common to all was emphasis upon woman's role as a passive mediatrix of (self-)knowledge to man. But unlike the medieval formulations, Renaissance discourses of love were significantly shadowed by another image of woman, one which did not confirm their focus upon masculine similitudes. Many literary texts influenced by these Renaissance attitudes are punctuated by anxiety that the beloved's passive power might suddenly seek active expression, in an assertion of her own feelings and desires which threatened to escape the rhetorical or imaginative control of the male lover. It is at such moments that the female beloved is no longer perceived merely as a lifeless mirror, but briefly metamorphoses into a figure who now dynamically combines spiritual and material attributes, as a nature goddess or queen of faerie. In this guise, the beloved threatens rather than affirms the emerging self-image of the lover, opposing his masculine narcissism with an alternative, feminine, self-centredness, and reminding him of the prominence in the natural world of precisely those forces he is struggling to transcend and deny: mutability and decay leading to death. As chapter 1 ends by pointing out, a myth which imaged this nagging doubt of the Renaissance lover most aptly was that of Diana and Actaeon, best known from Ovid's account in the *Metamorphoses*. In their multiple representations of the tragic fate of

Actaeon, the hunter who was metamorphosed into a stag and dismembered by his own hounds after he had inadvertently glimpsed the goddess of chastity and hunting naked in her woodland bath. Renaissance writers and artists explored their fear of some devastating reversal or *peripeteia* of the humanist desire to remake man in the image of god(dess) (plate 1).

These tensions within Petrarchism and Renaissance Neoplatonism became especially apparent when the Diana image was associated with their female beloved in literature and art which promoted the authority of the monarchies of late Valois France and Elizabethan England. Chapter 2 explores the curious formulations of kingship and masculine identity which were elaborated in an aesthetic strand of sixteenth-century French absolutist discourse. By means of the close reading of a range of French Renaissance literary texts, as well as reference to various paintings and sculptures, it argues that while the absolutist mode of political power emerged within an overtly patriarchal society, its conception of the relationship of a (typically male) ruler to a state or *respublica* which was implicitly gendered feminine contradicted conventionally patriarchal models of masculinity.

But chapters 1 and 2 also serve as preludes to the remainder of the book, which reinterprets the assembly of discourses which constituted a central element in Elizabethan absolutist ideology: the courtly 'cult' of Elizabeth I. Chapter 3 considers the absence of any emphasis upon gender within the influential account of this cult which still implicitly overshadows much Renaissance criticism: that of Frances Yates.[5] I point out that Yates' account of the cult overlooked the contest for sexual and political authority which motivated its initial formulation by Elizabethan courtiers, and argue that even some recent readings of literary representations of Elizabeth, while aware of gender issues, have none the less underestimated their importance. My interest is primarily in the problematic status of Elizabeth as a Renaissance woman ruler who was not only head of a secular state, but also 'supreme governor' of the English church. I argue that in spite of her position at the top of political and spiritual hierarchies which were androcentric, Elizabeth Tudor was not always necessarily represented as a passive emblem of patriarchal authority, a bearer of masculine power who just happened to be gendered female. An emphasis upon what one critic has termed 'the powers inhering in her blood' typically focuses upon Elizabeth's place in a chain of patrilineal descent (the Tudor dynasty).[6] In contrast to this view, I would contend that in order to understand her contradictory historical position *as a woman*, we have to consider the potentially subversive representation of Elizabeth as a Petrarchan or Neoplatonic beloved who also had both worldly and spiritual power. At the same time, we have to re-'member' and reinterpret Elizabeth's forgotten ties to other women, and reconsider the significance of her permanently censored relationship to the figure of her decapitated (because supposedly 'bad' – that is, adulterous) mother. The tragic life and death of Anne Boleyn overshadowed not only her daughter's childhood but also, by implication, her reign. In an early contribution to Elizabeth's literary cult, the 'April eclogue' of Edmund Spenser's *The Shepheardes Calender*, the importance of this relationship is obscurely hinted at, under the veil of mythological allegory. Here it is associated with a gynocentric model of Elizabethan courtliness which privileges ties between courtly women, rather than between female monarch and male courtiers, and which stresses the mysterious coexistence of spiritual power and a specifically feminine eroticism in the figure of Elizabeth as a chaste beloved.

The remaining three chapters delineate a diachronic study of Elizabeth's courtly cult, tracing its changing formulation in a range of literary texts produced over two decades. Interest in definitions of masculine courtiership and courtliness has been a prominent feature of contemporary Renaissance criticism; as chapters 4 and 5 demonstrate, a surprising range of alternative roles for the male courtier jostled for ideological dominance within the (relatively constricted) discursive domain of Elizabethan courtly literature, and each of these was informed by a slightly different interpretation of the roles of male lover and female beloved within Petrarchism and Neoplatonism.[7] Chapter 4 explores the elaboration and attempted manipulation of the idea of Elizabeth as a chaste beloved by a group of self-interested courtiers which began in the mid-1570s. This early version of the unmarried queen's cult used aristocratic pastimes to propose an active and assertive idea of courtiership, one with a strong militaristic as well as radical Protestant (or Calvinist) bias. During the decade of the 1580s, however, a more passive and contemplative model of Elizabethan courtliness was articulated in the courtly drama of John Lyly, which is analysed in chapter 5. We may infer that this formulation was more congenial to the political perspective of Elizabeth, in that it implied the surrender of the (political and sexual) initiative of the male courtier to his queen. Finally, in chapter 6, I argue that by the decade of the 1590s, frustration at the limitations which a courtly idealization of the queen was perceived to impose upon the search for masculine identity by male courtier or courtly poet was producing several texts which were deeply ambiguous in their representation of the ageing queen. I discuss Shakespeare's *A Midsummer Night's Dream*, George Chapman's *The Shadow of Night*, Sir Walter Ralegh's fragment of a narrative poem, *The Ocean to Scinthia*, and Spenser's epic poem *The Faerie Queene*; all these texts are marked in different ways and to different degrees by the profound anxieties which attended the reluctant recognition of the masculine subject that, as a woman possessed of power, Elizabeth could not ultimately be manipulated in the manner of other female objects of idealized desire. Implicit in these representations is the assumption that the unmarried queen's 'virginity' or 'chastity', which prompted her comparison to Diana or Cynthia, the Roman goddess of chastity, untamed nature and the moon, was not in fact an empty space, upon which might be inscribed the fruits of a search for the powers of masculine resemblance, but the sign instead of her own mysterious powerfulness, of a body and an identity which had somehow eluded successful appropriation by the masculine.

In its attempt to elucidate the interrelationship between Renaissance text and historical context, to unravel the political meanings encoded in a set of literary representations, this project has been influenced by the new historicist movement in Renaissance criticism, which as defined by Jonathan Dollimore is concerned to explore the relationships between the powers of the state and cultural forms.[8] In particular, like many contemporary Renaissance critics, I owe an especial debt to Stephen Greenblatt's pioneering study, *Renaissance Self-Fashioning*, which explored the limits imposed by ideas of secular and sacred power upon Renaissance constructions of identity.[9] But if new historicist criticism is frequently concerned 'to amplify . . . the marginalized voices of the ruled, exploited, oppressed and excluded', to undertake a study of representations of Elizabeth is apparently to speak for the ruler and oppressor, the embodiment of state power.[10] Yet by reading representations of the female monarch from a feminist perspective, it is possible to elucidate the curious conjunction of roles which Elizabeth had perforce to play (as oppressor and oppressed), the contradictory positions which she had to assume (centre-stage, and marginalized). When viewed from this angle, what is most striking about the queen, in vivid contrast to the repeated rhetorical emissions *about* her which were produced by many of her masculine subjects, is the dearth of texts which are indisputably authored by her alone. From the literary perspective, what chiefly remains of Elizabeth Tudor is her silence.

My feminist reading does not involve a detailed psychoanalytic study of the gender relations inscribed within Renaissance discourses of love. None the less, it has inevitably been influenced and informed by feminist psychoanalytic theory, and above all by the work of Luce Irigaray and Julia Kristeva. Both Irigaray and Kristeva have frequently pointed to the need to understand and unveil the Platonic and Neoplatonic assumptions which inform western philosophy so profoundly (as, indeed, did Jacques Lacan). Among repeated references by Irigaray, Kristeva, and Lacan to Platonic concepts, one of the most relevant for my project in this book was Kristeva's use of the Platonic term *chora* to explicate her reformulation of the pre-Oedipal stage of infantile development.[11] As I point out in chapter 1, this term was sometimes connected with the figure of a female Wisdom. While I consider that to propose an exact homology between the two discourses (of idealized love and psycho-analysis) would be to deny the historical specificity of the Renaissance texts, the parallels between the Renaissance attempt to elaborate masculine identity with reference to love and the psychoanalytic concept of the pre-Oedipal are quite striking. At the same time, I am indebted to one of Irigaray's most important contributions to feminist theory. This was her account of the patriarchal utilization of woman as a mirror of the masculine ego: according to Irigaray, this process of mirroring is occasionally interrupted by moments of crisis, when an 'other' image of woman intervenes in and disrupts this process of masculine speculariz-ation.[12]

The aggressiveness sometimes attributed to the female beloved of the love discourses seems to have been partly inspired by fear of an active female sexuality, which might elude the control and manipulation of the masculine subject. That this fantasy was closely connected with the disturbing possibility of woman taking narcissistic, and possibly even homosexual, pleasure in a female body is suggested by the recurrence of the figure of the goddess Diana in these discourses, whose association with close-knit communities of women from which men were usually excluded is stressed in so many of her myths.[13] The female beloved's paradoxical combination of maternal nurturance with a disturbing self-referentiality is vividly suggested in a painting of Diana executed by the Flemish artist Frans Floris around 1560 (plate 2 and cover). This painting is thought to have been owned by Elizabeth I early in her reign; that is, some time *before* she began to be complimented upon her own Diana-like 'chastity'. It is none the less interesting to speculate on the significance it may have possessed for its female owner, who as she approached 50 would have her political and spiritual authority exagger-ated yet simultaneously challenged by her own representation as the passive object of a collective masculine gaze. The right breast of Floris' goddess is presented as a source of nurturance and power, and hints at a parallel with the literary and artistic motif of drinking from the breast of Wisdom, which was associated in medieval iconography with the acquisition of mystical knowledge (plate 3). But at the same time, the auto-erotic gesture with which this Diana holds her nipple appears ironically to resist the desire of any male spectator to remould her in the image of his own fantasy.

Chapter one

Mirrors of masculinity: Renaissance speculations through the feminine and their genealogy

Various hypotheses have been advanced concerning the reason for the prominent role accorded to woman within the western discourses of idealized love. In my view, both their contradictory idea of a chaste female beloved, and the political significance of these discourses (in particular the implications of their appropriation by Renaissance absolutism), are best illuminated by reference to a theological source. Some scholars have attempted to relate the cult of the Virgin Mary to the rise of idealized attitudes to love, since the precursor of the Renaissance systems, medieval courtly love, reached its peak of greatest popularity and sophistication at a time when devotion to the Virgin was accelerating.[1] In fact, Mary had little in common with the idealized women of courtly love, whose unavailability was usually strictly temporary. But the emphasis upon chastity in both Petrarchism and Florentine Neoplatonism meant that there were more parallels between Mary and the beloved in these systems (this is anticipated by Dante's *Paradiso*, where Dante's vision of the Virgin is a culminating point in the process of growth initiated by his love of Beatrice). In the Christian monastic tradition, ascetic practices were seen as necessary for the attainment of an especial intimacy with God; however, the physical purity of Mary was of a different order. Its chief purpose in the religious scheme of things was not *her own* refashioning or rebirth, but the birth of a being of a completely new order, who was seen by Christian theology as constituting a vital link between a divine transcendent principle and a fallen natural world, since his incarnation was held to have initiated the process of that world's redemption. Just as Mary was seen as a selfless *material* mirror of heavenly purity, a 'speculum sine macula' worthy to be the *theotokos*, mother of God, so the idealized women of the love discourses were the nurses or receptacles of new men, intermediaries between their lovers as they were, and as they hoped to be.

Yet, on the other hand, the cult of Mary did not define her worship in terms of desire. It did not see her as a bestower of creative as well as worldly power. Nor was emphasis upon her physical and spiritual purity paradoxically juxtaposed with abundant natural imagery. These aspects of the idealized female beloved accord more closely with another concept, pre-Christian in origin but assimilated by Christian theology, whose genealogy was closely associated with those Platonic and Neoplatonic world views to which Petrarch as well as the Florentine Neoplatonists were indebted, and whose possession of masculine as well as feminine attributes more closely paralleled the sexual ambiguity which often characterized the female beloved in these systems. This was the idea of Sapientia or Sophia, the Wisdom of God (plates 3 and 4), who was described in Old Testament and Apocryphal texts as a female figure, and who often appeared in medieval texts as Lady Philosophy or Lady Reason.[2] As a bestower of wisdom she was most often connected with the Roman goddess Minerva or Pallas Athena in the Renaissance; but her links with an unfallen natural world, and her position as an object of desire, were paralleled not by Minerva but by Diana.[3] Wisdom arguably had a position of greater importance in medieval Christian theology than did the Virgin Mary, although some of her attributes were gradually assimilated by the Virgin's cult. There are some interesting parallels between the worldly powers of the Wisdom figure and those accorded the ladies of courtly love. It was not until the end of the middle ages, however, that her supernatural attributes were assimilated by the discourses of idealized love. At this stage, Wisdom's status as a transcendent symbol within Christian theology was no longer secure. Yet in fact the significance of Wisdom as symbol had always been somewhat ambiguous, probably because of her contradictory position as an image of supernatural feminine creativity and power within religious and philosophical systems whose fundamental assumptions were patriarchal. In spite of her importance, it had proved disconcertingly difficult to place Wisdom within the frameworks both of Neoplatonic and of Christian thought. For example, during the middle ages the figure was associated with the second as well as the third persons of the Trinity, with both Christ and the Holy Spirit.[4] In a rather similar fashion, the Renaissance attempt to accord fixed meanings to the figure of a desirable but chaste woman proved to be fraught with difficulties.

The Judaic sources of this figure were the 'Solomonic' or 'Wisdom' books of the Old Testament: these included Proverbs, Ecclesiastes, the Book of Job, the Song of Songs, and the apocryphal Ecclesiasticus and Wisdom of Solomon. The idea of wisdom was first explicitly connected with a female form in Proverbs, written in the fourth or third century BCE. The figure was here already much more than a mere personification of a divine attribute:

> Happy is the man that findeth wisdom. . . . She is more precious than rubies; and all the things thou canst desire are not to be compared unto her. Length of days is in her right hand, and in her left riches and

honour. Her ways are ways of pleasantness, and all her paths are peace. She is a tree of life to them that lay hold upon her; and happy is every one that retaineth her.[5]

Perhaps the most striking feature of the Wisdom figure as she appears in Proverbs is her claim that she was first of all God's creatures, possessing a divine origin prior to the creation, and assisting God at that event:

The Lord possessed me in the beginning of his way, before his works of old. I was set up from everlasting, from the beginning, or ever the earth was . . . when he appointed the foundations of the earth: Then I was by him, as one brought up with him: and I was daily his delight, rejoicing always before him.[6]

In this respect, Wisdom differs significantly from the human and historical figure of Mary. Like Mary, Wisdom is subordinated to the authority of a father God. But while Mary can only intercede with God (in the person of her son Christ) on behalf of sinful humanity, there is considerable emphasis upon Wisdom's own creative power in Ecclesiasticus and the Wisdom of Solomon (texts which were probably produced in the second and first centuries BCE) – which could be said to qualify, even to contradict, God's exclusive masculinity. She is 'the artificer of all things', and identified with the Torah or Law of God, as well as with the personal presence of the divine.[7] At the same time as being presented in some sense as God's consort, Wisdom is also depicted as the initial object of human desire in a mystical love quest for direct experience of God: 'I loved Her and sought Her from my youth and I desired to take Her for my bride, and I became enamoured of Her beauty.'[8] If these texts are interpreted in allegorical terms (a procedure which coincides with the exegetic strategies of early Christianity), Wisdom is depicted there as the means of salvation. In so far as she enjoys an especially intimate relationship to God, so to establish a relationship with her and to accept her tuition is to come closer to God. To court her is to court divine knowledge and revelation and the grace which these imply. Yet Wisdom does not merely *link* nature and supernature; she possesses the attributes of both these dimensions. In Ecclesiasticus and the Wisdom of Solomon, she is described as a dynamic embodiment of a highly eroticized natural world in which deity appears to be immanent (and which is therefore either prelapsarian or redeemed):

I was exalted like a cedar in Libanus,
And as a cypress tree on the mountains of Hermon.
I was exalted like a palm tree on the sea shore,
And as rose plants in Jericho,
And as a fair olive tree in the plain;
And I was exalted as a plane tree.

As cinammon and aspalathus, I have given a scent of perfumes;
And as choice myrrh, I spread abroad a pleasant odour;
As galbanum, and onyx, and stacte,
And as the fume of frankincense in the tabernacle.

As the terebinth I stretched out my branches;
And my branches are branches of glory and grace.

As the vine I put forth grace;
And my flowers are the fruit of glory and riches.

Come unto me, ye that are desirous of me,
And be ye filled with my produce.

For my memorial is sweeter than honey,
And mine inheritance than the honeycomb.

They that eat me shall yet be hungry;
And they that drink me shall yet be thirsty.

He that obeyeth me shall not be ashamed;
And they that work in me shall not do amiss.[9]

This passage combines Wisdom's transcendent purity, as 'unpolluted', 'an unspotted mirror of the working of God' (she is associated in Proverbs with the 'virtuous woman' whose price 'is far above rubies'), with a strongly physical dimension.[10] On the one hand her role can be seen as that of leading human awareness from the material world to the supernatural domain; on the other hand, she states that she can grant power over and within that material reality to her servitors. Sometimes this worldly authority extends to a conception of Wisdom as an attribute of kings: in the Old Testament and Apocrypha she is closely associated with both Solomon and David.

The combination of spiritual and material attributes in the Wisdom texts, especially the later ones, had been foreshadowed to some extent in the Song of Solomon, a much earlier text written around the fifth century BCE, and some later commentators connected Wisdom with the Shulamite/bride figure of that book.[11] But the apocryphal texts see Wisdom as beloved rather than lover, as the object of the spiritual love-quest, rather than the pilgrim or seeker. In other words, her role parallels that of the male beloved of the Song of Solomon, who was later to be equated with Christ as the *logos* or word of God in Christian allegorical commentaries: as symbols, both these figures are used to assert the existence of a close relationship between supernatural and natural dimensions, of God's presence in the world. (At the same time, belief in such a relationship was a necessary precondition for acceptance of their symbolic significance.) None the less, as I mentioned earlier, to describe a *female* figure in such terms implicitly called into question the inflexible masculinity of God. It has been speculated that the gradual personification of Wisdom as a female figure enjoying close ties with the natural world was motivated by the challenge posed to Judaism in the centuries just before the Christian era by the cults of the mother goddesses of the Near East, and of Egyptian Isis in particular.[12]

In the Hellenic Judaism which developed in the second and first centuries BCE, which produced not only the Wisdom of Solomon and Ecclesiasticus, but also the extensive and influential *oeuvre* of the Alexandrian philosopher Philo, this biblical concept was assimilated into the idealist philosophical tradition of Platonism. Philo followed the Jewish sapiential tradition in seeing Wisdom as a female life-principle which (somewhat paradoxically) assisted the supreme father God in his task of creation and in the administering of that creation. In some respects, this figure enjoyed the role of mother of creation, and Philo (and later, the Church Father Clement of Alexandria) associated her on several occasions with an enlarged definition of Plato's *chora* or nurse of material creation. But for Philo, Wisdom is the receptacle, not of earthly matter, but of the Platonic Forms or Ideas: 'Mother of all things in the Universe, affording to her offspring, as soon as they are born, the nourishment which they require from her own breasts'.[13] In other words, her former combination of natural with supernatural attributes was elided in Philo's account. He stressed the value of ascetic practices (including physical chastity) in preparing for the relationship with Sophia which would lead to union with God; the success of one's search for Wisdom, as he saw it, depended on estrangement from the body and from bodily desires. He seems also to have experienced some embarrassment concerning Sophia's feminine gender: for how could she be wholly feminine if she was mediator of the powers of a father God? At one stage in his definition of her spiritual function he had to state that she partook of the qualities attributed to both sexes:

> Let us then pay no heed to the discrepancy in the gender of the words, and say that the daughter of God, even Sophia, is not only masculine but father, saving and begetting in souls aptness to learn, education, knowledge, wisdom, good and laudable actions.[14]

The anxiety apparently felt by Philo over the implications of Sophia's gender was certainly compounded, at least in retrospect, by his use of another term from the Greek to describe her role as the instrument of God in the creation of the world. This was the idea of the *logos*, used by philosophers since Heraclitus to describe the principle of order in an apparently chaotic universe. At the time Philo was writing, the meaning of the term was being extended to encompass the idea of the mind or word of God. It was soon to figure in the definition of the role of Jesus Christ articulated by the gospel of St John, whose concept of the *logos* is now recognized by New Testament scholars to be considerably indebted to the biblical figure of Wisdom.[15] In Philo, the *logos* was often explicitly connected with Sophia.[16] His association of these terms was assimilated by Christianity in the first and second centuries CE, when the Christian Neoplatonists Clement of Alexandria and Origen equated Christ as *logos* not only with the *nous* (or Mind) of Plato, but also with the Jewish conception of Wisdom/Sophia as developed by Philo, and when the figure of a female creatrix named Sophia began to figure prominently in a range of Gnostic texts.[17]

In the third century CE, a Neoplatonic account of Plato's theory of creation was codified by the Egyptian philosopher Plotinus. The chief constituent parts of Plotinus' system were a trinity of principles or transcendent categories derived from the *Timaeus*, which he called hypostases. They were: the One (*en*) or the Good (*agathon*); Mind or intelligence (*nous*), a term which seems equivalent to Plato's craftsman god of the *Timaeus* as well as to the world of Forms or Ideas which he contemplates; and soul or the world soul (*psyche*), which is the universal life principle and includes all other souls. From the world soul emanates nature or the material world.[18] For Plotinus, both the world soul and the individual souls it encompasses risk losing contact with spirit through their descent into matter; yet while the world soul reaches down to the lowest levels of being, it also has affinities with *nous*. It is this double nature of the world soul and of individual souls which makes it the crucial bridge between the material world of becoming and the ideal world of being.[19] In its emphasis upon a return from material existence to a state of ideal being by means of contemplation, Plotinus' system undoubtedly privileged transcendence over immanence, spirit above matter, contemplation (*theoria*) over action (*praxis*). Yet his idealism was not as rigid as that of the Gnostics, who labelled all matter as bad; he stressed that an intellectual aspiration to the *nous* or One beyond it should be followed by a descent which had the goal of transforming or redeeming matter and the material world.

Plotinus too connected the quality of Wisdom with *nous*; however, he did not accord it a specifically feminine gender.[20] This was reserved for the third hypostasis, the world soul, whose close relationship with matter yet simultaneous impulse towards the divine he explained with reference to the myth of Eros and Psyche.[21] His association of Psyche with two different kinds of love, heavenly and earthly, paralleled the distinction between two Venuses made in Plato's *Symposium*, which would be taken up by the Florentine Neoplatonists; but, as we shall see, these later Neoplatonists would sometimes identify their two Venuses with *nous* and the world soul. Indeed, while we can see parallels to the biblical Wisdom figure's role as a bridge between spirit and matter in later accounts of the world soul as feminine, Wisdom's immaterial or transcendent qualities are echoed in medieval accounts of Lady Philosophy or Reason which identify this figure with the higher Platonic and Neoplatonic category of *nous*.

In a few texts, however, Wisdom's combination of material with spiritual attributes was more or less retained. When Boethius wrote his *De Consolatione Philosophiae* (Of the Consolations of Philosophy), he attributed the inspiration of his text to a version of the Wisdom figure, a Christian Muse called Lady Philosophy, who was queen of all the virtues. He claimed that she appeared to him while he was sick in prison, bearing a book in one hand and a sceptre in the other, and with a ladder embroidered on her gown (which had the Greek letter *pi* below it and above it, *theta*). According to Boethius, this figure nursed him like a mother; he imbibed wisdom with the milk from her breasts; this motif appears frequently in artistic representations of the Wisdom figure (plate 3), and appears to be the source of several Renaissance paintings, including the Frans Floris 'Diana' (plate 2 and cover). Lady Philosophy had also taught Boethius, through story and song. The Neoplatonic theme of an ascent from nature to a higher supernatural reality was implicit in the ladder embroidered upon her dress; she stressed the vanity of worldly concerns in a manner consistent with the dualism of Christian thought. Yet in so far as her ladder may be deemed to link earth and heaven, she partakes of the attributes of both these dimensions. Hildegarde of Bingen described Wisdom as follows:

> I am the highest fiery power, who has enkindled every spark that lives and breathes out nothing mortal. I distinguish all things as they are, surrounding the circle of the world with my superior wings; that is, flying about it with wisdom, I have ordered it rightly. . . . And I am Reason, and have the wind of the resounding Word through which every creature has been made, and I have given my breath to all these things so that none of them is mortal in its kind, for I am life. I am life whole and entire, not cut from stone, not sprouted from twigs, not rooted in the powers of a man's sex, rather all that is living is rooted in me. For Wisdom is the root, and in it blossoms the resounding Word.[22]

From the twelfth century, however, the idea of wisdom began to be defined in increasingly secular terms. Although there was not to be a fully coherent and successful defence of the *vita activa* until the advent of Renaissance humanism, we can see here the beginnings of an epistemological trend which would eventually challenge medieval philosophy's preference of the contemplative (spiritual/monastic/interior) life to the life of action, and would produce an ontology which defined man, not in relation to eternity, but within the context of secular human history.[23] But wisdom was only gradually transformed into an abstract concept. In some texts we still find it represented as a human and female figure, as

Lady Philosophy or Reason: in *La Cité des Dames* (The Book of the City of Ladies) of Christine de Pisan, for example, Wisdom (or Reason) is a bearer of poetic inspiration who can also be extremely practical. She is the chief of three female Muses or proto-feminist advisers who help Christine to build, with her pen, the City of Ladies. At the same time, a curious complement to increasing intellectual interest in the secular applications of wisdom as a depersonified concept can be found in the texts of medieval courtly love. Like Wisdom in the biblical texts, the lady whom the courtly lover serves is seen as the donor of a worldly wisdom and authority; but these secular attributes are not complemented by any supernatural or transcendent role.

Medieval courtly love was the site of certain closely interrelated intellectual and social processes. It emerged at a time of unprecedented social mobility in western Europe, when not only were men leaving the clerical class to write works of secular literature, but the lower aristocracy were seeking a means of articulating their own soon-to-be-realized aspirations for higher social status.[24] While there are reflective or introspective elements in much troubadour verse as well as in medieval romance, the courtesy (or *cortezia*) which had to be developed via service to an aristocratic woman was very definitely a social virtue, for on the one hand these texts idealized the active life of the knight and on the other they were especially concerned with the formation of 'gentil men' who would behave moderately and considerately within the courtly milieu.[25] This emphasis upon an explicitly secular love implicitly (and sometimes explicitly) challenged the priority accorded by orthodox medieval thought to the contemplative class of the clergy. Yet in so far as many courtly love texts depict a moment of illumination or conversion to right social behaviour they could be said to offer a secular parallel to the spiritual or religious code of conduct associated with Wisdom.[26] (In this connection it is significant that many of those who celebrated courtly love had either been clerics or had received a clerkly education.)

A prominent attribute of the biblical Wisdom figure, her power within the material world (of which she promises the fruits to her followers/ lovers in the Wisdom texts), was emphasized in literary and artistic representations of this figure during the middle ages and the Renaissance. Manuscript illuminations often depicted her holding the globe of the world (plate 4), thirteenth-century political treatises or 'mirrors of princes' defined her as a guiding principle of government, and even when depersonified, 'sapience' remained a key attribute of the prince or governor in Renaissance guides to good government.[27] This aspect of Wisdom was mirrored in the worldly power attributed to the lady of courtly love. This figure was often addressed in troubadour verse as 'midons' or my lord, and both in troubadour lyrics and in courtly medieval romances such as those of Chrétien de Troyes she was implicitly invested with the authority of a feudal lord (often her husband). Her service was most definitely associated with a potential improvement of social status for her lover, who deferred to her as her vassal and learned from her a code of courtly conduct. The terms *mesura, sabers* and *sens,* associated with the lady by troubadour poets such as Marcabru and Jaufré Rudel may perhaps be seen as secular and more socially meaningful correspondences to the Christian idea of Wisdom. The conception of *mesura* or the rational control of the senses, first used by the poet Marcabru, has been interpreted as the foundation of the code of courtly social conduct, *cortezia,* which the troubadours were helping to elaborate: 'De Cortezia .is pot vanar/Qui ben sap Mesur' esguardor' ('he can boast of courtliness who knows how to observe moderation').[28] When this principle is followed, the lady is seen as bestowing gifts very like those offered by the biblical Wisdom. Peire d'Alvernhe, for example, sings of the lady 'don sapiens/suy' (because of whom I am wise), and Peire Vidal says:

> E s'eu sai ren dir ni faire,
> Ilh n'aja .l grat, que sciensa
> Ma donat e conoissensa,
> Per qu'eu sui gais e chantaire . . .

> (If I speak and act worthily, it is
> thanks to her for she has given me
> the science and the knowledge
> to be joyful and to sing . . .)[29]

In stressing the lover's integration into the aristocratic class by learning 'courtly' behaviour from service to the lady, the proponents of courtly love subordinated the theme of individual subjective growth to that of social harmony: the lady's gifts were implicitly limited by the courtly emphasis upon the unity of the aristocratic class. This civilizing and socializing role of the idealized woman as a maternal instructress was to remain important in Renaissance conceptions of love; but the lover's *individual* growth was given more weight in these discourses. A heightened interest in individual self-determination was articulated in several Renaissance texts (such as Petrarch's *Rime Sparse*) in terms of the search for material success, for wealth and fame; in others, closer to the spirit of Florentine Neoplatonism (and also of Dante), interest was focused upon an active search for the mystical or philosophical fruits of that experience. The goal of this latter category of texts was the formation of a subjectivity which, while not defined in predominantly social and secular terms, as was that of Petrarch or of the courtly lover, was none the less distinguished in some important respects from the passive spiritual subject of Christian mysticism. The increased concern with *personal* progress (psychological as well as social) which characterized Renaissance discourses of love was therefore closely related to a more ambitious definition of the beloved's role. She was now associated with religious as well as secular powers which paralleled those of the Wisdom figure. But it was only with the revival of interest in Platonism, and with the dissemination of Platonic conceptions of love at the end of the fifteenth century, that her role as an earthly emblem of a higher, transcendent reality was given theoretical justification.

At the point at which supernatural or spiritual powers began to be attributed to a female object of desire, there was an attempt to erase all traces of active sexuality from this figure. This seems to have been motivated not just by the Christian connection of physical purity with spirituality, but also by the desire to make the sign of woman better capable of mirroring a transcendent dimension which, once contacted, could enable the male lover to forge a new and idealized identity. While the lady of courtly love was usually depicted as only temporarily unavailable, the female object of Petrarchan or Renaissance Neoplatonic desire was defined as unequivocally chaste. But just as the Wisdom figure had proved a somewhat disturbing presence within Christian theology, so the attempt to use the female beloved to legitimate the new self-consciousness of her male lover was not wholly satisfactory. In so far as she was represented as a bridge between the two opposing categories of spirit and matter, her bodily and material reality inevitably proved extremely difficult to elide beneath its attributed function of masculine mirror. For the most vital aspect of the beloved's role as mediator of a new masculinity, her chastity, had a disturbing habit of eluding or contradicting the significance accorded to it by the male lover as poet or philosopher. It often seemed to connote, not the negation of woman's bodily difference, of her own sexual desires, but rather the survival of a quality of feminine autonomy and self-sufficiency which could not be appropriated in the self-serving interests of the masculine subject. And behind the male lover's encounter with the elusiveness of woman's 'nature', as it appears to resist the meanings attached to it within these texts, we can trace the outlines of another emergent confrontation, scientific rather than erotic, whereby man attempts to transform the natural world which woman has so often signified into an obedient machine.

At the beginning of the fourteenth century Dante transformed the courtly love tradition by introducing a new conception of the female beloved.[30] In *La Vita Nuova* (The New Life), written around 1294, the figure of Beatrice began to be depicted in terms which were more religious than courtly. For example, he compared the difference between the mistress of Cavalcanti (a poet of courtly love) and his Beatrice to that between John the Baptist and Christ. This new conception of the lady which was beginning to take shape in Dante's mind was not to be concretized until the *Divina Commedia*. But before he began this great project Dante wrote a philosophical treatise entitled *Il Convito* (The Banquet). There he hymned the figure of Wisdom/Philosophy as a source of intellectual enlightenment which he affirmed could only be approached by means of love. His description of this figure was clearly derived from texts which included the Wisdom of Solomon as well as Boethius: 'She is the mother of every principle, . . . with her God began the world and especially the movement of the heavens, by which all things are generated, and from which all motion takes its origin and impulse.'[31] His exploration of the Wisdom figure clearly influenced Dante's conception of the role of (the spirit of) Beatrice in the *Divina Commedia*, who is frequently described in the language of the Wisdom texts.[32] Since she was conveniently dead, Beatrice could be depicted as an immaterial, indeed an angelic figure. By representing her in these terms, Dante removes any threatening traces of sexuality from her figure, and simultaneously separates her from nature and the material world. Beatrice performs a role similar to Wisdom in linking earth and heaven: she is the poet's guide from the Mount of Purgatory through the different levels of Paradise, and instructs him upon the metaphysical significance of the regions through which they are ascending. But she does not have the close connection with nature enjoyed by that figure (and which in spite of her chastity would later be an attribute of the Petrarchan beloved). Yet it is important to note that in stressing her angelic status Dante was by implication crediting her with a high degree of mystical achievement. The life of the Christian monk or nun who chose the celibate life was often described as the *vita angelica* in the middle ages, since it aimed at the eventual metamorphosis of sexed beings into the asexual state attributed to angels. And the poet's last address to Beatrice describes her enthroned among the company of saints in the Heavenly Rose of the Empyrean. The red rose, symbol of the female body in a courtly love text such as *Le Roman de la Rose*, has here become the white rose of mystical vision:

> Sanza risponder, li occhi su levai,
> > e vidi lei che si facea corona
> > reflettendo da sè li etterni rai.
> > > . . . e quella, sì lontana
> > come parea, sorrise e riguardommi;
> > poi si tornò all'etterna fontana.

(Without answering, I lifted up my eyes and saw her where she made for herself a crown, reflecting from her the eternal beams . . . and she, so far off as she seemed, smiled and looked at me, then turned again to the eternal fount.)[33]

Dante tells Beatrice: 'tu m'hai di servo tratto a libertate' ('It is thou who hast drawn me from bondage into liberty').[34] He attributes to her the gift of free will, the freedom to escape from the influence of fate which dominated medieval conceptions of human experience, and to remould himself and his life as he wishes. But the direction of Beatrice's glance, towards the fountain of light which Dante describes as God, stresses her role as an intermediary rather than active agent, as a mere mirror of this light, which she has guided Dante towards through his love for her, and which now, in the closing stages of his epic narrative, he can see without her mediation. Through this last act of contemplation, the process of Dante's own refashioning is apparently completed:

> per la vista che s'avvolarava
> in me guardando, una sola parvenza,
> mutandom'io, a me si travagliava.

(by my sight gaining strength as I looked, the one sole appearance, I myself changing, was, for me, transformed.)[35]

Dante's quest for self-determination has been accomplished at this moment. But in what likeness has he been remade? He says that within the blinding light was a circular design:

> Quella circulazion che sì concetta
>   pareva in te come lume reflesso,
>   dalli occhi miei alquanto circunspetta,
> dentro da sè, del suo colore stesso,
>   mi parve pinta della nostra effige;
>   per che 'l mio viso in lei tutto era messo.

(That circling which, thus begotten, appeared in Thee as reflected light, when my eyes dwelt on it for a time, seemed to me, within it and in its own colour, painted with our likeness, for which my sight was wholly given to it.)[36]

The image, in other words, is of Christ, of God made man.

In one sense Dante's entire poem has therefore enacted a circular process. Its poet protagonist has slowly moved from one version of masculine subjectivity, seen as fixed by fate, to another, freer, conception of himself which imitates or identifies with the figure of Christ, the god-man. (In this respect he anticipated the theological conception of *imitatio Christi*, which was not to be codified until 1418, in the work attributed to Thomas à Kempis – almost a hundred years after the composition of the *Paradiso*.) Yet Dante's account of his culminating encounter with God as absolute otherness is not entirely assimilable into a system of masculine resemblance. In the first place, his closing image of Beatrice is distinctly ambiguous. On the one hand she has been placed within a male-dominated hierarchy – the company of saints. But on the other hand, although as a disembodied figure she has ostensibly been removed from the domain of human sexual relations, Dante has attributed to her the experience of an intense and self-absorbing pleasure of a different order – the ecstasy of the mystic. That she turns away from Dante for the last time to look upon Being as a 'fountain of light' suggests that through the bliss of contemplation she could be seen as retaining an intense, if symbolic, relationship to the female body. The maternal attributes of this otherness are indeed hinted at in Dante's description of his attempt to speak the unspeakable:

> Omai sarà più corta mia favella,
>   pur a quel ch'io ricordo, che d'un fante
>   che bagni ancor la lingua alla mammella.

(Now my speech will come more short even of what I remember than an infant's who yet bathes his tongue at the breast.)[37]

Dante's *Divina Commedia* both foreshadowed and overshadowed Renaissance discourses of love. Significantly, his connection between woman as a source of supernatural inspiration for the male lover and woman as ecstatic and self-absorbed mystic was not repeated. None the less, while his attribution of spiritual powers to a desexualized version of the lady of courtly love was extremely influential, the tensions inherent in this formulation proved to be a source of mounting anxiety in both Petrarchism and Renaissance Neoplatonism.

The courtly poets of Southern France had written at a time when the degree of social mobility available to the poet who was not also an aristocrat was highly limited. As Florentines by birth, both Petrarch and Dante came from one of those Italian city states whose flourishing mercantile economy 'made Italy the weak link of Western feudalism', for the ruling elites of such cities were drawn from the mercantile classes rather than from an aristocracy of blood.[38] While Dante was born into a Guelph family of the lower nobility, Petrarch's father was a member of the legal profession. To this difference in class situation may be linked Petrarch's far more overt concern with fame and worldly success in comparison with the more contemplative (because more socially self-confident?) poetic persona created by Dante. The metamorphosis of earlier conceptions of love which occurs in Petrarch's work as well as in Dante's can obviously be related to the less 'courtly' social context with which they identified; however, the different manner in which each poet inscribed himself within his verse should serve to remind us that at this time Florentine society was neither homogeneous nor stable. (Dante was exiled from Florence from 1302 until his death; Petrarch grew up and began his literary career in Provence, following the exile of his father a year earlier.)

Petrarch's popularity in the Renaissance owed a great deal to the reception of one text, his *Rime Sparse*, sometimes called the *Canzoniere*, which was a collection of love poems written in Italian to a Madonna Laura. To a large extent this simply developed styles and themes of earlier verse: of the Provençal troubadours, of the Italian poets of the 'dolce stil nuovo', or of Latin love poets such as Ovid, Propertius, and Catullus; but Petrarch combined and codified these in a most accessible fashion. He also raised the (till then quite uncommon) idea of the poetic sequence or collection to new levels of sophistication and effectiveness. None the less, his far-reaching influence can be attributed to more than the perfection of a style. For the attitudes implicit in his discourse of love involved a rejection of certain key medieval attitudes still influential in the work of Dante and earlier poets. In the *Divina Commedia*, Dante's representation of Beatrice as disembodied angelic guide was certainly closely bound up with his own poetic ambition to achieve the highest levels of knowledge. Yet the poem is much more than an exploration of Dante's self-image. Its subjective element is situated within a complex religious scheme which has universal rather than merely personal implications. Petrarch too stressed the importance of contemplating the lady's 'angelic' beauty. But whereas Dante's conception of Beatrice in the *Divina Commedia* had been as guide to the universe of medieval Christianity, in which all things were related to each other and simultaneously to God, in the *Rime Sparse* the idealized woman becomes a means for man to know and affirm himself in his material environment rather than in relation to a transcendent order. She is the key to an androcentric rather than theocentric universe. The representation of Laura is indebted to a pre-Renaissance tradition of mystical and religious symbolism, and to the symbolic figure of Wisdom in particular; but as John Freccero has shown, Petrarch attempts to assimilate and redefine that symbolism in terms of a self-referential system.[39] In consequence there is a persistent tension within the *Rime Sparse* between the use of an image as symbol, and its more ambivalent application as sign.

Laura was accorded many of Beatrice's immaterial or 'angelic' attributes; indeed, she too was asserted by Petrarch to have died midway through his sequence. Like that of Beatrice, Laura's image is related to the second person of the Trinity, invested with attributes shared by Wisdom and Christ (although a connection with the Holy Spirit was also hinted at in Petrarch's punning on her name as *l'auro*, breeze or wind). Her chastity, her physical autonomy or absence, is closely linked with her possession of creative and inspirational powers which are comparable to those of Wisdom, or of Christ as *logos*: 'cria d'amor penseri atti et parole' ('She creates thoughts, acts and words of love').[40] Petrarch asserts that in loving her: 'Pasco la mente d'un sì nobil cibo/ch'ambrosia et nettar non invidio a Giove' ('I nourish my mind with a food so noble that I do not envy Jove his ambrosia and nectar').[41] Her golden, solar associations are also shared with Christ, with whom, like Wisdom, she is explicitly compared:

> di sé nascendo a Roma non fe'grazia,
> a Giudea sì, tanto sovr' ogni stato
> umiltate esaltar sempre gli piacque.
>
> Ed or di picciol borgo un sol n'à dato,
> tal che natura o 'l luogo si ringrazia
> onde sì bella donna al mondo nacque.

(He, when He was born, did not bestow Himself on Rome, but rather on Judea, so beyond all other states it pleased Him always to exalt humility.

And now from a small village He has given us a sun, such that nature is thanked and the place where so beautiful a lady was born to the world.)[42]

Here the poet attributes to Laura a creative power comparable to that of Wisdom and Christ; however, when he tells us early in the *Rime Sparse* that his love began at Easter, time of the resurrection of Christ: 'Era il giorno ch' al sol si scoloraro/per la pietà del suo fattore i rai/quando i' fui preso' ('It was the day when the sun's rays turned pale with grief for his Maker when I was taken'), he connects himself, rather than Laura, with that figure.[43] Dante's final recognition of identity with Christ, however personally liberating, had been placed within a religious framework. Petrarch, on the other hand, is simply drawing an analogy between his suffering and that of Christ. He does not seek a complete identification with this figure, an *imitatio Christi* which would require that his worldly identity, perhaps even his life, be sacrificed. For he is extremely afraid of death, doubtful that it will usher him into a Christian paradise or even purgatory: 'io temo che sarebbe un varco/di pianto in pianto et d'una in altra guerra' ('I fear that it would be a passage from weeping into weeping and from one war to another').[44] Instead, his poetic text attempts to formulate a secular equivalent to the religious narrative of God-as-man; he seeks godlike powers specific to himself. The sequence is simultaneously punctuated by anxiety over this error, this wandering or deviation from the Christian model of an identity founded in eternity rather than human history.[45] It was probably to protect himself from such charges that Petrarch concluded the *Rime Sparse* with a palinode or poem of recantation, in which he asserted that his love of Laura had been incompatible with religious orthodoxy.

At several other points in the *Rime Sparse* Petrarch appropriates images and attributes connected with Laura for himself. What is especially curious about this process is that it often *precedes* his more extensive identification of the same image with Laura. At the same time, we find that while he will frequently propose an exact symbolic correspondence between Laura and the image (a technique which connotes a Platonic world view), in associating the same image with himself Petrarch will favour the Aristotelian device of metaphor or analogy. By the retention of a suggestive gap between the two terms of the comparison connected with himself, his own identity never disappears beneath the image.[46]

For example, Petrarch's references to Laura as the fabled phoenix, immortal because capable of chaste reproduction on its funeral pyre, could be said to be qualified or undermined in that at an earlier stage in the text Petrarch had described himself in similar terms.[47] This earlier poem clearly announces the birth of a new subject, whose survival is paradoxically ensured as a result of the self-immolation required by love. The symbolic identification of Laura and phoenix as 'questa fenice', 'mia fenice' ('this phoenix', 'my phoenix') has been replaced by analogy: Petrarch affirms, with suggestive elusiveness, not that his new identity is that of the phoenix, but that in its longevity this new subject will be comparable or equal to this bird:

> Qual più diversa et nova
> cosa fu mai in qualche stranio clima,
> quella, se ben s'estima,
> più mi rasembra: a tal son giunto, Amore.
> Là onde il dì ven fore
> vola un augel che sol, senza consorte,
> di voluntaria morte
> rinasce et tutto a viver si rinova.
>   Così sol si ritrova
> lo mio voler, et così in su la cima
> de' suoi alti pensieri al sol si volve,
> et così si risolve,
> et così torna al suo stato di prima;
> arde et more et riprende i nervi suoi
> et vive poi   con la fenice a prova.

(Whatever strange and new thing ever was in whatever wondrous clime, if judged aright it most resembles me: to such a pass have I come, Love. There whence the day comes forth flies a bird that alone, without consort, after voluntary death, is reborn and renews itself to life.

Thus my desire is unique and thus at the summit of its high thoughts it turns to the sun, and thus it is consumed and thus returns to its former state: it burns and dies and takes again its sinews and lives on, vying with the phoenix.)[48]

Laura as phoenix is the symbol of a divine regeneration. When the image appears near the end of the sequence, it signifies her achievement, like Beatrice, of immortality after death (although the image, like Dante's description of God in the closing verses of the *Paradiso*, raises some doubts about deity's exclusively masculine gender). In contrast, Petrarch attributes the phoenix's capacity of self-regeneration to secular and historical (rather than spiritual) man.

We find a similar tension, between Petrarch's idealization of Laura on the one hand and, on the other, his affirmation of himself as an emergent subject of a distinctly new order, in his use of other recurring images. As has been pointed out by several critics, the *Rime Sparse* puns constantly upon various associations of Laura's name, metamorphosing her into a series of metonyms derived from her name.[49] These images, while they serve as metonymic substitutions for the figure of Laura, also had certain traditional symbolic meanings. But just as their use as metonyms displaces the human figure of Laura, so Petrarch replaced the established symbolic connotations of these images with other significations, of specific reference to his own poetic system and to the man he hoped to become. So Laura is the wind (*l'aura*) of poetic inspiration rather than of the Holy Spirit. The gold (*l'oro*) of her hair functions within the text not as a symbol of spiritual perfection but as the sign of Petrarch's hopes for material success. And most significantly, the laurel (*il lauro*) which usually symbolized the victory of a hero becomes the sign of Petrarch's desire for poetic achievement and fame. Given the importance which he accords this tree, Petrarch's presentation of his own metamorphosis into a laurel as a misfortune seems somewhat hypocritical. He says of the combined assault of Eros and Laura upon him: 'ei duo mi trasformaro in quel ch' i' sono,/facendomi d'uom vivo un lauro verde/che per fredda stagion foglia non perde' ('those two transformed me into what I am, making me of a living man a green laurel that loses no leaf for all the cold season').[50] Again we have the curious exchange of attributes between the object and the subject of desire, aptly signifying the poet's appropriation of this and other traditional symbols for his own ends. It is also notable here that while Petrarch stresses the evergreen nature of the laurel, for him this signifies the immortality conveyed by fame rather than spiritual salvation.

For implicit in Petrarch's emphasis on his individuality was a major redefinition of the relationship between ideas of action and contemplation. In focusing upon Laura as an image whose symbolic or transcendent significance was increasingly subordinated to worldly concerns, the poet was replacing a collective and religious idea of contemplation with an individual and secular process. To this emphasis upon success in the world, rather than its transcendence, can be related the predominant pastoral imagery of his work. Dante's encounter with Beatrice in a pastoral setting at the highest point of Purgatory was only the prelude to his vision of her as a guide to supernatural dimensions; in contrast, the poet of the *Rime Sparse* contemplates Laura's perfection within a predominantly green world, merging woman and nature in the laurel tree which is not just a metonym for Laura but also, more importantly, the sign of his desire for poetic fame. By his contemplative retreat to the hills of the Vaucluse near Avignon, where he wrote the *Rime Sparse* and other works, Petrarch was not rejecting the world, but rather sowing the seeds of his worldly success. His concern with the possibilities of transforming nature rather than transcending or rejecting it was also emphasized in his series of pastoral eclogues, *Bucolicum Carmen*. In the tenth of these eclogues he adopted the persona of Sylvanus, a Roman god of cultivated and uncultivated nature who was often connected with the folkloric figure of the wild man.

The overdetermination of Petrarch's discourse of love by worldly and material concerns is also apparent in the many references to the noble family of the Colonna in this collection of poems, ostensibly devoted to Laura's unique praise, for the Colonna patronage was helping Petrarch quite literally to translate poetic images of fame into a material reality. Laura often shares her pedestal with the figure of Cardinal Giovanni Colonna (who seems at times a human equivalent to the figure of Eros, manipulator/overseer of the courtly love-game):

> Carità di signore, amor di donna
> son le catene ove con molti affanni
> legato son, perch' io stesso mi strinsi;
>
> un lauro verde, una gentil colonna
> quindeci l'una et l'altro diciotto anni
> portato ò in seno, et giamai non mi scinsi.

(Devotion to my lord, love of my lady are the chains where with much labour I am bound, and I myself took them on!

A green Laurel, a noble Column, the latter for fifteen, the former for eighteen years, I have carried in my breast and have never put from me.)[51]

At the same time, Petrarch celebrates another, more diffuse object of love in these poems: the historical and geographical world in which he lived and wrote, and Italy in particular. In a well-known poem, he laments Italy's lack of peace as if this country, rather than Laura, were his beloved:

Italia mia, ben che 'l parlar sia indarno
a le piaghe mortali
che nel bel corpo tuo sì spesse veggio,
piacemi almen che' miei sospir sian quali
spera 'l Tevero et l'Arno,
e 'l Po, dove doglioso et grave or seggio.

(My Italy, although speech does not aid those mortal wounds of which in your lovely body I see so many, I wish at least my sighs to be such as Tiber and Arno hope for, and Po where I now sit sorrowful and sad.)[52]

Scattered throughout the text are numerous poems of topical interest, referring to events of the day and the leading political figures involved. Such references do not only indicate the extent to which Petrarch (as indeed Dante before him) was intellectually involved in the political events of the day; they also articulate his genuine literary interest in the figure of the active man par excellence, the hero, who achieves a secular immortality by positioning himself within human history. This interest had motivated an unfinished epic *Africa*, upon the life of the Roman general Scipio Africanus, as well as *De Viris Illustribus* (Lives of Famous Men), and was also suggested by his appropriation of the laurel of heroic victory to signify poetic fame. The preference for the active and worldly life implicit in these references was explored by Petrarch in more explicit terms in his *Secretum*, a work written in Latin in the form of an imaginary dialogue between himself and his intellectual mentor, St Augustine.[53]

The paradox inherent in Petrarch's use of a sublimated desire to articulate this involvement in the active life is aptly indicated by his use of colour. He tells us in several poems that colour is the key to feelings: 'Vedete ben quanti colore depigne/Amore sovente in mezzo del mio volto' ('You see well how many colours Love often paints in my face.')[54] The *Rime Sparse* is as brightly coloured as a Renaissance painting. He asserts that Love paints upon his face as a canvas, but within the context of his poetic text it is actually Laura that is the canvas, and Petrarch the (colourist) artist. Most of the colours in the *Rime Sparse* relate to Laura, who as the source of light in the poem is also apparently the means of its refraction. Two of these tints echo those connected with Beatrice when she appears to Dante at the end of the *Purgatorio*, 'sovra candido vel cinta d'uliva/ . . ., sotto verde manto/vestita di color di fiamma viva' ('girt with olive over a white veil, clothed under a green mantle with the colour of living flame').[55] White, green and red were the colours of the three evangelical virtues, faith, hope and love. But although Beatrice's colours of green and white recur constantly in Petrarch's description of Laura, along with her sunny or golden attributes (the colour of divinity), red is actually a more elusive colour in the Petrarchan text than some critics have implied. The supposedly 'characteristic' Petrarchan conceit, whereby the lady's beauty is described in terms of a contrast of red and white in a tradition that goes back to the Song of Solomon, is less common by far than the pervasive references to green, white, or green *and* white. In fact the colour red is named only four times in the text, and the many references to the (implicitly red) fire of desire are connected with Petrarch rather than Laura. If we read this imbalance in terms of the traditional symbolic connotations of these colours mentioned above, then it seems that Petrarch actually defined Laura's significance for him more in terms of faith and hope than of love.

It has been suggested that all colours stimulate the instinctual drives or the unconscious; but red is surely the most instinctual of colours, appealing directly to the sexual impulse.[56] Its connection with human (as opposed to divine) existence in Renaissance art is indicated by the fact that it was frequently the colour of the dress worn by the Virgin Mary beneath her characteristically blue robe (indicative of her spirituality). The green (as well as the golden) attributes of Laura were converted into signs of Petrarch's own future; her white veil or white skin (indicative of her chastity) became the space upon which he could inscribe his self-referential system of representation. But her red blood or her sexuality, the sign both of her physical creativity and of her own desires, is largely censored or repressed. Not only is Laura silenced within the Petrarchan text (in contrast to representations of the Wisdom/Philosophy figure and of Dante's Beatrice as speakers); not only is her figure metonymically displaced (as laurel, gold, or inspiration) or reduced by synecdoche to a part-object (hair, skin, lips, breast); it is also denied any material or sexual identity. This poetic evasion of Laura's bodily difference suggests Petrarch feared that recognition of her otherness, within a sexual rather than a sublimated love relation, would lead to the destruction rather than affirmation of his identity. In the framework of Christian theology, the *caritas* or love which red signified was inextricably connected with sacrifice, with the passion of Christ and of his martyrs.

None the less, the sign of Laura did occasionally elude interpretation and appropriation by the emergent masculine subject. At certain moments in the text, Laura's passive 'cruelty' in refusing the lover her favours is replaced by images of direct aggression. There are several brief but startling recognitions by Petrarch of her facial or bodily unity, as a Diana or Medusa figure whose menacing stare affirms an 'other' identity, a feminine difference, which has escaped his narcissistic process of poetic colonization. At an early stage in the sequence, Petrarch uses the Ovidian myth of Diana and Actaeon to describe a fantasized encounter between himself and Laura in which her active resistance to his erotic desires forces the poet to confront the baser 'animal' impulses from which he is trying to dissociate himself, by means of distance and separation from the beloved. His reference to Diana's metamorphosis of the hunter Actaeon into a stag when he accidentally saw the goddess bathing with her nymphs reminds the reader of the destructive power of lust: Actaeon's transformation from human to animal existence led to his pursuit and dismemberment by his own hounds. Again, Petrarch is identifying with an image which elsewhere in the sequence he associates with Laura, as 'that lovely cruel wild creature' ('quella fera bella et cruda') or 'a white doe' ('una candida cerva'). Within a tradition of Christian symbolism derived from commentaries upon the Song of Solomon, the beloved as a doe or hart is an allegory of Christ's incarnation. But Petrarch clearly does not wish to imitate the beloved in this guise. Unplanned mimesis of this sexual/sacrificial aspect of the beloved is seen as jeopardizing his quest for a worldly self-image, for it is followed by the threat of fragmentation and annihilation of identity. Of course, such an event would parallel the results of his own fetishistic and metonymic representation of Laura, as well as the crucifixion of Christ.[57] But Petrarch halts his fantasized repetition of the myth before this sacrifice is re-enacted:

> I' segui' tanto avanti il mio desire
> ch' un dì, cacciando sì com' io solea,
> mi mossi, e quella fera bella et cruda
> in una fonte ignuda
> si stava, quando 'l sol più forte ardea.
> Io perché d'altra vista non m'appago
> stetti a mirarla, ond' ella ebbe vergogna
> et per farne vendetta o per celarse
> l'acqua nel viso co le man mi sparse.
> Vero dirò; forse e' parrà menzogna:
> ch'i senti' trarmi de la propria imago
> et in un cervo solitario et vago
> di selva in selva ratto mi trasformo,
> et ancor de' miei can fuggo lo stormo.

(I followed so far my desire that one day, hunting as I was wont, I went forth, and that lovely cruel wild creature was in a spring naked when the sun burned most strongly. I, who am not appeased by any other sight, stood to gaze on her, whence she felt shame and, to take revenge or to hide herself, sprinkled water in my face with her hand. I shall speak the truth, perhaps it will appear a lie, for I felt myself drawn from my own image and into a solitary wandering stag from wood to wood quickly I am transformed and still I flee the belling of my hounds.)[58]

Laura as Medusa is associated with a different obstacle to Petrarch's clearly charted course of subjective development. This reference occurs in the final poem of the collection, the palinode or poem of repentance in which Petrarch addresses the Virgin Mary and 'recants' his irreligious love of Laura. He asserts that, like the Greek mythological figure of Medusa, Laura's petrifying gaze had threatened him with return to a more limited or a fixed identity, one comparable to that submission to fate from which Dante escaped at the end of the *Commedia*: 'Medusa et l'error mio m'àn fatto un sasso/d'umor vano stillante' ('Medusa and my error have made me a stone dripping vain moisture.')[59]

In both of these episodes, the poet presents himself as temporarily absorbed by the material and natural world which he has tried to control and transform through the figure of Laura. Implicit in Ovid's account was the suggestion that the tragedy was due to Actaeon's mistaken trespass within a sacred space or *temenos*: by failing to observe the difference between mortality and divinity, he violated natural law. As Diana and Medusa, therefore, Laura challenges Petrarch's desire for elevation to an heroic stature, for an immortality which would be the guarantor of lasting subjective unity. Just as her passive chastity had enabled his project of self-idealization, so these images of a more active and threatening assertion of female autonomy force a confrontation with his lower nature. These moments in the text disrupt Petrarch's fluid conception of the relationship between lover and beloved, in which ostensible differences of gender have not impeded a (one-way) exchange of attributes. Suddenly the boundaries between masculine and feminine are defined in menacing terms. In later Renaissance literature influenced by Petrarchism, there would be increasing emphasis upon this active and aggressive aspect of the beloved, which was frequently connected with representations of her as Diana, Roman goddess of chastity, hunting, and the wild. But the threatening ambiguity of the Petrarchan beloved was also to be an important theme in Renaissance Neoplatonism; and by the sixteenth century, Neoplatonic attitudes would frequently be combined with those of Petrarchism in literary representations of idealized love.

The highly subjective conception of love articulated by Petrarch was indirectly influenced, as had been the work of Dante, by Platonic and Neoplatonic ideas present in the work of Christian writers (and by St Augustine in particular). But in metaphorizing contemplation of the female beloved as a prelude to worldly success rather than to mystical experience, the *Rime Sparse* was in line with a materialist philosophical trend influenced by neo-Aristotelianism, which by the end of the middle ages had significantly undermined the still implicit influence of Platonism in western thought, and which was overshadowed by the work of Thomas Aquinas. Then, in the second half of the fifteenth century, a Platonic Academy was established in Careggi near Florence by Cosimi de' Medici, which was concerned with the translation and reception of certain key Platonic and Neoplatonic texts unavailable in the middle ages. The most important of these texts for Renaissance conceptions of love was Plato's *Symposium*, translated from Greek into Latin and commented upon by Marsilio Ficino in 1469 as *De Amore*; Ficino's translation of another rediscovered Platonic text about love, the *Phaedrus*, was published fifteen years later, in his *Opera Omnia* of 1484. In this new, Florentine, Neoplatonism, the idea of a contemplative process initiated by a chaste or sublimated passion occupied a position of central philosophical importance; in contrast with Petrarchan love poetry, however, this system stressed the mystical rather than the secular results of such a process. None the less, its conception of subjectivity had certain significant features in common with that explored by Petrarch. And the writings of Florentine Neoplatonists such as Ficino and Pico della Mirandola cast considerable light upon the ambiguous position of woman within Petrarchan poetics.

This new wave of Neoplatonism combined emphasis upon the contemplative role of the masculine philosophical subject as lover (who perceived in the material world and material objects of desire the trace of ideal meanings), with the theme of the restlessness, the ceaseless activity of consciousness. Ficino asserted that:

> the passion of a lover is not extinguished by the sight or touch of any body. For he does not desire this or that body, but admires, desires, and is amazed by the splendour of the celestial majesty shining through bodies. For this reason lovers do not know what they desire or seek, for they do not know God Himself, whose secret flavour infuses a certain very sweet perfume of Himself into His works.[60]

The Florentine Neoplatonists' definition of knowledge as contemplation therefore had the orthodox *telos* or mystical goal of union with God. Yet within this formula were the seeds of a new conception of man's relationship to the dimension of transcendence, that is, to deity. For although their philosopher–lover was described as being seized in the first instance by a Platonic *furor* or divine madness, he did not need, like the traditional Christian mystic, to wait passively for further gifts of divine grace. Instead, he could ascend the ladder of creation towards the Platonic One or God by the exercise of reason. Reason, according to Ficino, was the only faculty of the soul which was entirely free, and it consequently produced movement and change in the soul: 'That rational faculty which is the peculiar nature of the true Soul is not limited to one thing. For with a free movement it wanders up and down. . . .'[61] As Paul Oskar Kristeller has pointed out, this emphasis upon the extensive powers of the 'rational soul' was the cornerstone of Ficino's metaphysics, which placed the human soul at the centre of the hierarchy of the universe.[62] By stressing soul as self-moving through the exercise of reason, Ficino radically redefined the Platonic and Neoplatonic conception of contemplation or *theoria*. In one sense, this emphasis upon willed intellectual activity actually owed an important debt both to Aristotle and to his medieval disciple Thomas Aquinas; but it was also shaped by other Greek works, philosophical and occult, which had been brought to Europe after the fall of Constantinople in 1453, above all, by the compilation called the *Corpus Hermeticum*. This collection of texts was revered as especially sacred by Ficino and his fellow Neoplatonists, as well as by his Medici patrons; they believed (wrongly) that it was older than the writings of Plato (in fact the texts were really written in the second to third centuries CE), and so offered proof of the continuity between the wisdom of ancient Egypt and of Greece. It juxtaposed philosophical treatises with others on topics such as alchemy, astrology, and magic. As a result, Ficino considered the practice of 'natural magic' quite compatible with the pursuit of philosophy.[63]

Viewed from the perspective of medieval philosophy, where everything had a predetermined place and nature, this heroic and occult type of mystical ascent celebrated by Florentine Neoplatonism was profoundly hubristic. These Neoplatonists aspired, like Dante and Petrarch, to free themselves from subjection to fate through the sublimation of desire:

> The force of fate does not penetrate the mind unless the mind of its own accord has first become submerged in the body, which is subject to Fate . . . . Every soul should withdraw from the encumbrance of the body and become centred in the mind, for then Fate will discharge its force upon the body without touching the soul.[64]

Likewise, the discovery of man as godlike which this procedure was held ultimately to produce had to some extent been prefigured in Dante's transfiguration in the last verses of the *Commedia*. Ficino described the apotheosis of the philosopher–lover in these terms: 'the Soul is inflamed by the divine splendour, glowing in the beautiful person as in a mirror, and secretly lifted up by it, as by a hook, in order to become God.'[65] But Dante's personal metamorphosis had been qualified by being positioned within a rigidly structured and hierarchical view of the universe. In the thought of some of these Renaissance Neoplatonists, affirmations of man's godlike dignity appeared to claim for him an unlimited freedom. Kristeller pointed out that for Pico della Mirandola, man seemingly had no fixed place in the medieval hierarchy of being described in Dante's *Commedia*, but was somehow placed outside of that structure altogether.[66] A similar refusal of limits would later characterize the work of sixteenth-century Neoplatonist Giordano Bruno.[67]

Yet the theoretical (or contemplative) freedom and power claimed by the masculine philosopher–subject of Florentine Neoplatonism was not necessarily matched by these writers' material situations. Just as the

material wealth and power of the Colonna family had facilitated
Petrarch's image (re)making, so Ficino, the son of a doctor, translated
and wrote philosophy as the financial dependant of the Medici family.
(Pico della Mirandola, on the other hand, who elaborated even more
adventurously upon Ficino's system, was a member of a minor aristocratic
family and had private means.) Another apparatus of material authority
loomed behind Ficino also (somewhat paradoxically), in the shape of the
Catholic church, with whose doctrines he always asserted that his
philosophy could be reconciled. At 40 he took holy orders as a
Dominican monk, and was subsequently granted certain benefices in the
gift of the Medici. (In this respect his career was paralleled by the shorter
life of Pico, who was also buried in the Dominican habit.) The extent to
which Ficino's philosophical dualism was modified by other elements in
his work may certainly have been related to his ambiguous position as a
philosopher–client. While personally committed to the life of scholarship
and the melancholy rapture of theory-as-contemplation, he had at the
same time to make a recondite philosophy relevant to the more worldly
concerns of the Medici circle. Thus in some of his writings, Ficino
explored the theme of the balanced or tripartite life (*triplex vita*)
mentioned in Plato's *Republic*. This was a life in which the higher
functions of contemplation and worldly activity *could* be combined with
pleasure or the *vita voluptaria*. In elaborating this idea, Ficino may not
simply have been interested in the mystical properties of triads. The
potential relevance of the theme to his patrons is made clear in a letter to
Lorenzo de' Medici, where Ficino compliments him on the universality
which had resulted from his refusal to privilege any aspect of life over
another. Instead, Ficino asserted, Lorenzo combined wisdom, heroic
virtue, and pleasure – in other words, he was an admirable practitioner of
the *triplex vita*.[68]

So Ficino's Neoplatonism did not (could not?) renounce the material
world altogether. One wonders if he was implicitly sanctioning the
increasing political power of an elite – of his Florentine patrons – rather
than of man as a species (albeit a gendered species) when he indicated
that man's achievement of a godlike control over his own nature would
lead to his assumption of full authority over a redeemed or about-to-be-
redeemed natural world, as its undisputed lord:

> Man not only rules the animals by force, he also governs, keeps, and
> teaches them. Universal providence belongs to God, who is the
> universal cause. Hence man who provides generally for all things, both
> living and lifeless, is a *kind* of God.[69]

At this point Ficino seems uncertain about the precise goals of his
philosopher–lover: should they be spiritual or worldly? Such an ambiguity
was of course fundamental to Renaissance humanism. This fluctuating

attitude of Florentine Neoplatonism to matter is very much apparent in the curiously indeterminate status which it accorded to another 'material' factor in its promotion of a new and idealized subject. This was sexual difference.

Just as had Socrates and his disciples, the Platonic Academy at Careggi seems to have privileged a homoerotic ideal of noble friendship between intellectual men. For as Ficino expressed it: 'Likeness generates love.'[70] At several points in the Platonic texts, there was a distinction between an inferior carnal desire, which imprisoned soul in matter through sexual intercourse and physical procreation, and a chaste or spiritual passion, in which the intellectual sublimation of sexual desire led to spiritual transfiguration. In *The Symposium*, it was stressed that while both women and young boys could properly be the objects of the physical desire, the higher, chaste, and typically contemplative love could only be directed towards men (specifically, men who were either approaching or had arrived at adulthood), since it required a certain degree of intelligence as well as beauty in the beloved. (Of course, as I have already pointed out, a masculine subject or lover was assumed for both these kinds of love.) Yet in fact this gendered distinction between different modes of love corresponding to the polarity of matter and spirit was implicitly subverted at certain points in *The Symposium*. No women were present at the discussion which was described – even a flute-girl who had expected to provide some entertainment was sent away once the banquet which preceded the debate had ended. But whether intentionally or not, Plato inscribed in his text the trace of another kind of feminine presence, in the form of several passages which apparently contradicted Socrates' emphasis upon the higher love as a search for masculine similitude. And these passages appear to have influenced the subsequent development and application of these attitudes to love during the later Renaissance.

Firstly, in the passage which first elaborated the crucial distinction between two loves, a feminine gender was ascribed to *both* of these models of desire. In this speech, attributed to Pausanias, the two loves were described as two Aphrodites (Ficino substituted the name of Roman Venus for that of the Greek love-goddess). In Ficino's translation and exegesis of this passage, its distinction was amplified with reference to the Platonic categories of mind and world soul: concepts which, as I have mentioned earlier, had both been connected with feminine imagery in some early Neoplatonic texts:

> The first Venus, which is in the Mind, is said to have been born of Uranus without a mother, because *mother*, to the physicists, is *matter*. But that Mind is a stranger to any association with corporeal matter. The second Venus, which is located in the World Soul, was born of Jupiter and Dione. 'Born of Jupiter' – that is, of the faculty of the Soul

itself which moves the heavenly things, since that faculty created the power which generates these lower things. They also attribute a mother to that second Venus, for this reason, that since she is infused into the Matter of the world, she is thought to have commerce with matter.

Finally, to speak briefly, Venus is twofold. One is certainly that intelligence which we have located in the Angelic Mind. The other is the power of procreation attributed to the World Soul. Each Venus has as her companion a love like herself. For the former Venus is entranced by an innate love for understanding the Beauty of god. The latter likewise is entranced by her love for procreating that same beauty in bodies.[71]

Thus although there is an obvious attempt to separate the higher, contemplative love from the domain of the feminine, in the assertion that this Venus was 'born of no mother', the problem remains that both loves are personified by the same female deity, who is accordingly invested with an ambiguously double aspect.

And indeed, the second fissure in the Platonic text's emphasis upon masculine resemblance implicitly elided the opposition between these two loves, as well as the hierarchy of gender associated with them. For the fourth speech, attributed to the comic dramatist Aristophanes, raised the possibility that both men and women could be the subjects and objects of a desire which combined the sexual with the spiritual impulse. Aristophanes described love as aspiration to a state of double-sexed, androgynous or hermaphroditic unity, which he claimed men and women had once enjoyed. But he liberally proposed three different models of the fulfilment of desire in the union of two bodies and souls: these corresponded to the union of man with man, woman with woman, or man with woman. This theme of the androgynous goal of the search for identity was also present in some of the Hermetic texts, and it was given especial emphasis in the writings of Pico della Mirandola, who, like Philo and Origen before him, connected the image of the androgyne with the state of man before the fall.

It may have been under the influence of this Aristophanic formulation that, later in his commentary, Ficino modified a binary opposition once again, by the introduction of a third and mediating term. He said that between the two fundamental kinds of love or Venuses, which exist as 'daemons' in each individual soul, there were three lesser loves experienced by men: 'These three loves have three names: love of the contemplative is called divine; that of the practical man human; and that of the voluptuous man, animal.'[72] Divine and animal love seem merely the human expression of the two Venuses; but the third term, human love, appears to have been proposed both as a means of resolving the contradiction between these two extremes and as more appropriate than divine love to the life of the worldly man (or of the Medici nobility). In sixteenth-century applications of Neoplatonism, this middle term was to become extremely important, in connection with a new emphasis upon the combination of a sexual with a spiritual relation within marriage. But in fact the association of the same deity with the apparently irreconcilable extremes of spiritual and carnal love could be seen as obscuring the difference between them from the outset; this implicit problem was concretized as soon as a human woman began to be celebrated in terms of the higher, contemplative, or intellectual kind of love, as happened in so much Renaissance literature influenced by Florentine Neoplatonism (as well as by Petrarch).

Thirdly, and especially problematic, was the ascription of the culminating discourse of Socrates himself concerning a heavenly love beween men to a woman, Diotima of Mantinea (whom Ficino called a prophetess in his commentary). Socrates attributed to Diotima not just his ideas about love, but also supernatural powers – the delivery of Athens from a plague. The interpretive contortions to which this aspect of the text has reduced modern critics are extraordinary. Walter Hamilton, for example, while according the highest respect to Socrates' philosophy, finds it necessary to doubt his word on this point:

> It is almost universally and no doubt rightly held that Diotima is a fictitious personage, in spite of the apparently historical statements made about her by Socrates. It is not desirable here to go into the arguments in favour of this conclusion. . . .[73]

Naturally Diotima must be fictitious, an hallucination of the otherwise impeccably rational Master. For were she not to be a figure of fantasy, behind the text of *The Symposium* would loom the disturbing shadow of woman both as mystic and as original possessor of the Socratic *logos*. And how could a search for masculine identity through sublimated desire be reconcilable with a maternal, rather than a paternal source for this system? This final dissonance within the Platonic text was effectively compounded by Ficino's introduction to the speech of Socrates. There he described initiation into Diotima's mysteries (in other words, into this higher, contemplative love or Venus), in terms of service to two other goddesses, Diana and Pallas Athena:

> But you virtuous guests, and all others dedicated to Diana and Pallas, who rejoice in the freedom of a guiltless soul, and in the endless pleasures of the intellect; you are welcome to come and listen carefully to the divine mysteries revealed to Socrates by Diotima.[74]

This tension within Florentine Neoplatonism's conception of love survived in more popular and more literary sixteenth-century texts influenced by these ideas, which began to describe a sublimated desire of woman as the means to an idealized or contemplative love (a trend also due in part to the increasing literary influence of Petrarchism). In such texts, representation of an unobtainable woman as mediatrix of a masculine search for an identity founded on similitude was shadowed again and again by fear of a resistance to this process of transcendence, of an encounter with the woman's difference or material bodily reality which would disrupt her role as mirror of an idealized masculinity. For although designated as chaste, the female beloved was now often perceived as mediating between and combining these opposing modes of love, and so as uniting in her person the domains of spirit and matter with which they were associated, as did the biblical Wisdom figure. But although Leone Ebreo, in his *Dialoghi d'Amore*, gave a paradigmatic female beloved the name of Sophia, she was most frequently compared to Roman Diana: a goddess associated not only with female chastity and spiritual purity but also with matter, in the shape of wild nature. In such comparisons, the philosophical problems now inherent in this love discourse were often especially apparent. One of the first to popularize a Neoplatonic idealization of woman, Pietro Bembo (who at the climax of Castiglione's *Il Cortegiano* was made the spokesman for this view), followed Petrarch in using the myth of Diana and Actaeon to describe the perils which could overtake a lover. Bembo warned the lover not to allow the real woman to interfere with his fantasized image of her. He asserted that the occlusion of the transcendental signified of man-as-god beneath a stubbornly material and female sign would lead only to the negation of the lover's identity in death:

> For though believing that he was in love while he met his lady only in imagination, he has become like a solitary stag whom, like Actaeon, his hounded thoughts have pitifully torn; but he seeks to nourish rather than escape them, desiring to bring his life to an untimely end and not aware, apparently, how much better it is to be alive, on any terms, than dead.[75]

If the imaginary powers attributed to the idealized woman of the love discourses could cause such anxiety, then the combination of a fictive with a real authority must have been extremely alarming. When Petrarchan and Neoplatonic attitudes were assimilated by the aesthetic ideologies of French and English Renaissance absolutism, the female beloved was closely associated with the mystical body of the Renaissance state; and in the context of Elizabethan courtly literature, with the monarch herself. Some of the most detailed explorations of the effect upon masculine identity of this paradoxical sign of a chaste female beloved are accordingly inscribed within a Renaissance discourse of political power.

Chapter two

A curious conjunction: discourses of love and political power in the French Renaissance

In both Petrarchism and Renaissance Neoplatonism, the definition of masculine identity through or across a female figure had a secular as well as a spiritual dimension. Petrarch's *Rime Sparse* established a metonymic relationship between his private experience of love and the moulding of an objective public identity, as a successful poet. And Baldessare Castiglione's *Il Cortegiano* founded its definition of a 'courtly' aristocratic identity upon the Neoplatonic conception of love. But the impact of the love discourses upon the formation of social identity was not restricted to the poet or courtier; in some contexts it extended to the figure of the ruler. In the first half of the sixteenth century, Petrarchan and Neoplatonic attitudes were assimilated by the aesthetic strand of French absolutist ideology in order to forge a new image of the monarch. Both the biblical Wisdom figure and its medieval equivalent had often been depicted as the attribute of kings; French Renaissance literature and art briefly represented a Diana-like female beloved as the custodian, not merely of self-knowledge or of worldly success, but of absolute political power. The importance of this theme within French culture declined in the latter part of the sixteenth century; however, it was taken up and reformulated in courtly representations of Elizabeth I. In this gynocentric cult of an unmarried queen, the emphasis of the love discourses upon masculine subjectivity was to be seriously undermined. Yet the prominence earlier accorded Diana in French absolutism was an important prelude to this phenomenon.

A central theme which appears again and again in the ideologies of Renaissance absolutism relates to the divinely sanctioned power of their monarchs. As proof of this sacred character of their rule they were asserted to wield an especial authority over the natural world, comparable to that claimed by ecclesiastical authorities for the figure of Christ as a second Adam. Of course an emphasis upon the especial holiness of the Christian ruler was not new; it dated from the reign of the Emperor Constantine, and in France itself had been the basis of a cult of royalty in the high middle ages.[1] But the representation of Renaissance monarchs differed from that of their predecessors in two important respects. Firstly, these rulers justified their increased power by claiming that each one, individually, was inaugurating a second golden age in his territories. Secondly, in literature and art idealizing their sovereignty, a female rather than a male figure (and one derived from classical myth rather than from biblical sources), was often used to signify this new conception of their authority. The ruler's metamorphosis from ordinary man into a demi-god, which in religious terms was symbolized by the ritual of anointment at his coronation, was often implicitly attributed in French Renaissance literature and art to the transforming powers of a Diana-like beloved.[2] This paradoxical formulation was effectively at odds with a patriarchal conception of power. It would be taken further in literary representations of Elizabeth I, where use of the Diana image resulted in an exaggerated emphasis on the feminine gender of this sacred royal figure.

Frances Yates argued that there was one particular golden age myth which figured prominently in the Renaissance monarchs' idea of themselves: that connected with the figure of Astraea.[3] In fact, Astraea was not the only classical figure to appear in literature and art associated with Renaissance absolutism. In Renaissance France and England, while there are frequent references to Astraea, an especially prominent position was accorded to the Roman goddess Diana. Like Astraea, Diana was associated with an unfallen or redeemed natural world, signifying in her own bodily integrity the utopian possibility of a harmonious and undistorted relationship between spirit and matter. Her rulership of the moon suggested not only a quality of unearthly or heavenly purity, but also the ability to transmit this quality to the sublunary realm. In classical Greece, Diana's counterpart Artemis had shared with her brother Apollo the epithet *hagnos*: this conveyed the idea of a sphere of purity which was especially refined and sacred and was probably connected with these two gods' attributes of light.[4] Indeed, in the passage from Virgil's fourth eclogue which Yates cited as proof of the pre-eminent association of Astraea with classical ideas of absolute power, Astraea is only referred to indirectly, as 'Virgo', while both Diana and Apollo are mentioned by name. In her classical persona of Lucina, Diana was patroness of childbirth; in this passage, she is presented as the surrogate mother of a godlike ruler who will inaugurate a second golden age. This coming ruler is equated with her brother, the sun god Apollo. Yet he seems in this formulation to be *dependent* on his sister-as-mother, rather than her equal, for he requires her blessing to succeed in his task:

> Ultima Cumaei venit iam carminis aetas,
> magnus ab integro saeculorum nascitur ordo,
> iam redit et Virgo, redeunt Saturnia regna;

iam nova progenies caelo demittitur alto.
tu modo nascenti puero, quo ferrea primum
desinet ac toto surget gens aurea mundo,
casta fave Lucina: tuus iam regnat Apollo.

(Now is come the last age of the Song of Cumae; the great line of the centuries begins anew. Now the Virgin returns, the reign of Saturn returns; Now a new generation descends from heaven on high. Only do thou, pure Lucina, smile on the birth of the child, under whom the iron brood shall first cease, and a golden race spring up throughout the world. Thine own Apollo now is king!)[5]

Unlike the figure of Astraea, Diana was regarded as a maternal protectress of the Roman people long before the establishment of Imperial rule, as for example in a poem written by Catullus in the time of Julius Caesar, where he asked her: 'as of old thou wert wont, with good help keep safe the race of Romulus'.[6] Her prominence in the ideology of the Roman state dated back to its early republican history. Originally a local woodland goddess in the Italian region of Aricia, Diana's image was the second to be introduced in Rome, around 550 BCE (that of Jupiter came first).[7] Her Arician cult, centred upon the district of Nemi, appears to have appealed especially to women, but also to slaves and members of the plebeian class, and this non-patrician character of the pre-Roman goddess seems to have survived in her early worship at Rome. Her principal festival at Rome was on the thirteenth of August, when slaves were granted a holiday (this feast day was later transformed by the Christian church into the chief festival of the Virgin Mary, the day of her Assumption). Something of this popular character of Diana certainly survived in the middle ages, when in many treatises upon witchcraft she was referred to as the patroness of peasant women thought to be witches.[8] And as I shall show, even when reappropriated as a symbol of empire by certain Renaissance states, the figure of Diana retained a trace of ambiguity which often seemed at odds with the hierarchical and patriarchal power that her image was being used to affirm. But in spite of her popular and republican associations, Diana's political importance in Imperial Rome was considerable, and undoubtedly greater than that of the less complex figure of Astraea. In 17 BCE, when the Emperor Augustus reinstituted the Secular Games, a festival celebrating the preservation of the state, Horace's festival ode honoured Diana and her brother Phoebus Apollo above all the other gods of Rome, as protectors of the Roman state.[9] Also from the time of Augustus, Diana began to appear frequently on Roman imperial coinage, often in identification with some female member of the imperial family, and frequently in her persona of Diana Lucifera or Lucina, holding a torch to signify, on the one hand her connection with light, on the other her rulership of childbirth.[10] In other words, from her early role as a maternal guide and protector of the Roman state Diana came to be used, together with Phoebus Apollo, to assert the legitimacy of its imperial rulers. Later Roman emperors became increasingly identified with the sun–moon symbol.[11] They used this not only to define their power as divinely sanctioned, but also to justify their aspirations (and as directed by them, the aspirations of their state) to 'universal' power.[12]

The representation of the goddess Diana within the ideologies of French and English absolutism has certain features in common with their use of the image of Astraea, as discussed by Yates: Diana too is used to offer a spiritual legitimation of earthly power. Yet her significance is both more complex and more personal than that of Astraea, and affords a better insight into the curious conception of gender roles which underpinned this strand of absolutist ideology. Whereas Astraea was often used in the Renaissance to signify the public role of the absolute monarch and as a dispenser of a heavenly justice, Diana was used in both France and England to explore a more mysterious dimension to this role. For the absolute monarch's divine right was held to be dependent on their possession of a privileged mystical relationship with the *corpus mysticum* or immortal body politic of the state.[13] In religious and juristic terms, this mystical union was deemed to have been enacted at the coronation, where the chief prelate of the realm placed a ring on the new monarch's finger.[14] But in literature and art of the French and English Renaissance, the meaning of this union was re-explored through the mythology of Diana, whose chastity becomes the symbol for the inviolable sanctity of the state. The monarch's relationship to this goddess was used to define him or her as a contemplative figure who had an intimate experience of divine love, and who consequently possessed an inner spiritual purity consistent with the exaggerated powers which he or she claimed. This interior perfection was attributed, however, not to conventional religious practices, but to the cultivation of attitudes encoded in the love discourses. In France, the male ruler was represented as a type of Petrarchan or Neoplatonic lover, and his uneasy combination of human with divine attributes was figured by the different mythological guises in which he courted his realm as the goddess Diana. In Elizabethan England, Elizabeth's choice of 'marriage with my kingdom' united female monarch with feminine realm, and compelled consideration of the unsettling phenomenon of the feminine in relationship to itself. In each context, Diana was used to relate the monarch's private emotional, sexual, and spiritual identity to his or her political role and to his or her 'kingdom' – which in this context might justly be termed a 'queendom', in so far as it was gendered feminine.[15]

The powers of the French monarchs who were especially closely associated with the figure of Diana – François I and Henri II – were extensive.[16] Although the idea of the monarch's divine right was not articulated in France until the 1580s, there were some influential exponents of the doctrine of royal absolutism in early sixteenth-century France, and before the Wars of Religion the development of the French state in this direction seemed to be proceeding fairly smoothly.[17] By the end of the fifteenth century, the French realm included all the feudal provinces of medieval France under a single monarch, although it did not yet amount to a fully centralized state. There had also been a considerable increase increase in the French crown's control of French ecclesiastical affairs. The Concordat of Bologna, signed between François I and Pope Leo X in 1516, increased the king's power to nominate to French bishoprics and abbeys; during the reigns both of François and of Henri II, royal control of the ecclesiastical hierarchy in France was virtually complete. For this reason, neither François nor his son had need of the Reformation to strengthen their hand in religious matters. In fact, during Henri's reign, literary references to his connection (through his mistress, Diane de Poitiers) with Diana's virtuous chastity often seem connected with his vehement persecution of Protestants: a policy of militant Catholicism – or intolerance – which Diane de Poitiers and her relations the Guise family did much to encourage.[18] Ironically, when the idea of religious purity was implied in comparisons of Elizabeth I to Diana a few decades later, the religion in question was Protestantism rather than Catholicism.

While strengthening their powers at home, both François I and Henri II were eager to expand their territories and their self-images as monarchs. Their nostalgia for the code of medieval chivalry resulted in several costly and fruitless wars in Italy, but testified to the concern of both father and son to affirm their importance upon the international as well as the national scene. It seems to have been partly due to such imperialist urges that sixteenth-century French kings were frequently connected with the figure of the Greek hero Hercules, often used in the Renaissance to signify an engagement with the active life as privileged by humanism.[19] Yet Hercules had other, more complex connotations in Renaissance mythography. He was seen as an emblem not only of man's physical powers, but also of an unrestrained phallic sexuality, signified by his massive club. As such he had a connection with the lustful satyr or wild man of Greek and medieval folklore, and in some contexts, with the figure of Actaeon.[20] At the same time, he was linked with the sun god Apollo, in his guise of Hercules Musagetes, for this was Apollo's title as leader of the Muses.[21] Both of these seemingly contradictory associations, on the one hand with an earth-bound masculinity overdetermined by genital heterosexuality, and on the other with a fiery spiritual being, centred in a transformed or resurrected body, are implicit in Hercules' description in Castiglione's *Il Cortegiano*. In the culminating speech

attributed to Pietro Bembo, the mythical hero is cited as an example of
the purification of man's fallen nature through the fire of a divine or
Platonic passion, which metamorphoses man into god:

> And therefore, as commune fire trieth gold and maketh it fyne, so this
> most holye fire in soules destroyeth and consumeth whatsoever there is
> mortall in them, and relieveth and maketh beawtyfull the heavenlye
> part, whyche at the first by reason of the sense was dead and buried in
> them. This is the great fire in the whiche (the Poetes wryte) that
> *Hercules* was burned on the topp of the monntaigne *Oeta*: and through
> that consumynge with fire, after hys death was holye and immortall.[22]

The representation of Diana in connection with these kings referred in
different ways to many aspects of their rule. For example, when she is
connected with the French nation, her chastity implicitly stresses not just
the immortality of its mystical body, but also its recent unification by the
Valois. At the same time, she is also used to elaborate a new image of the
king's identity, suited to the expansion of his political authority as also to
the increase in his control over religious affairs; an increasing emphasis
upon the religious or spiritual role of the monarch appears to have been a
necessary prelude to the emergence of a full-blown theory of divine right
in both France and England. In fact, much of the importance attributed
to the Diana figure within the discourse of French absolutism appears to
be due to the capacity of this image to function as a link or mediating
term between the two different ideas of the male monarch to which I
referred above. In her role as an object of desire, Diana relates the
persona of the monarch as a Hercules or Actaeon, an active and virile
man, to his emergent but still ill-defined role as another Apollo, 'le roi
soleil' – a figure accorded contemplative and godlike attributes consistent
with the claim that his rule is divinely legitimated. Thus in French
'courtly' representations of his courtship of a Diana figure, the male
monarch was often identified with the aspiring lover of Petrarchism and
Neoplatonism, as another Actaeon; and this role was also hinted at in his
connection with Hercules. Yet he was also equated with the lover's
ultimate goal, the Platonic One whose light was mirrored by the idealized
beloved and who was often compared to Apollo as the sun.

In that the king was simultaneously seen as below and beyond his
Diana-like beloved, as a servant who was also a master, this use of
Petrarchan and Neoplatonic attitudes appears to reaffirm the masculine
self-reflexivity of those systems. But although Diana's beauty and
brilliance is often stated or implied to be dependent upon her royal lover,
it is usually her figure which is most clearly represented and defined in
these representations. The monarch's identity (whether as human lover or
supreme transcendent principle) is typically gestured towards and evoked
through her. This indirect construction of the masculine subject as ruler,

through the mediation of this feminine image of state power, parallels the formulations of Petrarchism and Neoplatonism proper. On one level, the circuitous mode of representation invests the monarch with an elusive and immaterial quality appropriate to his identification (as another Apollo) with the Platonic One. None the less, it accords to the primary signifier of his political authority, a Diana-like beloved, an importance she had not formerly enjoyed in the discourses of love.

The first example that I have been able to find of Diana's appearance within the discourse of an emergent French absolutism occurs in Pierre Gringore's pageants for the entry of Mary Tudor into Paris in 1514, as the new bride of Louis XII. (Given the later prominence of the same image within the cult of the last Tudor monarch, it is interesting to note that this reference appears in a pageant to celebrate the entry of the French king's English and Tudor bride, who was sister to Elizabeth I's father, Henry VIII.) The choice of Diana to signify the French nation was clearly related in part to her classical role as a patroness of nature. But her association with the moon was also important for Gringore's comparison, since this attribute meant that her reflection of the light of her brother Phoebus Apollo (as the sun) could be presented as an image of the idealized relationship which was held to exist between France and her monarch. The interpreter of Gringore's sixth pageant explained the presence of Phoebus and Diana as follows: 'par Phebus humble et doux/ Dyana est en terre reluysant/. . .Phoebus est roy qui domine sur nous./Et Dyana est France la fertille.'[23] ('Through the humble and gentle rays of Phoebus, Diana shines on earth . . . Phoebus is the king who rules over us, and Diana is fertile France.') No connection was made here between Diana and Mary (understandably, given her English nationality); instead the foreign queen was compared to 'stella maris', a star of the sea which receives light from both Phoebus and Diana as sun and moon. Nor was Diana seen here as an object of idealized love. Some twenty years later, in the 1533 entry of Eleanor, queen of François I, to Lyons, the queen was herself identified with Diana, but this comparison was still uninformed by Petrarchan or Neoplatonic attitudes.[24]

Then during the 1530s what was possibly the first artistic representation of Diana in the French Renaissance appeared at the king's rebuilt hunting lodge of Fontainebleau (plate 5): this was a painting by the Italian artist Rosso within one of the cartouches in the château's Galerie François Ier.[25] Rosso's 'Diana' was subsequently painted over, but in the 1540s the goddess became a dominant image in the art of Fontainebleau. Around the middle of that decade, Benvenuto Cellini's 'Nymph' was completed; this bronze figure of Diana, nude and embracing a stag, which appears to have been influenced by the painting of Rosso, was placed on the main gate of the château, the Porte Dorée. Within the château, the fabulous Galerie d'Ulysse included thirteen panels depicting Diana; while in its

Appartement des Bains, the decorative theme was the story of Callisto, a nymph of Diana who was seduced by Jupiter and discovered by the goddess to be pregnant while she was bathing. The designs of both these rooms were part of a decorative programme conceived by another Italian painter, Primaticcio, who replaced Rosso as artistic director at Fontaine-bleau in 1540.

Like earlier Italian art of the Renaissance, the decorations of Fontainebleau appear to have been influenced by Petrarchan and Neoplatonic attitudes; by the 1540s these had begun to make a significant impact upon French literary culture.[26] In Maurice Scève's *Délie* (1544), the first French poetic text (that is, the first one written in the vernacular rather than Latin) to be influenced by these attitudes, Diana was used as a persona for the Petrarchan or Neoplatonic beloved. Two years previously, in 1542, Castiglione's *Il Cortegiano* had been translated into French. In fact, this book had made a fundamental distinction between the roles of courtier and monarch, for the skills that it recommended to the courtier (which included the art of Neoplatonic love) were designed to further the humanist aim of influencing the prince or ruler. At Fontainebleau, however, it was François who was placed in the role of lover, with Diana as the most frequent and most venerated object of his devotion. As a hunting lodge, the palace was of course dedicated to that art which Diana patronized, and which was then a favourite diversion of the French aristocracy. None the less, given the idealizing emphasis of absolutist ideology, it is somewhat surprising to find that the mythological associations of Diana with activity and aggression (which so often proved problematic when treated in Renaissance literature), figured prominently in the art of Fontainebleau, although usually these were treated indirectly. The recumbent form of Rosso's 'Diana' and Cellini's 'Nymph' appears at first sight to present Diana as a passive object of pursuit or desire. But her embrace of the stag which she usually hunts reminds the observer of the goddess' metamorphosis of Actaeon, and so of an alternative hunt of love, in which she has the initiative. Later artists of the French Renaissance produced numerous images of a reclining Diana who often embraced a stag ('Diane caressant un cerf') or a hound (plate 6). Equally popular were representations of the goddess bathing, which inevitably recalled the occasion upon which Actaeon observed her naked body, and which sometimes inserted the figure of the royal lover himself as Actaeon, as in François Clouet's 'Le Bain de Diane' (plate 7). Here the contemporary attire of Henri II, juxtaposed with the nymphs and satyrs who surround his mistress Diane de Poitiers as another Diana, asserts an uneasy homology between mythic and historical event.[27]

The privileging of the female nude within the art of Fontainebleau points to an important difference between the literary articulation of Neoplatonic and Petrarchan attitudes and their appropriation by a visual system of signification. The idealized masculine identity elaborated within Petrarchan poetics and Neoplatonic philosophy required the mediation of a female beloved; but the power of their masculine subjects depended on an evasion of the female body as erotic object. The mere fantasy of seeing Laura's nakedness had filled Petrarch with fear that he would suffer the punishment of Actaeon. Bembo too, in *Gli Asolani*, had used this myth to warn against a failure of sexual sublimation on the part of the Neoplatonic lover. In contrast, the introduction of female nudes into paintings which appear to explore the Platonic meanings of certain myths suggests not the sacrifice of body to spirit, but a disturbing fusion of these two dimensions. The aristocratic patron for whom they were painted is consequently constructed both as privileged voyeur (another Actaeon) and as an interpreter of divine mysteries. The multiple repetitions of the encounter of Diana and Actaeon in the art of Fontainebleau push this apparent contradiction to its limit, by representing the tabooed object of sexual desire in relation to the very myth which told of the punishment of this transgression.

The 'absolute' masculine subject which is addressed and implicitly reconstructed through the art of Fontainebleau, while defined as a type of Neoplatonic or Petrarchan lover, is consequently formed through an encounter with that principle of sexual difference, of female otherness, which literary Petrarchism and Neoplatonism were most concerned to avoid. This artistic emphasis was probably indebted to religious recuperations of the Diana–Actaeon myth in fourteenth- and fifteenth-century commentaries upon Ovid's *Metamorphoses*, which had interpreted Actaeon's fate as an allegory of Christ's incarnation.[28] Behind them seems also to lurk the biblical text of the Song of Solomon, whose explicit sexual imagery had been explained by Christian commentators as an allegory of the union of Christ with the soul. Not only had this text compared the male beloved to a roe or hart, it had described him in curiously feminine terms. But the conception of the monarch's identity implied in the art of Fontainebleau foreshadows the version of Neoplatonic love which would be formulated by Giordano Bruno only later in the century. In Bruno's *De Gli Eroici Furori* (The heroic frenzies), the 'heroic' role of the male lover involves the annihilation of a masculine identity founded on a specifically phallic sexuality. This requires him not to *evade* but to directly *encounter* woman as alien and other. The lover's re-enactment of the myth of Actaeon leads to his refashioning in the image of his desire (in that the stag was one of the totemic animals of Diana):

Actaeon represents the intellect intent upon the capture of divine wisdom and the comprehension of the divine beauty. . . . Therefore Actaeon, who with these thoughts, his dogs, searched for goodness, wisdom, beauty and the wild beast outside himself, attained them in this way. Once he was in their presence, ravished outside of himself by so much beauty, he became the prey of his thoughts and saw himself converted into the thing he was pursuing.[29]

It seems that it is only after this traumatic experience of loss, in which the male is 'ravished' in place of the female – that the aspiring lover can arrive at 'the principal god, Apollo, who with his unborrowed splendor transmits his arrows in every direction, that is, his rays, which are the innumerable species and marks of the divine goodness, intelligence, beauty and wisdom'.[30] For the restrictive definition of self founded on the singular power of the phallus is substituted a more complex image of masculinity and its possible pleasures. This involves a diffusion or extension of identity and of desire in multiple directions.

It is interesting to note, however, that although the imagery of François I's Fontainebleau persistently gestures towards the apotheosis of the monarch, its attention is directed more to the means of such a transformation – the mystical encounter with a Diana-like beloved – than to the end of his Platonic quest. Apparently the idea of 'le roi soleil' was still in its infancy. Only in Primaticcio's Galerie d'Ulysse did Diana's brother Apollo receive as much attention as Diana herself. There, as well as appearing separately in several works, brother and sister were depicted together in five different paintings.[31] One of the three central ceiling panels in the gallery was of Apollo with the Muses upon Parnassus, probably in compliment to François I's superlative performance of the courtly role of Renaissance patron of the arts.[32] But Apollo was most often represented in the Galerie d'Ulysse in his role of sun god: a reminder of the king's claim (shared with other 'absolute' monarchs of the Renaissance) to be ushering in a new golden age. Following the accession of François' son, Henri II, in 1547, this idea of 'le roi soleil' was to be somewhat further developed in several literary and artistic works which made more explicit use of Neoplatonic and Petrarchan attitudes in order to compliment a male monarch. Yet in that context the dependence of this idealized image upon the female beloved was still more apparent: the cult of Henri II as an 'absolute' monarch was integrally related to the many extravagant visual and literary compliments which compared his mistress, Diane de Poitiers, to the classical goddess.

The French critic Françoise Bardon suggested that the historical figure of Diane de Poitiers was both the centre and source of French Renaissance interest in Diana.[33] There is in fact some evidence that Rosso's lost Diana was originally a compliment to this woman, who was a leading favourite at the court of François I before she attracted the attentions of the then Dauphin Henri (some twenty years younger than herself). However Bardon neglected to note that the goddess Diana was associated with France as early as 1514; in fact she gave no indication that the image's cultural prominence might have been determined by a complex of political as well as aesthetic considerations. In the personal case of Diane de Poitiers, celebration of this lady as Diana was by no means a 'natural' phenomenon, but a highly artificial act of propaganda. If the accident of her name allowed a convenient identification with the goddess already identified with France, none the less this identification seems to have been quite deliberately promoted. In the first instance, this may have been as part of an attempt to elide the fact of her clearly unchaste relationship with the Dauphin (she bore him several children), and to arrest the flow of satiric attacks upon the favourite, which dated from 1538, the beginning of her influence upon Henri.[34] Many of these attacks emphasized the gap of twenty years which divided the couple. The poet Clement Marot, for example, asked: 'Que voulez, Diane bonne,/ Que vous donne?/Vous n'eustes, comme j'entens,/Jamais tant d'heur au printemps/Qu'en Autonne.'[35] ('What, good Diana, do you wish to be given? You never had, as I hear, as much happiness in the spring of your years as you have in your life's autumn.')

In the mid 1540s, Diane de Poitiers' position of influence became ever more secure. In his 'Eclogue sur la naissance du filz de Monseigneur le Dauphin', written in 1544 shortly before Henri's accession, Marot had clearly abandoned his earlier attitude towards the royal mistress. It is she, rather than the mother of Henri's son, Catherine de' Medici, who is complimented in the poem. Marot associates the child's birth with the advent of a new golden age, and although the figure of Astraea is mentioned, it is Diane de Poitiers as the goddess Diana who is accorded the role of chief dea-ex-machina:

> Or sommes nous prochains du dernier aage
> Prophetizé par Cumane, la saige;
> Des siecles longs le plus grand et le chef
> Commencer veult à naistre de rechef.
> La vierge Astrée en bref temps reviendra;
> De Saturnus le regne encore viendra;
> Puis que le Ciel, lequel se renouvelle,
> Nous ha pourveuz de lignée nouvelle.
> Diane clére ha de la sus donne
> Faveur celeste à l'Enfant nouveau né
> D'Endymion; à l'Enfant voyrement
> Dessoubz lequel fauldra premierement
> La Gent de Fer, & puis par tout le Monde
> S'eslevera la Gent d'Or pur et munde.[36]

(Now we approach the last age which the wise Cumaean Sybil prophesied. The greatest and the chief of many centuries is impatient to burst suddenly into life. The virgin Astraea will soon return,

Saturn's reign will come again; for a new day has given us a new line of kings. Bright Diana has here on earth bestowed a heavenly blessing upon the child recently born to Endymion: behold the child during whose rule there will arise first the race of Iron and then, throughout all the world, the pure and chaste race of Gold.)

Since Henri was not yet king, he is described here not as Apollo but as Endymion, whose love of Diana was often interpreted in the Renaissance as a Platonic allegory of divine inspiration.[37] The poem also echoes the passage from Virgil's *Eclogues* quoted earlier, where Diana's role in the restoration of the golden age, in her persona of Lucina, patroness of childbirth, and in association with Apollo, was stressed. After Henri's accession, his mistress was often associated with this role of Diana Lucina or Lucifera, as a light-bearer who was also mother of creatures and so patroness of childbirth – a classical equivalent to the folk-tale figure of the fairy godmother. This poetic displacement of the real mother was based on fact: Henri had made his mistress 'gouvernante' of the royal children, so that it was she, rather than the queen, who engaged their tutors and nurses and generally supervised their upbringing. Marot's intriguing suggestion, that the 'divine' qualities of Henri's children (in other words, their dynastic claims) derive from their nursing or fostering by a Diana figure, was elaborated visually in several paintings. These transferred the medieval motif of Sapientia dispensing wisdom from her breast to the representative of the classical goddess. François Clouet painted a picture of 'Diane de Poitiers donnant une nourrice au Duc d'Alençon devant la cour de France', and a similar study of 'Diane de Poitiers et la famille de Henri II' was produced by an anonymous artist of the Franco-Flemish school. The same motif was introduced into several portraits of half-naked ladies at their toilettes (works which could also be seen as variations upon the theme of 'Diane au bain' so popular among artists of the School of Fontainebleau), and it seems also to be played upon, albeit with slightly different connotations, in the picture of 'Diana' reproduced on the cover of this book. Thus in the cult of Diane de Poitiers, the maternal attributes of the female beloved which the love discourses had censored or elided emerge into startling prominence.

Throughout the reign of Henri II, Diane de Poitiers as the goddess Diana was seen in both literature and art as an extremely powerful mediator of the king's authority. These representations were in general much more explicit than those created at Fontainebleau during the reign of François I. In Henri's spectacular entry to the city of Lyons in 1548, Diana tamed a lion (intended to represent the city) in imitation of Hercules, and presented this to the king. In other words, she symbolically usurped the Herculean role often favoured by French monarchs. And as at least some of the onlookers must have been aware. Henri used the lion as his own heraldic device.[38] At Rome, later the same year, the goddess appeared in triumphs celebrating the birth of Henri's second son. When the king entered Rouen a year later, one of the episodes in the spectacle presented to him was of Orpheus taming animals with his music, and singing 'le chante de Diane': 'Ne seras-tu pas compagne/O Diane/A louer la majesté/Du Roi, qui ton croissant porte/Et supporte ta vertu de chasteté?'[39] ('Diana! Will you not help me to praise the majesty of that king who bears your crescent moon, and who protects your virtuous chastity?') The reference here is to Henri's adoption of the goddess' emblem of the waxing crescent moon as his personal device. This royal device appears to have had several forms. In *Le Recueil des inscriptions* of Etienne Jodelle, three different versions were listed: a crescent moon lying on its back; three interlaced crescents; a crescent moon merging into a sun disc animated by a face.[40] The motto of the first device was usually given as 'Donec totum impleat orbem.' ('Until it fills the whole globe.') Jodelle gave the motto of the last device as 'Quum plena est, fit aemula solis.' ('When it is full, it becomes the rival of the sun.') These mottoes offer a good illustration of the expansionist aspirations (religious as well as political) which were connected with this privileging of the figure of Diana in Henri's reign.[41] But they also reveal the extent to which his image as a male monarch was subordinated to a feminine symbol, by its more frequent identification with the figure of Diana than with her solar brother.

Diane de Poitiers herself certainly did her utmost to increase the importance of the goddess Diana in the mythology of French absolutism, by means of a highly self-conscious identification with the classical figure. From 1549 onwards, the best architects, artists, and sculptors were summoned to her new château of Anet (a gift from her royal lover) to inscribe Diana's mythology there: on canvas, on tapestry, and on stone. A faintly ironic view of this project is indicated in a sonnet by Joachim Du Bellay, which ostensibly compliments both Anet and its mistress:

De vostre Dianet (de vostre nom j'appelle
Vostre maison d'Anet) la belle architecture,
Les marbres animez, la vivante peinture,
Qui le font estimer des maisons la plus belle:

Les beaux lambriz dorez, la luisante chappelle
Les superbes dongeons, la riche couverture,
Le jardin tapissé d'eternelle verdure,
Et la vive fonteine a la source immortelle:

Ces ouvrages (Madame) à qui bien les contemple,
Rapportant de l'antiq' le plus parfait exemple,
Monstrent un artifice et depense admirable.

> Mais ceste grand' doulceur jointe à ceste haultesse,
> Et ceste Astre benin joint à ceste sagesse,
> Trop plus que tout cela vous font emerveillable.[42]

(The fair architecture, the lifelike statues and vivid paintings at your 'Dianet' (for I call your château of Anet by your name), make it esteemed as the fairest of houses. The beautiful gilded panelling, the gleaming chapel, the superb turrets, the fine roofs, the garden carpeted with an unfading green, and the living fountain of immortal life: these works, madam, which offer a perfect example of the antique style, are proof of wonderful contrivance and expenditure. But it is your joining of great sweetness with nobility, and your kindly Star combined with such wisdom, that makes you especially worthy of admiration.)

In the two quatrains which comprise the sonnet's octet, the artistry of the château is praised for its naturalness. Du Bellay describes Anet as a place where Diane (as Diana) has restored paradise and the spiritual gift of immortality associated with man's pre-lapsarian existence, by a magical use of art. At the same time, his description of the fountain as a source of eternal life would have inevitably reminded a reader of the widespread speculations that Diane used witchcraft to preserve her appeal to a lover twenty years younger than herself. Although the sestet contains an implicit comparison of Diane to Astraea ('your kindly Star'), together with compliments to her wisdom and nobility, it also makes it clear that Anet's naturalness is an illusion, created by 'a wonderful contrivance and expenditure'. While complimenting Diane's *imitation* of the antique style, Du Bellay refuses to identify her completely with the classical world she has tried to recreate at Anet. The château may resemble paradise, yet in Du Bellay's eyes Diane is clearly a goddess of art (and artifice) rather than one of nature.

Decorated with images reminiscent of the ideals of medieval chivalry as well as many from classical myth, Anet certainly situated the relationship of king and royal favourite within an artificial version of history, one from which the imperfections of a nation's lived historical reality had been excluded. Over the gateway of the château was placed Cellini's Nymph of Fontainebleau; in its two courtyards were fountains with figures of Diana. Inside were numerous tapestries and pictures treating different aspects of the figure's mythology, and numerous engravings of the symbols and devices associated with the goddess: in particular, the crescent moon which had now become a royal device. Sadly, little of this decorative enterprise now survives. The sculptures which were made by Jean Goujon and Germaine Pilon for the gateway and fountains respectively still remain, along with some of the smaller pieces of craftsmanship contained in the château – for example, six plates engraved by Etienne Delaune with the history of Apollo and Diana. We know that the tapestries which decorated many of the château walls probably included a series treating the mythology of Diana designed by Jean Cousin, as well as a famous sequence, conceived by Etienne Duvet, which associated Henri and Diane, not with Diana and Actaeon, but with a medieval tale which closely paralleled the classical myth, that of the virgin and the unicorn. But there is no detailed record of the paintings which hung there, and our knowledge of the engraved work at Anet is entirely dependent upon the records made by the architect, Philibert de l'Orme.[43] We do know, however, that one of Diane de Poitiers' clients, the scholar Gabriel Symeoni, conceived a series of emblematic images for the château, several of which depicted the relationship of Henri and Diane as that of Apollo and Diana. He left a description and interpretation of three sculptures placed in the lower galleries around part of Anet's garden.[44]

The first of the sculptures described by Symeoni was of a woman in a chariot drawn by a stag and a boar. He said that the woman represented the grounds of Anet, the animals its denizens (proof of the château's suitability for hunting, a favourite pursuit of Diane and Henri, like most members of their class). The second sculpture was of the king, with a sunburst about his head, in a chariot drawn by a lion and a lamb. Symeoni described the two animals as representing Henri's combination of the kingly qualities of force and gentleness, and apparently the imagery was also related to aspects of the king's horoscope; however, the juxtaposition of these two animals also had apocalyptic overtones. The third figure was of the goddess Diana, in a chariot drawn by a hind and a bull, and holding a globe or golden apple in one hand, a torch in the other. According to Symeoni, the globe represented Diane de Poitiers' wealth and power, the torch the radiance of the goddess Diana (in her persona of Lucifera); but this symbolism also closely parallels the orb and sceptre of the monarch. Again, it is the goddess (and her human namesake), rather than Henri himself, who is the bearer of royal authority. In connection with this sculpture's theme of worldly power, it is noteworthy that both the globe and the torch often appeared in medieval representations of the Wisdom figure. At the same time, the mistress' fantasized usurpation of royal status is indicated here by Diana/Diane's presence in a 'char de triomphe' similar to those used in royal entries and festivals: triumphal processions where in reality she occupied a position inferior to that of the queen, Catherine de' Medici.

A similar conception to that implied in Symeoni's sculpture, of Diana–Diane as the active agent of her lover's royal power, was explored in a sonnet written about Diane de Poitiers by the leading court poet of the day, Pierre de Ronsard:

> Tout ainsi que la Lune en s'aprochant aupres
>   Du Soleil prend clarté, vertu, force & puissance:

> Puis s'eslongnant de luy, d'une douce influence
> Et Ciel, & Terre, & Mer elle nourrist apres:
> Ainsi nostre Soleil, vous ornant de ses rais,
> Vous fait par tout verser un bon heur en la France. . . .[45]

(Just as the moon, by coming close to the sun, receives brightness, virtue, strength, and power, and as she moves away from him, with her gentle beams nourishes the sky, the earth, and sea, so in the same way our sun, by adorning you with his rays, enables you to spread happiness all across France. . . .)

The relationship described here between Apollo and Diana, or sun and moon, differs slightly from that delineated in Gringore's 1514 pageant, since in Ronsard's poem Diana does not represent France itself. Instead, in her lunar role she is depicted as an intervening veil or mirror between king and country, sun and earth: the vital transmitter of the French Apollo's light to his subjects.

As Terence Cave has shown. Ronsard was especially interested in the mythology of Apollo, whom he saw as 'le roi des poètes', and to whom he often compared himself: 'Je resemble . . . au Prestre d'Apollon.' ('I am like Apollo's priest.')[46] The emergent idea of the king as comparable to a god who was also, after all, leader of the Muses, certainly created a *potential* identity of interest between male poet and male monarch. Yet the absence of any developed poetic use of this image in relation to Henri suggests some dissatisfaction with his actual performance as a patron of the arts and of humanism – a role which his father François I had played admirably. In his 'Ode au Roy Henri II', Ronsard's comparison of the king to Apollo is a direct appeal for patronage: 'Mais, ô Phebus, authorise/Mon chant, & le favorise.'[47] ('But Phoebus, sanction my poetry: give it your blessing.') When Joachim Du Bellay appealed to Diane de Poitiers (as 'holy Diana') to stimulate the king's patronage of the arts, he contrasted this (implicitly undeveloped) aspect of the king with his virtue and his martial courage: 'Faites, Diane saincte/Que ce roy vertueux/Après la force, ésteinte/De mars l'impetueux,/Escoute quelquefois/Des neuf muses la voix.'[48] ('Holy Diana, once the impetuous vigour of Mars has been expended, encourage this virtuous king to listen occasionally to the voice of the nine Muses.') Of course there is a sexual innuendo in this appeal. Just as their sexual union enabled Venus briefly to dominate Mars, according to Renaissance interpretations of the classical myth, so it is when Henry's physical 'force' has been exhausted in erotic pleasure that he is likely to be submissive to his mistress' 'holy' control. Perhaps he may then be willing to transfer his attention from phallic sexual conquest to a different mode of pleasure, centred on the receptive organ of the ear.

While Henri was apparently not enough of an Apollo in his attitude to the arts, he seems to have taken the god's association with the spiritual or religious aspects of kingship more seriously. But even this expressed itself in rigid and indeed martial terms, through a violent defence of Catholic orthodoxy. Perhaps Henri's lack of comprehension of the humanist ideas to which many contemporary intellectuals subscribed (Catholic as well as Protestant) was partly responsible for his ferocious persecution of French Protestants. None the less, this policy was vigorously encouraged by his much more cultivated favourite, and by her kinsmen the Guise. It made the royal mistress extremely unpopular in certain circles. But as I mentioned earlier, while the courtly idea of Diana implicitly focuses on her destructive powers, these were seldom dealt with directly. At François' Fontainebleau, images of Diana had largely avoided the attributes of the goddess associated with her persona of Hecate, goddess of the waning moon, of death, the underworld, and witchcraft. Two exceptions to this rule, however, were paintings executed by Primaticcio for the Salle du Bal at Fontainebleau: 'Diane dans un char attelé de dragons' and 'Diane–Hecate avec Cerbère et l'Amour'.[49] During the reign of Henri II, artistic representations which emphasized the connection between Diana and Hecate were still rare. But poetic interest in this aspect of the female beloved had developed following the publication of Maurice Scève's *Délie* in 1544.

Although Scève had occasional interactions with the world of the court, *Délie* was not a product of court patronage; this left the poet free to explore the figure of the female beloved in terms which were not consistently idealizing.[50] The sequence was influenced by both Petrarchism and Neoplatonism. But Scève's poetic emphasis on the bodily reality of woman paralleled the image of Diana privileged within the framework of French absolutism; indeed, it could be said to be its underside. Scève's unifying theme, of the moon's ever-changing cycle, invests his Délie with a sinister quality which is closely connected with her psychological and bodily mutability, and with a mysterious sexuality which he seems unable to control. One of his poems, for example, used the image of a 'stained' moon to suggest a variety of meanings, from a simple change of mood which mirrors the lunar phases to a more physical metamorphosis. Here the colour red, which appeared so rarely in Petrarch's *Rime Sparse*, is briefly privileged, as the possibility of his beloved's concealment of some sexual intrigue taints Scève's idea of her 'white' purity and faithfulness The spotting of Délie's moon (or womb) with blood suggests on one level her continued chastity (or refusal to conceive), as manifested in the event of menstruation. Yet as her 'stained faith', it also hints at Scève's suspicion of a possible end to that chastity, in a sexual initiation from which he has been excluded. Whatever its hidden meaning, Délie's feminine stain or wound is displaced to become an image of the hurt it inflicts on the lover:

Quant de ton rond le pur cler se macule,
Ta foy tachée alors ie me presage:
Quand, pallissant, du blanc il se recule,
Ie me fais lors de pleurs prochaines sage,
　Quand il rougit en Martial visage,
I'ouvre les ventz a mes souspirs espaiz:
　Mais ie m'asseure a l'heure de ma paix,
Quand ie te voy en ta face seraine
Parquoy du bien alors ie me repais,
De quel tu es sur toutes soveraine.[51]

(When your pure clear orb becomes spotted, I have a presentiment of your stained faith; when, as it wanes, its white colour fades, I remind myself that tears are near; when it reddens with a warlike expression, I breathe thick and gusty sighs. But I am certain that a peaceful hour will come, when I see you with a serene demeanour; on that good face I feast my soul, the face which sets you above all others.)

At the close, the poet is able to use the regularity of the moon's lunar cycle to affirm that 'a peaceful hour' will return, when the moon is clear and full and bright; none the less he recognizes that he cannot permanently separate this from the other, less pleasing, faces of his beloved. Scève's poem thus offers a striking comment upon the problematic duality of a Petrarchan beloved who is both red and white: a flesh and blood woman as well as an idealized concept.

A French Renaissance poet who seems to have been strongly influenced by Scève's view of the beloved was Etienne Jodelle, who made Diana's more aggressive attributes central to several poems. In the following sonnet, he presented the goddess as overriding masculine authority in the domain of Greek myth. It invests the hunt of Diana with a macabre and gloomy menace, and with a seemingly gratuitous cruelty:

Des astres, des forets, et d'Acheron l'honneur,
Diane, au Monde hault, moyen et bas preside,
Et ses chevaulx, ses chiens, ses Eumenides guide,
Pour esclairer, chasser, donner mort et horreur.

Tel est le lustre grand, la chasse, et la frayeur
Qu'on sent sous ta beauté claire, prompte, homicide,
Que le haut Jupiter, Phebus, et Pluton cuide,
Son fondre moins porter, son arc, et sa terreur.

Ta beauté par ses rais, par son retz, par la craincte
Rend l'ame esprise, prise, et au martyre estreinte:
Luy moy, pren moy, tien moy, mais hélas ne me pers.

Des flambans forts et griefs, feux, filez et encombres,

> Lune, Diane, Hecate, aux cieux, terre, et enfers
> Ornant, questant, genant, nos Dieux, nous, et nos ombres.[52]

(Diana is goddess of the stars, of the forests, and of Acheron. She rules the upper, the middle and the lower world. She sends her horses, her dogs, and her Furies to inspire, to pursue, and to bring death and horror. Such is the great light, the hunt and the dread which one senses beneath your bright, startling and murderous beauty, that Jupiter's thunder, Phoebus' bow and Pluto's terror seem less forceful. Your beauty, with its rays, its nets, and its dread, takes the startled soul prisoner, and condemns it to martyrdom. Enlighten me! Seize me! Keep me! But alas! do not destroy me with your fierce and tormenting torches, with your fires, your nets, and your traps. Luna, Diana, Hecate, ruler of sky, earth and hell! Who ornaments, then pursues, then tortures our Gods, us, and our shades.)

Jodelle's Diana is a goddess whose supernatural powers transcend conventional distinctions between good and evil, masculine and feminine; thus she is no longer even superficially subordinated to a masculine figure. The poet's use of parallelism and repetition to structure this experience increases rather than reduces our impression of Diana's boundless power. The parallel between her triple aspect (as Luna, Diana, and Hecate) and the three gods (Jupiter, Phoebus Apollo, and Pluto) suggests a definite tension between male and female deities. Yet the balance of power is tipped in favour of Diana; it is she who controls the three worlds of heaven, earth, and hell, inhabited by 'our Gods, us, and our shades'. Jodelle speaks of the impact of the goddess' aspect of pitiless and terrible destroyer upon the lover's soul. But the imagery of 'torture' and 'martyrdom' joins soul to body, and conjures up the spectre of a ceaseless subordination of masculine to feminine sexual desires in an upside-down otherworld.

Jodelle's poem did not associate Diana with Diane de Poitiers, but was written about another aristocratic woman, Claude-Catherine de Retz. Even in poetic compliments to the king's mistress, however, references to the death-dealing powers wielded by the classical goddess occasionally appeared. The poet Clement Marot, for example, might have exchanged a satiric for an ingratiating tone once Diane de Poitiers' power was secured, but some ambiguity appears to survive in this epigram:

> Le cler Phebus donne la vie & l'aise
> Par son baiser tant digne & precieux,
> Et mort devient ce que Diane baise.
> O dur baisser, rude & mal gracieux,
> Tu faiz venir ung desir soucieux
> De mieulx avoir, dont souvent on desvie.

>   Mais qui pourroit parvenir à ce mieulx,
>   Il n'est si mort qui ne revient en vie.[53]

(With his noble and precious kiss, bright Phoebus gives life and grace; one kissed by Diana dies. O harsh kiss, difficult and unfortunate favour, you create a painful longing to renew an experience which one should avoid. But one who can obtain this happiness will not perish without being restored to life.)

Marot's initial opposition between the clear and benign light of Phoebus as the sun and the fatal and sinister light of Diana as the moon hints at a desire to separate the qualities attributed to the monarch from those identified with his favourite, to focus directly on a masculine object of desire rather than its feminine mirror. The close of this opening sentence '. . . one kissed by Diana dies', implies a somewhat ironic perspective, not just on the destructive desires of the royal mistress, but on her role in their relationship: in other poems, Marot sometimes used 'baiser' in its crude colloquial sense of penetration.[54] Did he perhaps intend the meaning of his epigram to slide between courtly compliment and ribald speculation, between celebration of a mystical or Platonic union and satirization of a more earth-bound relationship, where the mistress was physically (rather than spiritually) 'on top'? In spite of the attempt in the last lines to idealize this imagery of death, the poem certainly leaves the reader in doubt as to the character of an erotic encounter with Diana. Does the death caused by her 'favour' really lead to Platonic renewal? Or merely to the res-erection of the male sexual member?

In 1559, Henri II died after a fatal jousting accident (he was 42). This brought the cult of his favourite to an abrupt end; however, it considerably enhanced the political power of another woman. His widow, Catherine de' Medici, exercised extensive influence during the reigns of her three sons, who proved to be the last Valois kings: François II, Charles IX, and Henri III. Diana was still occasionally associated with women close to the monarch: both Marie Touchet, the mistress of Charles IX, and Gabrielle d'Estrées, mistress of Henri IV, were identified with Diana at different times, as was the second wife of Henri IV, Marie de' Medici, and even his sister upon one occasion. As late as the reign of Louis XIV, the king's mistress Louise de la Vallière was painted as another Diana. Several later uses of the classical image were mere repetitions of earlier representations, however; for example, Gabrielle d'Estrées was painted as Diana in settings which exactly resembled those used for Diane de Poitiers.[55] Literary and artistic emphasis upon the king's role as another Apollo continued in the second half of the sixteenth century; indeed it was at this time that the legal and political theory of royal 'divine right' was codified.[56] But the long Wars of Religion which began in 1562 and continued intermittently until near the end of the century revealed that the monarch's authority was by no means as secure as that enjoyed by Henri II and François I. In *Les Amours de Diane*, a collection of Petrarchan sonnets by Philippe Desportes, the Diana image was used in a radical exploration of the crisis faced by French absolutism during these years.

Desportes' sequence was published in 1573, the year before the last Valois king, Henri III, succeeded his brother Charles IX. Desportes was Henri's secretary while he was duke of Anjou (and briefly, king of Poland), and retained his favour after his accession, when he became the leading court poet. Some critics have suggested that *Les Amours de Diane* refers to one or several of the future king's mistresses; but in fact Henri III was not reputed for his interest in heterosexual pleasures. He preferred the company of his male 'minions', and was much attracted to transvestism.[57] This makes one wonder about the gender of the Diana figure in Desportes' sequence; in Marlowe's *Edward II*, the erotic masque Gaveston plans to offer the homosexual king includes 'a lovely boy in Dian's shape'.[58] In any case, the lover whom Desportes describes can be associated with Henri. The disordered (or transgressive?) relationship which the sequence explores may therefore refer to the future king's rejection of conventional masculinity for homosexuality. But although *Les Amours de Diane* was composed before Henri's accession, Desportes' representation of the relationship between this lover and his Diana-like beloved suggests that the figure of Diana still retained something of her earlier connection with the French nation. Thus it can also be read as an allegory of the new, more unstable relationship between monarch and state which this third Henri was soon to inherit. The year before the publication of Desportes' sequence, 1572, had seen one of the worst incidents in this intermittent conflict: the bloody massacre of St Bartholomew's Eve, when French Protestants (or Huguenots), assembled in Paris for the wedding of the Protestant Henri of Navarre (the future Henri IV) to the Catholic Marguerite de Valois, were murdered *en masse*. Yet in fact the loss of 'masculine' initiative which Desportes explores merely develops to an extreme the trend implicit in earlier representations of Diana in connection with François I and Henri II.[59]

Les Amours de Diane combines insistent and realistic imagery of war with an exaggerated emphasis upon the passivity of the male lover in relation to the aggression of his beloved, who closely resembles the sadistic Diana figure of Jodelle's poem. Love and war have become inseparable, as the unorthodox roles of the lovers are related to the political paradox of civil war, in which country overwhelms king. The Petrarchan conceit of love as a battle is here combined with a series of macabre images which emphasize horror rather than beauty, for both Mars and Cupid inhabit the world of these poems: 'Le Dieu Mars et

L'Amour sont parmy la campagne:/L'un au sang des humains, l'autre en leurs pleurs se bagne:/L'un tient le coutelas, l'autre porte les dars. . . .'[60] ('Mars and Cupid are about; one bathes in the blood of humans, the other in their tears; one holds a sword, the other, arrows. . . .') The apparent opposition between these male deities (war and love) is united by Desportes in the figure of Diana, who mercilessly dominates her lover. His complaint: 'Je suis le champ où vous faites la guerre' ('I am the field where you do battle') equates his subordinate role with that of his wounded nation.[61] The pastoral innocence associated with Diana in earlier representations is forgotten; her classical role of a huntress, who kills within the bounds of natural law, is now seen as excessive and sinful: she is a 'belle meurtrière' ('fair murderess').

This exaggeration of the Petrarchan theme of wounding invests the love experience which the poem explores with an insistent physical dimension: do the sequence's repeated references to an apocalyptic ending suggest an orgasmic close to sexual pleasure, as well as a moment of historical closure? That the relationship is sexual is also suggested by the fact that the theme of apocalypse is linked, not with hopes for the re-establishment of a golden age, but with ideas of hell and damnation as the rewards for sin: 'apres la mort, qui les beautez efface./Je tiens que nous irons a l'infernal torment'.[62] ('After death, which destroys beauty, I am sure we will experience the torments of hell.') Yet the apocalypse the lover here anticipates is also a vivid present experience; the sequence is dominated by Diana's aspect of Hecate, ruler of the underworld and death, and in this underworld imagery it seems to hint at forbidden pleasures centred on the anus, an illicit homosexual 'torment': 'Tous les tourmens d'Enfer à moy seul sont donnez:/La Justice de Dieu tourmente les damnez./Et je suis tourmenté d'une injuste Déesse.'[63] ('I alone experience all the pains of hell. It is God's justice that torments the damned; but an unjust goddess tortures me.') At the same time, the morbid concern of the sequence with ideas of perdition also foreshadows the taste Henri III would reveal for masochistic religious penances during his reign. He later devoted much of his energy to organizing penitential processions through the streets of Paris, which he would join wearing no distinguishing signs of his kingship.[64]

Ironically, both Henri III's exaggerated piety and his ambiguous sexuality were extreme versions of the idea of kingship which had formerly been explored through the figure of Diana. But while those earlier representations had gestured towards the *idea* of a metamorphosis of a phallic masculine sexuality, the unpopularity of Henri III during his reign illustrated the need to maintain a gap between mythic ideal and historical reality. Indeed, in one of the sonnets of *Les Amours de Diane*, an identification with the raw masculine force of Hercules is implied to be the only way in which the lover can control the Diana figure who is both unruly France and his dominant beloved. She is compared to the Hydra which Hercules had to slay as one of his twelve labours: 'J'accompare ma Dame au serpent furieux,/Que le divin Thebain surmonta par la flame;/Ce serpent eut sept chefs, et ma cruelle Dame/A sept moyens vainqueurs des hommes et des dieux. . . .'[65] ('My lady resembles the fierce serpent which the immortal Theban hero destroyed with fire. That serpent had seven heads; my cruel mistress has seven ways to conquer both gods and men. . . .') It is clear, however, that for him to assume such a role is now out of the question. The Diana figure once identified with the king's capacity to restore a golden world in France is now the serpentine agent of a tragic fall in which it is the male lover and future monarch who plays the part of Eve.

Three-personed queen: the courtly cult of Elizabeth I and its subjects

By associating a female object of desire with the transmission of political power, French Renaissance literature and art proposed a curious modification to the masculinity of its rulers; none the less, Salic law made it impossible for a female heir to inherit the French throne. Only a male monarch could perform the mystical marriage with his kingdom.[1] Much more potentially problematic, however, was the figure of the female ruler. Even now, Renaissance criticism continues to elide the problem posed by Elizabeth I's government. Louis Adrian Montrose, who has contributed significantly to critical understanding of the complex power relations at the Elizabethan court, and who in several recent essays has acknowledged the importance of gender to an analysis of literary representations of Elizabeth, has none the less remarked that: 'Because she was always uniquely herself, Elizabeth's rule was not intended to undermine the male hegemony of her culture. Indeed, the emphasis upon her *difference* from other women may have helped to reinforce it.'[2] Although reformulated in the terms of the new historicism, this recuperation of Elizabeth's gender simply mirrors that effected by the traditionalist scholarship of Frances Yates, whose deleterious influence on views of the unmarried queen I will discuss shortly. (Perhaps significantly, Montrose has not addressed the issues raised by feminist criticism directly. Nor has he attempted to define his own relationship to feminism, as several other male critics interested in issues of gender have recently begun to essay.)[3] Elizabeth's presence on the English throne for forty-four years certainly did not end the patriarchal structure of English society; none the less, in certain respects it *was* a radical event – and in Elizabethan literature, it was increasingly perceived as such.

Elizabeth's reign has been perceived through the distorting lens of patriarchal attitudes, which characterize history as composed of the actions and experiences of men, and which, when they consider women at all, define them in relationship to men. Her refusal to marry freed her from subordination to a husband; although at times it seemed merely a tantalizing deferral of marriage (for twenty years!) as England engaged in numerous diplomatic manoeuvres with the foreign governments whose princes were the queen's suitors. But when her unmarried state began to be accepted and even idealized in courtly literature, some fifteen years after her accession, it was as the unattainable *object* of masculine desire that Elizabeth was represented, in an assimilation of Petrarchan and Neoplatonic attitudes by English absolutism which was significantly different from that effected in France. Early representations of Elizabeth in these terms effectively deny that independent self-determination which had presumably motivated her to remain unmarried; they also deny her any active political role: both she and the twin realm she now embodies (as ruler of church and state) have become the passive vehicles of masculine fantasy. This formulation of her queenly role was certainly not fashioned by Elizabeth herself; instead, it was fabricated by a group of male courtiers who attempted to use it to further their own political and personal ambitions. None the less, in the discrepancy between the initial version of this 'cult' and its formulation in the last decade of the reign may be discerned, if not the influence of Elizabeth herself, still an increasing sense of her capacity to elude or unmask such masculinist manipulations. Her courtly cult gradually introduced modifications to the status of lover and beloved within the discourses of love which were even more radical than those implicit in French absolutism. At the same time, it revealed further ambiguities in the mythological figure of Diana, which became the primary signifier of this courtly conception of the queen as a chaste beloved.

Frances Yates and Elizabethan imperialism: some long-lived critical misconceptions

The phenomenon which has been termed the cult of Elizabeth was first discussed in depth by E.C. Wilson in *England's Eliza*; subsequently it was analysed by Frances Yates in two articles, 'Queen Elizabeth I as Astraea' (1947), and 'Elizabethan chivalry: the romance of the Accession Day Tilts' (1957), which were republished in *Astraea: the Imperial Theme in the Sixteenth Century*.[4] Yates' views later formed the basis of several studies by her former student Roy Strong, most notably *The Cult of Elizabeth*.[5] Wilson's thesis was based primarily on a survey of literary materials which were both popular and courtly. He assembled an impressive amount of evidence to support his argument concerning the cult's existence; however, his analysis was founded upon an idealist and (old) historicist notion of the historical moment as an extractable 'essence'. As a result, Wilson was unable to explain the emergence of Elizabeth's cult as anything other than a natural phenomenon, declaring that: 'The concept of England's Eliza grew inevitably from the spirit of the age in happy conjunction with the unique character and achievement of its queen."[6] Yates, writing somewhat later, saw the cult in more artificial terms, as a deliberate but successful ideological manoeuvre (although she did not describe it in these terms), the motivations of which were both political and religious. For her, the cult was vitally linked to the search of European absolutist monarchies for a glamorous self-image, which she argued was found in the 'imperial' idea.

A significant feature of Yates' work was its demonstration that idealization of the queen as an absolute monarch was linked with her role as a restorer of the 'true' religion, Protestantism. Thus although she never articulated this point directly, Yates' work illustrates the extent to which Elizabeth's cult was founded on her *joint* rulership of both church and state. This is often forgotten by contemporary Renaissance critics, who frequently assimilate the specifically religious aspect of the monarch's authority into a focus upon her political role. Yates showed how Elizabeth's cult adapted the apocalyptic and Golden Age imagery favoured by European absolutism in the service of the English Protestant Reformation. She argued that an idealization of the female monarch was an important element of Protestant worship from the 1570s onwards. The absolutist conception of the monarch's rule as divinely determined, and as having effected an apocalyptic transformation of English society equivalent to restoration of the classical writers' Golden Age or of the biblical Eden, was connected by Yates with the mythological figure of Astraea, the 'imperial virgin', which she saw as the cult's central classical image. While this figure had appeared in compliments to other Renaissance monarchs, Elizabeth's combination of feminine gender with an unmarried state meant that she could herself be identified with Astraea.

Yates' work provided literary critics and historians of culture working in the Renaissance with a valuable starting point for consideration of the relations between different elements of Elizabethan culture and the society's specific ideologies of political and religious power. It is strange, however (especially when one considers how much innovative work has appeared in the field of Renaissance scholarship since the 1960s), that her thesis has yet to be challenged fundamentally. For it was flawed in several important respects. In the first place, she saw the Elizabethan cult as essentially unified. Yet in fact there is no coherent, 'base' ideology of the cult of Elizabeth; it rather was comprised of a loose collection of discourses, which accorded different weight to various ideas of Elizabeth and which defined the female monarch in relation to different 'subjects'. For example, the two areas of the cult which interested Yates most, Protestant ideology and the courtly pastime, were influenced by the concerns of two quite distinct groups (the Protestant clerical class and the courtly aristocracy). As a result, Yates failed to accord the literary dimension of the cult any specificity at all; in her relating of texts to historical context she often implied that such texts amounted to nothing

more than reflections of a pre-existent ideology. But in fact, representations of Elizabeth within the work of professional writers offer another
set of variations on the ideological themes of her cult. While they cannot
be distinguished completely from other articulations of the cult, and are
related especially closely to its courtly discourse, in several of these
literary representations we can trace the influence of attitudes and
interests which conflict with those of the court, and which thus suggest the
formation of a third interest group: that of the professional writers who at
that time were beginning to affirm their own importance and identity in
the face of significant economic disadvantages.[7] Yates also presented the
cult as having no real history or chronology (in terms of different moments
or phases), but simply as reiterating the same basic message within a
variety of discursive contexts. This is certainly not true of its courtly
dimension, where the respective roles of female monarch and male
courtier were defined very differently during the course of two decades.

Yates' theory of Renaissance absolutism stressed its expansionist
character; she assimilated all features of absolutist ideology under an
imperialist banner. It was this perspective which led her to privilege the
imperialist figure of Astraea as the primary signifier both of Elizabeth's
cult and of Renaissance absolutism as a whole. Certainly Elizabeth's reign
has always been seen in imperialist terms: as the age which saw the birth
of the English navy and the (very brief) establishment of English colonies
in America. This idea of the English state was certainly fantasized by
several of Elizabeth's male courtiers during the latter part of her reign;
since then, it has exercised the imaginations of many generations of male
historians. Yet while emphasizing the religious dimension of the
Elizabethan cult, Yates overlooked the fact that this aspect of absolutist
ideology could sometimes contradict its expansionist strand. For as is
clear from the case of French Renaissance absolutism, emphasis on the
private and interior (emotional/spiritual) life of the monarch did not
always reinforce an imperialist definition of their role. Although
imperialist motifs often figure in Elizabeth's portraiture, many literary
texts produced in the latter part of her reign present her as implicitly
disinterested in such endeavours, as an introspective and contemplative
figure rather than an aggressive colonialist. Yates stressed the shared
objectives of monarch and aristocracy; but these later representations of
Elizabeth as a Petrarchan beloved often highlighted their conflicts rather
than their agreements.

Yates' view of Elizabeth's cult was seriously distorted by this focus
upon Elizabethan imperialism, and upon comparisons of the queen to
Astraea. Had she looked more carefully at representations of Elizabeth
as another Roman goddess, Diana or Cynthia (which, somewhat
paradoxically, given her neglect of the analogy, she admitted to be 'the
most popular of all the figures employed by Elizabeth's adorers'), Yates

might have seen that at the heart of this cult were numerous depictions of a woman *with other women.*[8] Instead, her emphasis on Elizabeth's *difference* from all other women, as an 'imperial virgin', a unique woman occupying a man's world (a view reiterated by Montrose, and by many other contemporary Renaissance critics), enabled Renaissance scholarship to displace the fundamental problem of the queen's gender. Perceived as both more and less than a woman, because a woman supposedly purged of sexual desire, she is either asserted or implied to reinforce rather than disturb the political and religious hierarchies of the patriarchy, *and her ties of blood, friendship, and affection with other women are thereby elided.* Leonard Tennenhouse, for example, has asserted that:

> The English form of patriarchy distributed power according to a principle whereby a female could legitimately and fully embody the power of the patriarch. Those powers were in her and nowhere else so long as she sat on the throne. They were no less patriarchal for being so embodied as a female, and the female was no less female for possessing patriarchal powers. In being patriarchal, we must conclude, the form of state power was not understood as male in any biological sense, for Elizabeth was certainly represented and treated as a female. The idea of a female patriarch appears to have posed no contradiction in terms of Elizabethan culture.[9]

What Tennenhouse has omitted to consider is the centrality both of marriage and of patrilineal descent to the survival of patriarchal authority. It depends upon woman subordinating herself to a husband and accepting her reproductive role: by this means she provides the vital biological link in that chain of social, political and economic power which centres upon the transmission of the name of the father to his son. Tennenhouse thereby implies, as do so many other critics, that Elizabeth's chastity was seen as unthreatening, as a lack rather than a positive choice. But as an autonomous woman with political authority Elizabeth was inevitably unsettling; even more disturbing to a sixteenth-century mind would have been her possession, as a Protestant monarch, of an absolute authority in spiritual affairs which her Catholic sister Mary had not claimed. This role made all the more pronounced Elizabeth's difference not just from the conventionally masculine monarch, but also from the figure of Christ, with whom even a Catholic monarch (who could not claim to be head of his national church) was identified. As in the case of the biblical Wisdom figure, Elizabeth's combination of spiritual authority with a feminine gender indirectly contaminated the masculinity of the God whose regent she was deemed to be.

Elizabeth was apparently sensitive to the Protestant clergy's anxiety over her rulership of the church from the very beginning of her reign, for she did not take the title of 'supreme head' of the English church which her father Henry VIII had created, but assumed instead the title of 'supreme governor'.[10] Yet it is interesting to note that she used a religious definition of her government to legitimate her chastity (and so to justify her retention of sole political authority); in a speech delivered by proxy to Parliament in 1558, on the subject of her marriage, she defined her power in spiritual rather than secular terms:

> I have made choice of such state as is freest from the incumbrance of secular pursuits and gives me the most leisure for the service of God: and could the applications of the most potent princes, or the very hazard of my life, have diverted me from this purpose, I had long ago worn the honours of a bride. . . . I have long since made choice of a husband, the kingdom of England, . . . charge me not with the want of children, forasmuch as everyone of you, and every Englishman besides, are my children and relations. . . .[11]

What this speech does not acknowledge, however, is that Elizabeth's unmarried state was in conflict with Protestant ideology, which had removed the option of a celibate monastic life from both men and women, and which had commenced a propaganda campaign on the importance of marriage several years before Elizabeth's accession.[12] As early as 1549, *The Book of Common Prayer* produced under Edward VI stated of matrimony that it was: 'an honourable estate, instituted of God in paradise at the time of man's innocency, signifying unto us the mystical union that is betwixt Christ and his church'.[13] One of the most immediate results of this Protestant sanctification of marriage was the appearance of married clergy. But while Edward had legalized this situation, Elizabeth never gave it her official sanction. By the middle of her reign, however, this emphasis upon marriage at the level of religious ideology was being reinforced in the cultural sphere, via handbooks of courtly etiquette imitating French and Italian models which were influenced by the ideal of *amore humano* or a humane married love. In *The French Academye* of Pierre de la Primaudaye, for example, which was translated in 1586, it was asserted that: 'The societie of wedlocke is the seminarie and preservation of all society.'[14]

Less obviously problematic than this issue of marriage, but significant none the less, was the fact that the spheres of both secular and religious activity with which Elizabeth could claim an intimate relationship were *not* gendered masculine in political theory and theology; and this is a point which I believe has been overlooked in discussions of the 'two bodies' of the unmarried queen. The 'two bodies' concept of monarchy was first explored by Ernst Kantorowicz, who described how, from an idea of the mystical and immortal body of the church (*corpus ecclesiae mysticum*) explored in medieval canon law, was developed an idea of the immortality of the secular state (*corpus reipublicae mysticum*).[15] More recently, Marie Axton analysed the use of this concept in a debate about the Elizabethan succession which was carried on in legal as well as literary texts, and which was partly prompted by Elizabeth's refusal to marry.[16] An important point which neither Kantorowicz nor Axton emphasized, however, but which is clear both in the Latin terminology and in the notion of representation by means of a symbolic marriage (performed by priest or king), is that both these institutional apparatuses – *respublica* and *ecclesia* – were gendered feminine. In other words, the power of male monarch or priest depended on the union of their 'natural' or mortal masculine body with the symbolic female body of the immortal state or church. It was however as a female head of both church and state that Elizabeth performed a double symbolic marriage with both these feminine domains. Strictly speaking, therefore, (although in the post-Reformation era these two mystical bodies had been united in a single 'body politic') Elizabeth as queen had a triple rather than a dual aspect, like the triune God of Christian theology. So, of course, did the moon goddess Diana, to whom she was so often compared in the latter part of her reign; while the three Graces were described by Renaissance Neoplatonists as 'unfolding' the hidden enigma of Venus.[17] In this respect, Elizabeth's rule figured *the feminine in a mystical or symbolic relationship with itself*, and when viewed in these terms, the many comparisons of her to Diana in late Elizabethan literature take on a deeper significance than they have formerly been accorded. It seems to have been precisely this similarity of gender that led Elizabeth to be more closely identified with both state and church than any male Renaissance monarch, Catholic or Protestant, since she was of course able to 'represent' these 'mystical bodies' much better than a man. But acknowledged or not, it must also have made her an extremely disturbing figure.

Thus although this study would never have been produced without the impetus provided by Yates' path-breaking work, I dispute her account of the Elizabethan cult on a number of grounds. This persuasive analyst of European absolutism discovered what she wished to find in the narratives which these monarchies wove about themselves: images of national unity and of political consensus. She was consequently blind to the ideological and political problems inherent in the rule of an unmarried female monarch. At the same time, she did not observe that the courtly legitimation of that rule, which was effected by the use of Petrarchan and Neoplatonic attitudes, ultimately exaggerated rather than resolved the problem of Elizabeth's gender. And she bequeathed many of her erroneous assumptions to later generations of critics.

The mythic figure of the female monarch: one of a monstrous regiment

Given the reservations which had been expressed about government by a
woman by one eminent Puritan only shortly before Elizabeth's accession
to the English throne in 1558, it is indeed extraordinary that by the
middle of her reign her cult was openly privileging an image of feminine
power. In *The First Blast of the Trumpet against the Monstrous
Regiment of Women*, published in 1558, the Scottish Puritan John Knox
argued that a woman ruler could only retain power by a monstrous
combination of usurpation, seduction, and witchcraft, which would
involve a debasement of her male subjects paralleling the metamorphosis
of the companions of Ulysses by the enchantress Circe. Knox imagined
the shocked reactions of the Greek philosophers to this unnatural event:

> I am assuredlie persuaded, I say, that suche a sighte shulde so
> astonishe them, that they shulde iudge the hole worlde to be
> transformed into Amazones, and that such a metamorphosis and
> change was made of all the men of that countrie, as poetes do feyn was
> made of the companyons of Ulisses, or at least, that albeit the
> owtwarde forme of men remained, yet shuld they iudge that their
> hartes were changed from the wisdome, understanding, and courage of
> men, to the foolishe fondness and cowardise of women . . . he that
> iudgeth it a monstre in nature, that a woman shall exercise weapons,
> must iudge it to be a monstre of monstres, that a woman shal be
> exalted above a hole realme and nation.[18]

Knox's theme, supported by classical references to the Amazons and to
the sorcery of Circe, was that to give a woman political power was to
change the order of nature in a way which posed a serious threat to
conventional ideas both of masculine and feminine identity. The female
ruler undid a political and sexual hierarchy at a single blow. And this
point is given added emphasis by his use of women from myth to illustrate
his argument: the implication being that there existed no historical
precedent for the monstrous dominance of the female ruler. Although it
would later be regarded in more positive terms, Elizabeth's connection
with the domain of myth would remain a constant theme in representations of her authority. The effect of such an emphasis was to displace the
female monarch from the historical arena. In literary texts, she was
increasingly represented as an 'unmoved mover' or first cause, thus as
existing beyond the mutable and 'fallen' mode of time in which ordinary
mortals, and men in particular (as the agents of history), lived and
moved. While the myth of the masculine woman was occasionally
idealized in the literature of this period, there is no doubt that the idea of
this fiction being translated into reality was intensely threatening.[19]
The increasing assertiveness of contemporary English women was a topic

of satire during Elizabeth's reign as well as in that of James I.[20] In 1583, for example, the Puritan Philip Stubbes referred to women who favoured the new more masculine style of attire, in which the bodices of dresses resembled men's doublets, as 'Hermaphroditi; that is, Monsters of bothe kindes, halfe women, halfe men'.[21]

In fact, Knox's invective had been aimed at the Catholic queens Mary Tudor of England and Mary queen of Scots. When a Protestant queen ascended the English throne, later in the same year that Knox's tract had been published, the Protestant camp had hurriedly to modify Knox's argument, making of Elizabeth a notable exception to what they still maintained was the general rule of disastrous female rulers. The opinion expressed by John Calvin in response to a letter from the new queen's chief advisor, William Cecil, was to be the core of the new apologia:

> Two years ago John Knox asked of me, in a private conversation, what I thought about the Government of Women. I candidly replied, that as it was a deviation from the original and proper order of nature, it was to be ranked, no less than slavery, among the punishments consequent upon the fall of man: but that there were occasionally women so endowed, that the singular good qualities which shone forth in them made it evident that they were raised up by Divine authority.[22]

But at base, Calvin's remarks failed to resolve the contradiction posed by a figure such as Elizabeth. In fact they offer a good illustration of the difficulty of justifying woman's rule with reference to scripture. It is noteworthy that this leading representative of a movement which turned so frequently to scripture to confirm its programme of religious reform did not produce a biblical text to legitimate Elizabeth's rule, although some precedent could have been found in the career of the Hebrew 'judge' and prophetess Deborah. Even if he was critical of Knox's extremism, perhaps Calvin too preferred to depict Elizabeth as a truly exceptional case. He resorted to a vague reference to the mysterious operations of 'Divine authority'.

In spite of this deficiency in the modified Puritan or Calvinist argument, the change of attitude suggested by Calvin's letter was quickly taken up by the propagandists of the new government, for a hastily composed reply to Knox was promptly published: John Aylmer's *An Harborowe for Faithfull and Trewe Subiectes* (1559). Here was articulated for the first time the view that Elizabeth had a crucial role to play in the coming Protestant apocalypse, and had indeed been chosen by God for this very purpose. Aylmer imagines God's reply to male critics of Elizabeth's rule: 'What letteth, that she may not as well represent my maiestie, as any of you all?'[23] But to uphold this view was to imply that a woman could represent the *logos*, the Word of God made flesh. This was obviously a dangerous line of argument, not least because it threatened the exclusive masculinity of the Christian priesthood, where the priest was seen as Christ's representative. And indeed, Puritan anxiety about the precise extent of Elizabeth's power in spiritual affairs was also apparent in Aylmer's text. Knox's attack had been upon women as bearers of political power; he had refused even to contemplate the possibility of a woman being invested with supreme religious authority. Aylmer attempted to define (and so to limit) Elizabeth's highly controversial status within the church, by dividing ecclesiastical government into two parts: spiritual ministry and formal jurisdiction. He argued that her 'governorship' only extended to the second domain, since on the evidence of the New Testament, a woman could not be a priest.[24] This argument was reaffirmed a year later, in Bishop John Jewel's *Apology of the Church of England*. The question of the precise extent of Elizabeth's powers over the church would remain a highly contentious issue for the remainder of the reign. Yet the most direct challenge to that authority, which occurred in 1577 over the queen's suppression of Puritan 'prophesyings', ended in abject failure, with her suspension of the Puritan-inclined archbishop of Canterbury, Grindal.

Aylmer's attempt to combine his justification of Elizabeth's authority within the English Protestant church with her exclusion from its ecclesiastical or priestly domain was effectively subverted, however, in a passage from the work of his more famous successor as apologist for the Elizabethan Reformation: John Foxe's *Acts and Monuments* (often referred to as the 'Book of Martyrs'), which was published in England in 1563. Foxe stressed Elizabeth's narrow escape, during the reign of her Catholic sister Mary I, from the same death by decapitation formerly meted out to her mother. He represented her as a sacrificial figure, whom God had spared the death of a Protestant martyr in the reign of her Catholic sister in order that she might perform an especial religious task:

> And therefore as we have hitherto discoursed the afflictions and persecutions of the other poor members of Christ comprehended in this history before, so likewise I see no cause why the communion of her grace's afflictions also . . . ought to be suppressed in silence. . . . And though I should through ingratitude or silence pass over the same, yet the thing itself is so manifest, that what Englishman is he which knoweth not the afflictions of her grace to have been far above the condition of a king's daughter. For there was [nothing lacking] to make a very Iphigenia of her but her offering upon the altar of the scaffold.[25]

At one level, this passage may have assuaged Puritan anxiety about Elizabeth's authority over the church, in that it emphasized a time when she had been, not a queen regnant, but vulnerable and powerless. Yet the narrative from classical myth which Foxe used here to illuminate Elizabeth's tribulations, the story of the virginal Greek princess

Iphigenia, had some rather contradictory associations. Euripides'
Iphigenia at Aulis dramatized the sacrifice of Iphigenia to Artemis by her
father, king Agamemnon, in order to persuade the goddess to grant fair
winds to the Greek fleet, which she was preventing from departing for the
Trojan war. But a sequel to this tragedy, which was most probably known
to Foxe, had been presented in Euripides' *Iphigenia at Taurica*. In this
play, it was revealed that Iphigenia had not in fact been killed. Instead,
at the crucial moment, she had been enveloped in a thick cloud and
carried away to become Artemis' chosen priestess. at her temple in the
desolate region of the Tauric Chersonese. Thus the Greek myth had two
parts: the first related to the apparent sacrifice but miraculous rescue of a
virgin from death; the second concerned her subsequent dedication to the
service of deity, in payment for the life which had been saved. Foxe's
meaning here might accordingly be construed as follows: just as the
Greek Iphigenia had been spared from the sacrificial altar by Artemis,
and had survived to serve her, so Elizabeth had been spared from
martyrdom by the providential intervention of God, and thereby
possessed some kind of especial spiritual status. It is possible that Foxe
intended this analogy to support Elizabeth's assertion that she would
eschew marriage in order the better to serve God and her country.
Interestingly, he anticipated the association of Elizabeth with the
mythology of Diana (the Roman counterpart to Greek Artemis) by more
than a decade. But his comparison of the unmarried queen to a woman
who became a pagan priestess, the servant of a goddess rather than a god,
was not perhaps the best way to allay concern about her ecclesiastical
powers – in a church, moreover, which refused her sex even the highly
restricted religious vocation of the nun.

At the same time, an uncannily appropriate feature of the Iphigenia
myth chosen by Foxe was the fact that the princess' special destiny was
part of a complex family tragedy. It had prompted the sexual betrayal and
murder of her father Agamemnon by his wife Clytemnestra, and the
subsequent act of matricide committed by her son Orestes. Inevitably, the
accession of the new queen prompted recollection of another, not too
dissimilar, collapse of familial affection, which had occurred some twenty
years previously: the well-known and sensational story of her mother
Anne Boleyn's supposed adultery, which was followed not only by her
tragic death by beheading but also by Henry VIII's rejection of his two-
year old daughter, in a declaration of her illegitimacy (he never revoked
this decision, although his will named Elizabeth as one of his heirs).
Elizabeth inherited the throne as 'a king's daughter', regardless of the
aspersions formerly cast on her paternity. Yet it is noteworthy that the
Iphigenia myth emphasizes the bond between mother and daughter; while
the father betrays his daughter, it is the mother who revenges her, and a
surrogate mother figure. Artemis or Diana, who protects and preserves

her. For in fact Foxe's text was one of the primary sources of a new image of Anne Boleyn, articulated from the beginning of her daughter's reign. Foxe attributed to Anne the same religious dedication which he claimed for her daughter:

> There were in this Quene besides the comelinesse of her forme and beauty, many other giftes of a well instructed minde, as gentlenes, modestye, and piety toward all men, besides a fervent desire in her hart unto the true and sincere religion, so that during her life, religion happely flourished and went forward.[26]

Although some of Foxe's more detailed claims for Anne's religious zeal were exaggerated, it is now considered that his picture of her as a convinced evangelical, an active proponent of the English Reformation for its own sake (rather than as a means to her marriage), was essentially accurate.[27] Thus while Elizabeth's political status stemmed from her father, her mother could genuinely be regarded as a key figure behind her claim to authority over the Protestant church, and Foxe appears to recognize this dual lineage.

We have no concrete evidence of Elizabeth's feelings for her two parents. None the less it is important to recognize that by refusing to marry she knowingly ended the Tudor patriliny which had so obsessed her father and paternal grandfather: a dynasty then only in its third generation. One of her biographers, Paul Johnson, has also pointed out that she ignored the request made in Henry VIII's will, that his body should be laid alongside that of his third wife, Jane Seymour, in an expensive tomb. Although he was placed in Jane's existing tomb at Windsor, his own was never finished. Elizabeth discussed the possibility of completing this project at the beginning of her reign, but in the end she did nothing.[28] Johnson likewise asserted that she 'never displayed any posthumous affection for her mother'.[29] It is hardly surprising, given the circumstances in which she grew up, that there is no record of anything Elizabeth ever said about her mother; but in fact her actions on her accession suggest she felt a strong bond to this side of her family. The young queen gathered around her many of Anne's Boleyn and Howard relatives.[30] For example, she appointed her grand-uncle lord Howard of Effingham as her lord chamberlain (his son Charles would later be admiral in command at the time of the Armada), and her cousin by marriage, sir Francis Knollys, as her vice chamberlain. Her former governess and long-term confidante, Kat Ashley, was already married to a Boleyn cousin; Elizabeth now chose many women from this side of her family as ladies-in-waiting. One of these, Kate Carey (whose grandmother was Mary Boleyn and who later married lord Charles Howard), is thought to have been Elizabeth's closest female friend during a long period of service.[31] But Elizabeth promoted her mother's former ecclesiastical protégés also. Matthew Parker, for example, who had been one of queen Anne's chaplains, became her first archbishop of Canterbury.[32] Another of those chaplains, William Latimer (who wrote a manuscript life of queen Anne in this reign, perhaps intended for her daughter), became one of the new queen's chaplains and clerk of her closet.[33] And Anne's biographer, E.W. Ives, has noted several important continuities between the imagery associated with mother and daughter. Not only did several themes of Anne's coronation procession appear again in Elizabethan iconography, the new queen also used several of her mother's badges, most notably the falcon and the armillary sphere.[34] The latter emblem appears in several portraits both of Elizabeth and of her courtiers, for example in the 'Ditchley' portrait as an earring and on the sleeve of the queen's dress in the 'Rainbow' portrait.[35] This last Tudor monarch, then, this odd unmarried woman, who claimed an especial vocation to rule, seems to have identified as much with the lineage of her murdered mother as with that dynasty of kings whence she derived her royal authority.

A cult for courtiers: Elizabethan absolutism and the new aristocracy

Ties of kinship enabled several of her Boleyn and Howard relatives 'to flourish mightily' under Elizabeth.[36] But others among the nobility had no certain passport to security at the new court, and had to shift for themselves. Some of them elected to play the game of courtliness for all it was worth, in an attempt to renegotiate their relationship to the 'absolute' monarch in terms more favourable to themselves. Indeed, what particularly distinguishes Elizabeth's courtly cult as an articulation of absolutist ideas is the prominent role of members of her aristocracy in its formulation. Norbert Elias has described the absolutist court as: 'at the same time an instrument for controlling the nobility and a means of sustaining it'.[37] Although it is generally agreed that the English nobility were in the throes of a profound political and economic crisis in the late sixteenth century, their status under absolutism is now thought to have been stronger than formerly estimated.[38] In the courtly version of Elizabeth's cult, we are offered an intriguing insight into one highly specific example of the ambiguous and charged relationship between monarch and nobility which was characteristic of Renaissance absolutism. As Alan Sinfield has remarked: 'We should . . . perceive the Elizabethan state not as a static totality whose power structure is revealed in the ideology of monarchy, but as diverse and changing, the site of profound contradictions.'[39] Within the courtly strand of Elizabeth's cult (as I have mentioned, it also had a specifically religious as well as a more popular discourse), ideas drawn from medieval courtly love as well as from Petrarchism and Neoplatonism were used to formulate several competing models of courtly subjectivity. For example, while one idea of courtliness privileged the perspective of the male courtier, another questioned his centrality to the courtly experience, which was defined rather in terms of ties between courtly women. This predominantly literary debate certainly affords the Renaissance critic an important insight into one aspect of the power struggle which was waged not only between Elizabeth and her nobility, but also between different factions and groups within that class; it also reveals the complex role played by gender in this conflict.

Several historians have suggested that the crucial political conflict at this historical juncture was not between the aristocracy and an emergent bourgeoisie, but between groups within the aristocracy itself.[40] As a class it was divided into *nobilitas maior* (traditional titular peerage) and *nobilitas minor* (knights, esquires, and upper gentry who had coats of arms).[41] But throughout this period, the peerage was in serious decline; Hugh Trevor-Roper pointed out that: 'of the sixty-two members of Elizabeth's peerage in 1560, thirty-seven had titles conferred since the accession of her father'.[42] While Elizabeth was markedly reluctant to promote to its ranks, she also withheld significant favours from this ostensibly elite group:

> the peers, who, as hereditary royal councillors, were accustomed to expect great offices, and based their way of life upon that assumption, were during the reign of Elizabeth, or at least after the aristocratic revolts of 1569–72 which discredited them with the Queen, largely excluded from such office. . . .[43]

It was chiefly members of the *nobilitas minor*, or individuals who had only recently risen out of it, rather than the traditional peerage, who benefited most substantially from the various rewards of royal favour, chief among which was the holding of office. Trevor-Roper described the members of this new group of successful royal servants as 'court-gentlemen' as opposed to 'country-gentlemen'; more recently, the group has been defined as a 'meritocracy' or 'new aristocracy'.[44] The difficulty of characterizing it accurately is clear when one considers that it included not only the Boleyn and Howard relatives who prospered most under Elizabeth, but also such widely differing personalities as William Cecil, later lord Burghley, and Robert Dudley, later earl of Leicester, who for most of Elizabeth's reign were the leaders of the two major political factions on her privy council. The group's members have been described as sharing many of the business interests of the commercial gentry, as well as playing an important role in the remodelling of the English parliament, which Wallace T. MacCaffrey believes to have been very much the instrument of their purposes at this time.[45] Many of its members were committed to the furtherance of the Puritan cause (although there were some notable exceptions to this trend, such as lord Burghley, sir Christopher Hatton, and sir Walter Ralegh), and as a group it was also influenced by humanism in its interest in education and culture. It was mainly members of this group who built the great Elizabethan houses for which the latter part of the reign is famous: monuments by means of which they signalled – and sometimes terminated – their prosperity. Ties of blood aside, the most significant characteristic of the group was the fact that the power and status of each individual member depended to a hitherto unprecedented degree upon the continuing goodwill of the queen. It was certain members of this group (who can be said to have constituted a distinct faction within it) who first elaborated Elizabeth's courtly cult in the 1570s.

Frances Yates and Roy Strong pointed out that in the early 1570s Elizabeth's Accession Day, 17 November, began to be widely celebrated both in various parish churches and at court: festivities which can probably be interpreted in part as supportive responses to the queen's excommunication in 1570. But it was not until the Kenilworth entertainment of 1575, staged by the earl of Leicester, that there was the first hint of that idealization of Elizabeth's unmarried state which would become the central element in courtly and popular expressions of her cult.[46] Of course, by the middle of the 1570s, to celebrate the queen's chastity was in a sense to make a virtue of necessity. In 1575 she was 42, and must therefore have been approaching her menopause. Five or so years later, during the courtship of the duc d'Alençon, it was maintained that she was still fertile; none the less it must have seemed highly unlikely that a royal marriage would now provide a Tudor heir.[47] Moreover, English Protestants had not forgotten the St Bartholomew's Eve massacre of Huguenots in Paris in 1572, and were alarmed about the political implications of a French alliance.

The entertainments and tilts presented before the queen in the late 1570s and early 1580s, by members of the Leicester–Walsingham faction, were the first articulations of a specifically courtly cult of Elizabeth. But as several critics have demonstrated, highly complex motivations could lie behind Elizabethan courtiership.[48] On the one hand, these events celebrate the favours enjoyed by the courtiers who have organized them, and in the case of the entertainments, they relate Elizabeth's supposed restoration of a golden age to her gifts of property to a favourite such as Leicester. But the pastimes did not simply demonstrate (and attempt to secure the continuance of) the good fortune of individuals; they also sought the queen's support for certain quite specific political and religious objectives.[49] Their initial acceptance and celebration of Elizabeth's unmarried state was integrally related to the desire of this group of courtiers for a foreign policy in which they could play key heroic roles. The pastimes' conception of chivalry was derived primarily from the medieval Arthurian romances, but in the first instance it was also defined in terms of a commitment to international Protestantism. The Leicester–Walsingham faction appears to have used these elaborate (and expensive) compliments to the queen to promote its aim of military intervention on behalf of beleaguered Protestants in the Netherlands and in France: 'Yet say, I wil abide hers to command,/where so adventures hard shal carry me,/Not leaving Love by sea nor yet by land,/though that I love, I never hap to see. . . .'[50] Thus Elizabeth's identification in these events with an unfallen natural world signified not only the personal prosperity which her favour conferred on a propertied elite, but also the purity of the reformed religion, whose re-establishment is implied to have made England a restored paradise. And while the courtier's self-image as knight stressed his membership of a class entitled to such privileges, this role was also seen in religious terms. These early pastimes imply that only military action can secure the Protestant golden age, and bring history to its promised apocalyptic end. By this means, they also attempt to free the male courtier from complete subjection to the queen and English state, by defining his necessary sphere of action as existing beyond the boundaries of Elizabeth's 'queendom'.

Not until the 1580s was there an explicitly imperialist aspect to courtly demands for military intervention abroad, a shift of emphasis which seems at least partly to have been indebted to Giordano Bruno's imperialist conception of Elizabeth in *Cena de le ceneri* (1584):

> If her earthly territory were a true reflection of the width and grandeur of her spirit this great Amphitrite would bring far horizons within her girdle and enlarge the circumference of her dominion to include not only Britain and Ireland but some new world, as vast as the universal frame, where her all-powerful hand should have full scope to raise a united monarchy.[51]

A figural parallel to this formulation was offered by John Case's engraving in *Sphaera Civitatis* (1588), where Elizabeth was depicted as containing all the planetary spheres within her body (plate 8). This aspect of her iconography resembles that of the medieval Wisdom figure. In fact, Bruno's formulation depends on a metaphoric subversion of that idea which was already central to Elizabeth's cult, her chastity; in an unusual reversal of the usual Renaissance description of territories in feminine terms, Elizabethan imperialism is defined in terms of a symbolic penetration of the queen (as the body politic of England/'Britain') by 'some new world'. But in sir Walter Ralegh's courtly poetry, and in certain other representations of the queen, both popular and courtly, which were produced in the latter part of the reign. Elizabeth's chastity was stressed along with expansionist themes:

> Beta, long may thine altars smoke with yearly sacrifice,
> And long thy sacred temples may their sabbaths solemnize;
> Thy shepherds watch by day and night,
> Thy maids attend the holy light,
> And thy large empire stretch her arms from east unto the west,
> And Albion on the Apennines advance her conquering crest.[52]

Yet the military objectives behind many courtly compliments to her unmarried state never won Elizabeth's unequivocal support. In his *Fragmenta Regalia*, sir Robert Naunton remarked of the heroic aspirations nurtured by many of Elizabeth's favourites:

> And it will be a true note of Magnanimity that shee loved a souldier, and had a propension in her Nature to regard, and alwaies to grace them, which falling into the Courtiers consideration, they took as an invitation to winne honour togeather with their Mistris favour by exposing themselves to the warres . . .; for we have many instances of the sallies of the nobility, and Gentry, yea and of the Court, and of her prime favourits, . . . so predominant were their thoughts and hopes of honour growne in them . . . whose absence and their many eruptions were very distasteful unto her.[53]

Elizabeth's reluctance to pursue the militant policies urged upon her by these courtiers was undoubtedly motivated in part by anxiety concerning the increased power which might be gained by the leader of such an expedition. In spite of the emphasis in the Elizabethan entertainment upon her active role, it was obvious that as a woman she could not lead these forces herself (despite her rousing speech to the assembled troops at Tilbury in 1588, which ironically was made *after* the Armada had been dispersed, although danger still seemed imminent). The aggressivity symbolically attributed to her as another Diana would have to be acted out on the historical stage by men. Such concerns almost certainly influenced her lengthy procrastination concerning Leicester's proposed Netherlands expedition, as well as Essex's campaigns in Rouen and Ireland.[54] Problems such as these, which were of course specific to Elizabeth's situation as a woman ruler, may at least partly explain why several later contributions to her cult stressed contemplation, rather than militant activity, as its *leitmotif*.

In Renaissance France, the figure of Diana was used to mediate between two images of the king as courtly lover, and also between two different ideas of masculinity. Much emphasis was placed upon her metamorphosis of a phallic sexuality, as represented by the 'wild man' figures of Hercules or Actaeon. In the Elizabethan courtly pastimes which

first complimented Elizabeth as another Diana, the wild man as a persona
of the male courtier was idealized: it was Hercules who kept the gate of
Kenilworth castle in 1575, and another wild man offered her his service
later in her visit. The erotic innuendo implicit in these encounters (the
entertainments often cast Elizabeth as the May or Summer queen who
was the wild man's consort in European folk tradition) suggests that if she
will not submit to the *sexual* power of the erect phallus – emblematized
by his weapon of a club or uprooted tree – then her 'taming' of masculine
desire requires her at least to grant it sublimated expression in the
political sphere. The male courtier is apparently not prepared to sacrifice
his phallic self-definition altogether to his queen. This idea of courtliness
would later be given extended expression in Spenser's epic poem *The
Faerie Queene* (1590, 1596), where both the hero prince Arthur and the
knight of justice, sir Arthegall, are compared to Hercules: 'Who all the
West with equall conquest wonne,/And monstrous tyrants with his club
subdewed;/The club of Iustice dread, with kingly powre endewed.'[55]
Yet as Spenser's lines make clear, Hercules' heroic force involves a claim
to kingly power inappropriate in an Elizabethan courtier.

In the succeeding chapter, I consider the implications of the wild man's
dominance as a model of courtiership in the early stages of Elizabeth's
cult, and the degree to which, even in the courtly pastime, it was
challenged by other ideas of courtliness. Several critics have noted the
opposition of two courtly roles, forester (alias wild man) and shepherd, in
sir Philip Sidney's courtly entertainment, *The Lady of May*, performed
before Elizabeth in 1578.[56] But they have failed to interpret this conflict
in terms of sexual politics. Yet once it is recognized that the debate about
courtiership involved a conflict of sexual as well as political authority, the
figure of the unmarried queen (which has been marginalized by analyses
of courtliness focused upon the male courtier) becomes of central
importance. Thus at one point in Spenser's *The Shepheardes Calender*
(1579), celebration of the courtiership of the shepherd (by whom the wild
man's phallic power is redirected to poetic activity) is subordinated to yet
another mode of courtliness, one which is located in an exclusively
feminine domain.[57] In the first place, the poem's April eclogue represents
Elizabethan courtliness in terms which exclude the male courtier as wild
man or Herculean hero from knowledge of its innermost mysteries. But it
also implies that even the relinquishment of a sexuality focused upon the
phallus would not gain the male courtier full admission into the hidden
centre of the courtly world – although unlike Actaeon, this more
receptive type of courtier could at least testify to the mystical significance
of its holy of holies. As Spenser represented it here, the exclusive inner
circle of Elizabethan courtliness was a mysterious space dominated by ties
between women, where the queen existed not for and in relation to men,
but in intimate association with her own sex. Perhaps most importantly,

the tabooed figure of the queen's mother is metaphorically represented in this eclogue, and for her terrible death is substituted a mystical metamorphosis which has enabled her to usurp the place and function of the wild man's phallus.

The hollow phallus of the mother: the hidden centre of Elizabethan courtliness

The *noblewoman* or lady-in-waiting has characteristically been elided from contemporary critical views of the Elizabethan court; yet as the 'Procession Picture' attributed to Robert Peake reveals, the shadowy presence of these women always hovered behind the male-defined idea of the female monarch (plate 9). By implication, Spenser's eclogue shifted the focus of courtly service from the semi-public spaces of the Elizabethan court – the privy chamber, and the presence chamber, in which male courtiers predominated – to a more secluded and feminine courtly domain: the queen's private apartments (the withdrawing chambers), where she was served by her maids-of-honour and ladies of the bed-chamber.[58] In the April eclogue, the solid phallic authority claimed by the male courtier in the pastimes, and emblematized by the wild man's club, has been replaced by a different mode of sexual power, attributed to a maternal rather than a paternal figure. At the same time, we are offered an apotheosis of Elizabeth as another Wisdom figure, a female *logos* or Christ, who unifies heaven and earth in her own person. Eliza 'Queene of shepheardes all' is the virginal *daughter* of a virgin birth, whose paternity is marginalized even as it is asserted: 'For shee is *Syrinx* daughter without spotte,/Which *Pan* the shepheards God of her begot.'[59] The phallic instrument in this unusual mode of conception was the nymph Syrinx, a follower of Diana; after she was metamorphosed into reeds as she fled his sexual advances, Pan tied some of these reeds together and placed them within the orifice of his mouth, making the music which Spenser equates with Eliza. The phallic club of the wild man or satyr, of whom Pan is yet another type, is here hollowed out and transferred to the female. It is now the emblem of a maintenance of feminine autonomy, via the miraculous obstruction of a rape, and via the immaculate conception of a female saviour: that song which is Eliza.

French Renaissance representations of the male monarch as Actaeon had implied his relinquishment of a phallic masculine identity in a privileged yet sacrificial relationship to Diana. In Spenser's eclogue, the place of the decentred and sexually thwarted father, Pan, is assumed by his own persona of the shepherd poet Colin Clout. Like Pan, Colin has replaced phallic sexual desire with the pipes of Pan: the hollow and musical maternal phallus (which is also multiple rather than singular). Only by such a substitution, Spenser implies, can one obtain a more detailed knowledge of the Petrarchan or Neoplatonic beloved: that is, of her hidden, enfolded relationship to a feminine and maternal space. His poetic gaze can consequently afford to linger on the tabooed object of the female body. As was Diana in her famous appearance in Ovid's *Metamorphoses*, Eliza is naked, clad in the 'Scarlot' and 'Ermines white' of her own skin. This colouring, together with the green of her pastoral setting, makes her a combination of love, faith, and hope, like Dante's Beatrice:

> See where she sits upon the grassie greene
> (O seemely sight)
> Yclad in Scarlot like a mayden Queene,
> And Ermines white.[60]

But significantly, although he calls upon his readers to 'see', Colin himself is excluded from the eclogue. His song about Eliza is sung in his absence by the shepherd Hobbinoll. Her nakedness emphasizes the fact that Spenser's queen is attended only by feminine companions: by the Muses conventionally associated with Apollo, but also sometimes linked with his sister Diana; and by the three Graces, whose tripartite perfection she clearly embodies in her own person, as another Venus.[61] For the Neoplatonist Ficino, the three Graces had symbolized the unity of contemplative, active, and voluptuous love, and this theme is recapitulated in the eclogue's emblem, *O quam te memorem virgo?*, stressing Eliza's paradoxical union of Venus and Diana, love and chastity (it is a line from Virgil's *Aeneid* which describes Venus' appearance to her son Aeneas dressed like Diana).[62] This, together with Spenser's poetic emphasis upon the colour red (notable by its absence from Petrarch's *Rime Sparse*) should alert us to the fact that even if the male is excluded from this scene, it is none the less far from devoid of sexuality.

Various other 'nymphs' and 'shepheards daughters' come at the end of the poem to dress Eliza with flowers:

> And whither rennes this bevie of Ladies bright,
> raunged in a rowe?
> They bene all Ladyes of the lake behight,
> that unto her goe. . . .
>
> Ye shepheards daughters, that dwell on the greene,
> hye you there apace:
> Let none come there, but that Virgins bene,
> to adorne her grace. . . .
>
> Bring hether the Pincke and purple Cullambine,
> With Gelliflowres:
> Bring Coronations, and Sops in wine,
> worne of paramoures.

Strewe me the ground with Daffadowndillies,
And Cowslips, and Kingcups, and loved Lillies:
    The pretie Pawnce,
    And the Chevisaunce,
Shall match with the fayre flowre Delice.[63]

Unlike the golden world of the Elizabethan pastimes, which testified to the prestige and the ambitions of certain male courtiers, this paradisal environment is exclusive to women. The description of Eliza's nymphs as 'Ladyes of the lake' associates them with the fairy women of Arthurian legend, inhabitants of an otherworld dimension who are the motivating springs of the actions of Arthur and his knights. The flowers with which Eliza is adorned, together with the eclogue's calendar theme of the month of April, reinforce this motif of faery, as well as emphasizing her maternal bonding, for they connect her with the spring goddess Persephone, a female saviour restored to her mother Demeter every springtime who was often linked with the faery queen in medieval English literature.[64] Both Persephone's abduction by the ruler of the underworld, Pluto, and her subsequent annual return from her husband's to her mother's kingdom, were associated with flowers. She also seems to have had some connection with music in the Renaissance; she was certainly implicated in the mythology of the poet and musician Orpheus, who descended to the underworld in search of his wife Eurydice, and who is thought to have been used by Spenser as a poetic model in this poem.[65] Indeed, while she is initially revealed in a posture of contemplative repose which resembles that of the 'Nymph' of Fontainebleau, Spenser's Eliza is surrounded by female figures involved in intense creative activity: by the music of the Muses and the dancing of the Graces, as well as by the more mundane business of the young women who act as her tiring-maids.

The status of the male in relation to this elite and gynocentric conception of Elizabethan courtliness is ambiguous. On the one hand, his relinquishment of an explicit phallic authority has marginalized him like the mythic father and archetypal poet, Pan; of course this was Spenser's literal situation, as a courtly poet rather than a courtier *per se*. On the other hand, in so far as they are presented through the agency of his art, he also claims to possess a knowledge of feminine mysteries which the other, more masculine (and superficially more privileged) mode of courtiership cannot rival. The courtly poet's paradoxical combination of physical exclusion with knowledge was repeated in the parallel conception of the male courtier as hermit or pilgrim, a figure withdrawn from the royal beloved and the court, yet possessing an especial knowledge of her secrets. This formulation of the role of the absent courtly lover introduced a distinctly Catholic nuance to the cult of Elizabeth. The courtiers bent on military exploits had justified such fantasies in terms of the Protestant conception of holy warfare, while in the notes to *The Shepheardes Calender* the pastoral figure of the shepherd was connected by Spenser with a Puritan idea of correct priesthood. Yet in a poem probably written in the 1590s, after his fall from favour with Elizabeth, sir Walter Ralegh compared the court to the former Catholic shrine of the Virgin Mary at Walsingham (which incidentally was close to the birthplace of Anne Boleyn at Blickling Hall in Norfolk): 'As you came from the holy land/Of Walsinghame/Mett you not with my true love/By the way as you came?'[66]

Thus my argument in the ensuing chapters is that alongside the first version of Elizabeth's courtly cult, which dates from the Kenilworth entertainment of 1575, and which affirmed the ambitions of the male courtier, there developed interest in another, more private, sphere of the cult, one which was less compatible with the assertive identity desired by the masculine courtly subject, and which represented Elizabeth as retaining rather than delegating her powers as a female *logos* or saviour. During the last years of the reign this hidden feminine dimension of Elizabethan courtliness received increasing attention in contemporary literature, with Elizabeth frequently represented as another Diana surrounded by her nymphs: '"Hey, down, a down!" did Dian sing,/Amongst her virgins sitting;/"Than love there is no vainer thing,/For maidens most unfitting". . . .'[67] While the female beloved of Petrarchism and Neoplatonism was a figure whose gender was largely elided by the narcissistic masculine subject of those discourses, these late Elizabethan representations allied emphasis upon Elizabeth's combination of female-ness and physical autonomy with an implied recognition of her close ties to other women. In these texts, the queen's extensive powers in the political and spiritual spheres are related to and overshadowed by another mode of power, one altogether more enigmatic and secretive, which was signified by the motif of chastity: a power over her own body. But at the same time, several of these texts reveal a growing anxiety about this unorthodox image of the queen, as certain Elizabethan writers began to realize the threat posed by this idea of Elizabeth to the literary formulation of a stable and assertive masculine identity.

Plate 1 Titian, *The death of Actaeon*, mid-sixteenth century

Plate 2 *Diana* by Frans Floris, *c*. 1560

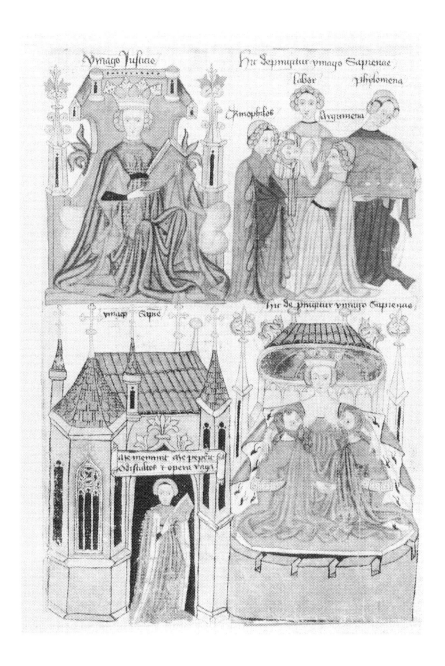

Plate 3 *Sapientia (as nursing mother) with Justitia*, fifteenth-century manuscript illumination

Plate 4 *Sapientia with globe*, detail from a fifteenth-century tapestry

Plate 5 *The Nymph of Fontainebleau*, sixteenth-century engraving by Pierre Millan after a painting by Il Rosso

Plate 6 *Diana resting after the hunt*, sixteenth-century engraving by L.D. after a painting by Primaticcio

Plate 7 François Clouet, *The bath of Diana*

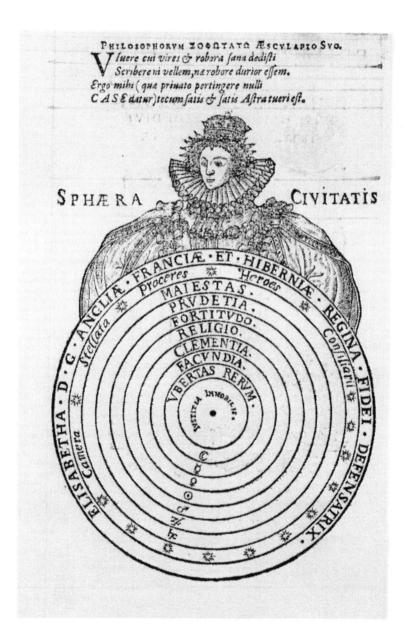

Plate 8 *Queen Elizabeth I as the English state*, from John Case, *Sphaera Civitatis*, 1588

Plate 9 *The procession of Queen Elizabeth I*, attributed to Robert Peake the Elder

Plate 10
Queen Elizabeth I and the Pope as Diana and Callisto, engraving by Pieter van der Heyden

Chapter four

Carnival at court: contests for authority in Elizabethan aristocratic pastimes

Both Petrarchism and Neoplatonic love philosophy exhibited a distinct ambiguity towards the natural world. Did the lover's impulse towards an idea of perfection require the rejection and transcendence of nature, or was it possible that it could itself be redeemed? In spite of the dualistic attitudes which had shaped these systems, they both articulated some hope of the transformation of man's earthly environment. In terms which paralleled biblical descriptions of the Wisdom figure, the love discourses represented the female object of a chaste desire as a vital point of intersection between a fallen and mutable material world and a transcendent and unchanging realm, equivalent to the Platonic World of Ideas. Petrarch's Laura was represented within an earthly paradise (like Dante's Beatrice when he first encountered her in the *Purgatorio*); the Neoplatonist Giordano Bruno described Elizabeth I as engirdling the new world of the Americas. Thus paradoxically, while the fear of sexuality which was central to these systems (especially the sexuality of woman) involved a rejection of the materiality of the body, the female beloved also emblematized in her person the possibility of a golden age in which spirit would once more be immanent in matter.

As I have already indicated, the emphasis of the love discourses was usually on the meaning of this figure for an individual masculine subject. In this context, she mediated between the male lover's fallen self, unable to master his own destiny or his environment, and his desire to become an heroic or angelic being, with the power to control his own life, to shape himself according to his own desires and consequently to impose his will upon nature. In other words, the beloved conferred upon him the equivalent to a religious state of grace. Within the discourse of Renaissance absolutism, however, a similar female figure was accredited with a collective rather than an individual experience of earthly paradise, in the form of the benefits conferred by the absolutist state upon its members. Thus we find pastoral and golden age motifs being used to legitimate a particular political and social order. In Elizabethan absolutism, the paradisal theme was lent especial emphasis by the female gender of the monarch: 'Rudenesse it selfe she doth refine./Even like an Alychymist divine:/Grosse times of yron turning/Into the purest forme of gold.'[1] In the literary discourse of French Renaissance absolutism, Diana, as an idealized representation of the French nation, was subordinated (at least in theory) to the authority of the male monarch as her lover/consort. But as is clear from her developing association with nature in courtly literature, Elizabeth emblematized the state which she also ruled. Her role as an earthly incarnation of the immortal body politic of England was used to emphasize the corporate identity of the state, along with a new sense of its religious integrity: 'In her shall last our *State's* faire Spring./Now and for ever flourishing,/As long as Heaven is lasting.'[2] This political metaphor was given a specific application within the discourse of Elizabethan courtiership, where representations of the queen as the centre and source of an evergreen pastoral world were used to affirm the existence of a 'natural' order in which the new hierarchy of the absolutist state, which conferred privileges on its aristocratic members, was implied to be divinely ordained. But the precise definition, both of these privileges, and also of the renewal of the English state held to be emblematized by Elizabeth's chastity, was a contentious issue. In discussions of sir Philip Sidney's *The Lady of May*, several critics have demonstrated that Sidney used the trope of a restored golden age as the ground for a contest of political authority between female monarch and male courtier which was also a contest at the level of religious ideology.[3] Yet when this conflict is viewed within the complete series of aristocratic pastimes which first idealized the queen's unmarried state, it becomes apparent that it was also, most importantly, a contest of sexual authority.

Representations of Elizabeth as a figure deemed to link earth and heaven were implicated in a courtly debate influenced by humanism and Protestantism, concerning the relative merits of contemplation and action. As I have mentioned in earlier chapters, while the *vita contemplativa* and an ascetic withdrawal from the world was typically privileged in medieval thought, the impact of humanism had led to a growing emphasis upon man's capacity to transform the world through action.[4] Calvinist doctrine had developed this emphasis upon the *vita activa* and the Erasmian idea of the Christian soldier to formulate an idea of Christianity as militant activity.[5] And within the early Elizabethan pastime, ideas of a pastoral transformation centred upon the figure of the female monarch were combined with an ambitious interpretation of the male courtier's identity which was influenced by these humanist and Calvinist concerns. He was represented as committed to a Protestant programme of militant activity in a world deemed to be on the verge of apocalypse. In other words, while presenting himself in Petrarchan and Neoplatonic terms, as her rejected lover, he desired to imitate and equal Elizabeth's role as creator of a restored paradise in the English state, by

claiming the task of extending this English golden age to the international scene. The Kenilworth entertainment of 1575, presented to
Elizabeth when she was the guest of the earl of Leicester, introduced this
new style of courtly response to the queen. Its assumptions, extended and
refined in entertainments at Ditchley (1575) and at Wanstead (1578), and
in a tilt entitled 'The Four Foster Children of Desire' (1581) were
reiterated in other courtly pastimes throughout the rest of the reign.
Elizabeth's saturnalian reversal of gender roles is aptly figured by her
comparison in the aristocratic pastime to the May queen of folk tradition.
In subtle ways, however, the male courtiers who devised these events also
attempted to challenge Elizabeth's powers as a Lady of Misrule – that is,
as a female monarch.

The Elizabethan entertainment shared certain features with other
species of courtly pastime, with medieval disguisings or mummings, as
well as with the Renaissance masque; but its typically out-of-doors and
daytime location also distinguished it from these forms, which were
conventionally performed at night in a hall or banqueting chamber.[6] It
comprised, not a single dramatic performance, but a string of different
dramatic episodes, usually of an apparently impromptu character, staged
for the queen at intervals during her visit to a great house on one of her
summer progresses about the country. The entertainment therefore had
an exclusive and predominantly aristocratic audience. The tilt, on the
other hand, was a more public affair, designed to demonstrate to a crowd
of non-courtly onlookers the collective power of both queen and nobles.[7]
At base, however, both Elizabethan entertainment and tilt were
introspective, since both were primarily concerned with affirming a new
and special accord between absolute monarch and certain members of her
aristocracy. This relationship was now defined in terms of the *desire* of
courtier for monarch (or for the state of spiritual perfection which she
was held to embody). Both these species of pastime stressed Elizabeth's
capacity to redeem a fallen world because of her physical self-sufficiency
or chastity. And to reinforce the theme of activity, the queen was
constructed as a participant in, as well as spectator to, the entertainment;
it represented her as actively initiating the new golden age during the
course of her visit.

A desire for Elizabeth to play a militant role as a Protestant queen
seems to have had popular currency from the very beginning of her reign.
The final tableau in her coronation entry to the city of London in 1559
compared the new queen to the biblical Deborah, and emphasized this
heroine's gift of guidance from God in time of war:

> In war she, through gods aide, did put her foes to flight,
> And with the dint of sworde the bande of bondage brast.
> In peace she, through gods aide, did alway maintaine right
> And judged Israell till fourty yeres were past.[8]

This theme appeared again in civic entries organized for Elizabeth's visits to Bristol in 1574 and Norwich in 1576. At Bristol, the main event of the entry was the siege of a small fort called Feeble Policy by hostile troops. Here Elizabeth was seen as an active upholder of peace, sending sufficient aid to the just cause (which seems to have represented the Netherlands Protestants, currently resisting Spanish troops).[9] At Norwich, Deborah again appeared, and told the queen to: 'Continue as thou hast begun, weed out the wicked rout,/Uphold the simple, meeke and good, pull downe the proud and stout,' while another biblical virago, Judith, cited the example of her own valour and appealed to Elizabeth to 'hold for aie a noble victor's part'.[10] The appearance here of St George, a saint closely linked with the medieval crusades, reinforced this message of Christian militancy.

The focus of the Elizabethan entertainment on the queen as an active figure was therefore not restricted to or devised by aristocratic circles. But the new courtly formulation of this idea differed from that found in these entries in several respects. In the first place, classical and medieval chivalric motifs rather than biblical images were used to articulate the idea of Elizabeth as a warrior queen, and to combine this idea of female militancy with the theme of chastity (this was absent from the civic entries to London and Bristol; its presence in the Norwich entry suggests the influence of the courtly entertainments staged the previous year). The Roman goddess Diana, with whom Elizabeth was increasingly associated by her courtly cult (and to whom she was compared in the first of these events, the Kenilworth entertainment), figured a state of pre-lapsarian harmony with nature; she was also, as a huntress, equipped with the weapons and powers to defend it. In fact Elizabeth appears as Diana in a propagandistic Dutch engraving, which depicts the queen as a key defender of international Protestantism against Catholicism (plate 10). And Diana had close affinities with the figure of the Amazon or woman warrior.[11] Not only did the entertainments often accord Elizabeth her favourite sporting role of huntress; in a striking departure from the formulae of medieval chivalric romance (a departure presumably indebted to the female knights of Renaissance romances such as *Amadis de Gaule* and Ariosto's *Orlando Furioso*), these events also represented Elizabeth herself as a questing knight, committed to extending her own state of perfection through aggressive action.[12] Yet while the attribution of this role of warrior to a woman ruler challenged conventional ideas of proper feminine behaviour (especially in its Amazonian combination of agressiveness with chastity), still it is important to note that it did this only in imaginative terms. The entertainment may have held Elizabeth up as the literal model and inspiration of a new style of aristocratic chivalry, but it was only men who could translate this fiction into real terms. In other words, Elizabeth was being used to mime (and so to legitimate) the ambitions of certain of her male courtiers. In emphasizing the links between Elizabeth's cult and heroic action, these courtiers seem to have been interested less in her role as queen than in their own identities as courtly servants. What distinguishes the approach of the courtly pastime to the theme of militant action from that of the civic entries is that it does not simply promote a political strategy via its mythologization of the female monarch; it also articulates the mounting self-consciousness of various members of Elizabeth's court.

A central figure in the group of new aristocrats who sponsored the idealization of Elizabeth in the courtly pastime was Robert Dudley, earl of Leicester. The use of these events as a vehicle for the queen's cult was in the first instance closely linked to the last phase of Leicester's long-standing personal relationship with her, which dated from the beginning of her reign and which had prompted a great deal of speculative gossip (as indeed did her relations with several other favourites, such as sir Christopher Hatton and sir Walter Ralegh). The earl's courtship of his monarch was a central theme of the entertainments presented before her by Leicester, his protégé, sir Henry Lee, and his nephew Philip Sidney, at Kenilworth, Woodstock, and Wanstead in 1575 and 1578. But it is difficult to know how to interpret this theme. The combination of erotic innuendo with compliments to the queen's decision not to marry which characterizes these events offers yet another example of the paradox whereby Elizabeth's chastity was often represented in implicitly sexual terms, as a state of physical autonomy rather than physical virginity. For by this time, sixteen-odd years after the beginning of this courtship, it seems extremely unlikely that Leicester had any expectation of it leading to marriage. The repetition of his earlier pleas for consort status in these events seems to refer instead to his desire to retain an especial relationship with the queen – the privileges of his personal 'golden age' as chief favourite. It was also probably connected to the fact that at some time prior to 1578, he had begun to consider marriage to Lettice Knollys, countess of Essex. Fearing the queen's anger at the match (rightly!), Leicester's reiterated courtship in these pastimes may have been so that he could later argue that the marriage was due to pique at his continued rejection by Elizabeth. But the representation of the earl in these entertainments as a virile lover intent on action indicates that his suit also had political motivations. In the 1570s, Leicester had his finger in many pies; on the one hand he was a leading supporter of the growing 'Puritan' opposition to the Elizabethan religious settlement; on the other hand he was firmly committed to an active English foreign policy inspired by radical Protestant ideals.[13] The privy council faction which he led with sir Francis Walsingham was pressing Elizabeth ever more insistently to adopt a foreign policy of military intervention in order to assist Protestants in France, Scotland, and the Netherlands, and specific reference to the

Netherlands issue was made in the Kenilworth entertainment.[14]

Leicester's marriage to the countess of Essex, shortly after the Wanstead entertainment of 1578, might have been expected to signal the loss of his own influence with the queen and a corresponding decline in the power of his faction. In fact, the end of his individual suit made it possible for Elizabeth to be served with Petrarchan devotion by not one, but a whole group of courtiers. The association of courtiership with activity which he had promoted survived in both tilt and entertainment until the end of the reign, although it was challenged in certain other contributions to Elizabeth's cult. In other words, these courtiers were attempting to justify their social climbing (which had taken Leicester in particular from one level of the aristocracy into the other, from the *nobilitas minor* to the *nobilitas maior*) with reference to the military role which had defined the feudal aristocracy. And just as the status of the medieval knight had been enhanced by a religious definition of his role during the Crusades, as a 'miles Christi', so a commitment to radical Protestant or Calvinist ideology was now used to legitimate the military aspirations of this group of aristocrats. This religious definition of their role also equated their class privileges with membership of a spiritual elite. As early as 1563, the Protestant theologian Lawrence Humphrey had suggested that true nobility depended on spiritual grace rather than heredity. He called upon the English nobility to

> prove themselves, descended of that reverende, auncient, and Goddishe race: which for the excellencye of her vertue, and manye merites of mankynde, is deemed to have had heavenlye byrth, and glyded from the skyes: and as the Saviour and preserver of mankynde, is honored with the tonges, and pennes of all men.[15]

The prominence of the wild man motif in the early entertainments connected with Leicester foregrounds this theme of social mobility legitimated through politico-religious action; in medieval romance, the wild man is an outsider to the status quo but none the less is usually depicted as having a great deal to teach it.

But within the context of Elizabethan absolutism, the most important justification of their status made by this group was their claim that only *they* could accurately interpret the sign which was Elizabeth and so have greatest access to the earthly paradise which she personified. In the entertainment, the restored green world of the absolutist golden age is specifically equated with private property – with the courtly residences which were the settings for these events.[16] This generation of aristocrats was of course among the first to abandon the old fortified castles of feudal times for more gracious dwellings, dedicated to purposes of leisure rather than of defence. The great 'stately' homes of the Elizabethan age – Leicester's Kenilworth, lord Burghley's Theobalds, sir Christopher

Hatton's Holdenby – offer eloquent proof of the power and affluence enjoyed by Elizabeth's most favoured servants.[17] They justified these prodigious examples of conspicuous consumption, however, by the argument that their houses were either modernized or built to entertain the queen and her vast retinue in the course of her summer progresses.[18] But not only were these 'prodigy houses' signs of their owner's devotion to and benefits from Elizabeth, they were also emblems of a new social order, and the different social relations which this prescribed, for in their carefully delimited gardens and parks we see the new Elizabethan aristocrats gradually separating themselves from the country scene. They often did this, of course, by the notorious practice of enclosure, for they fenced in the 'commons' not just for agricultural purposes but also to provide themselves with enlarged parks, warrens, and chases for their homes. Burghley, for example, writing to Hatton after a visit to his Holdenby, praised its magnificence, and commented upon the 'large, long, straight fair way' that led to the house.[19] The house had an elaborate formal garden, described in the seventeenth century as 'adorned with several long walks, mounts, arbors and seats, with curious delightful knots', and planted with fruit trees. There were orchards, fish ponds, bowling alleys, spinneys planted with ash, and 'a variety of delightful walks'.[20] House and garden encompassed 38 acres, while the dimensions of the park which encircled it were around 500. It is these extensive gardens and parks, rather than the unconfined reaches of nature that lie beyond, which correspond to the idealized context of Elizabethan pastoral. R.H. Tawney pointed out that: 'The gentle Sidney's *Arcadia* . . . was composed, if we may trust tradition, in the park at the Herbert's country-seat at Washerne, which they had made by enclosing a whole village and evicting the tenants.'[21]

The nature which Elizabeth encountered in the Elizabethan entertainment was thus highly constrained, represented either by the emblematic designs of the formal garden, or by parks and chases whose fences or walls cautiously excluded all signs of the harsher reality of country life, where the monarch and her courtiers could hunt without venturing into the open countryside. In these exclusive Edens, the aristocracy affirmed the sanctity of property and simultaneously separated themselves from all evidence of the fact of labour. Yet the courtier who presented himself to Elizabeth within this enclosed green world was a curiously paradoxical figure, torn between impulses to identify with, or to tame and so transcend nature – much as were the Petrarchan and the Neoplatonic lover.

The shepherd is traditionally viewed as the most important inhabitant of the perpetually green world of pastoral convention. But although this role was sometimes mimicked by courtiers in Renaissance pastoral literature, it was primarily a poetic persona, adopted in emulation of the pastoral poets Theocritus and Virgil. The shepherd's relationship with nature was consequently defined in terms of art. On the other hand, in medieval romances, and in works of Renaissance literature influenced by medieval chivalry, the figure of the wild man was closely involved with an aristocratic search for identity via an epic encounter with a wild and harsh nature untamed by art. In contrast to the shepherd, he inhabited the wilder, and usually wooded borders of the pastoral world. The notable prominence accorded to this figure in the first Elizabethan entertainment, at Kenilworth in 1575, suggests that the enclosed green world of Elizabethan courtliness was already conceived there as part of a wilder, epic landscape. Thus a sojourn in the earthly paradise is implied to be a prelude and inspiration to heroic endeavour in an untamed natural world, which lies beyond both the aristocratic estate and the idealized body politic of England. The wild man links the idea of courtliness as pastoral retreat with an active commitment to the extension of that green world, through 'golden age' absolutist politics. Yet this figure is not only used to affirm the search for masculine identity through military action; he also defines courtiership and the benefits it can confer not in terms of a sublimated or transformed sexuality, but as dependent on the erotic authority of the erect phallus, symbolized by the wild man's club. As an emblem of sexual misrule within the polity of a female monarch, the challenge posed by Leicester's wild man is both to her authority and to her supposedly self-sufficient sexuality. In later entertainments, however, this carnivalesque persona was sometimes replaced by those of shepherd or hermit, both of whom had different associations with nature and sexuality, and who figured more submissive modes of male courtliness.

Wild man, shepherd, hermit: pastoral roles for the courtier

The medieval wild man (*wodewose* or green man) had a prominent place in European folk tradition (although he may originally derive from Celtic myth). Usually depicted in deliberately grotesque terms, covered with a thick coat of hair, or with moss and ivy, and carrying an uprooted tree or club, he was presented as an image of primitive man, who lacked any knowledge of a Christian God. The typical emphasis upon the lustfulness of this figure points to a connection with the unconscious and all the terrors it concealed; his association with instinctual desires is also implied by the fact that the wild man was a forest dweller rather than (as was the shepherd) an inhabitant of open tracts of land adapted for agricultural purposes.[22] His frequent description as a 'carl' or 'vilain' in medieval literature also seems to indicate fear of the peasant class, and this theme survived in certain English Renaissance representations which connected the wild man with 'masterless men' or vagrants.[23] It was presumably this association with a threat to the established order of society that led to the wild man's prominence in popular festivity and carnival: he had obvious affinities both with the Robin Hood figure who was 'king' of the May Day festivities, and also with the wintertime lord of Misrule.[24] Yet in aristocratic literature and entertainments during the twelfth century, he also became important in developing ideas of courtliness. In this context his role was primarily as an emblem of the anti-social or instinctual human state which medieval courtly love attempted to refine and control; however, his presence in the discourses of medieval courtly love also points to the links between this emergent courtly code of behaviour and the new degree of mobility which was then occurring within the different levels of the feudal aristocracy.

European medieval romances such as Chrétien de Troyes' twelfth-century *Yvain* and *Lancelot* set representations of the wild man as external antagonist alongside others of the wild man as inner experience, as a psychological state *temporarily* experienced by the courtly lover. The best-known of these transformations was that of Yvain:

> Lors li monta uns torbeillons
> El chief si granz, que il forsone,
> Lors se descire et se depone
> Et fuit par chans et par arees. . . .
> Les bestes par le bois agueite,
> Si les ocit et si manjue
> La veneison trestote crue
> Et tant conversa et boschage
> Come hon forsené et sauvage. . . .

> (A whirlwind broke loose in his brain
> So violent that he went insane,
> and clawed himself, tore off his clothes,
> and fled across the fields and rows. . . .
> Once in the woods, he lay in wait
> for animals, killed them, and ate
> their flesh uncooked, completely raw,
> like a wild man. . . .)[25]

It seems to have been due in part to this altered conception that the wild man became a popular emblem in medieval heraldry. The convention gained in strength in Renaissance romances such as Ariosto's *Orlando Furioso*, where the wild-man-like insanity inspired in the knight Orlando by unrequited love is a central element of the plot. Paradoxically, this state of mania, or 'love madness', which led to the knight living like a wild man in nature, was interpreted as part of his progress towards an ideal of courtly behaviour, as a training ground where he must be overwhelmed by, then learn to control, his powerful instinctual drives.

Just as love (or lust) was usually seen as the cause of this mania in a knight, so it was often posed as the solution: a typical visual image of this process was of a maiden leading a 'tamed' wild man in chains.[26] This motif resembles yet differs from Diana's metamorphosis of Actaeon in classical myth, for the taming/chaining suggests the encircling or direction of the wild man's exaggerated phallic potency within the female womb or vagina – unlike Petrarchism and Neoplatonism, courtly love often aimed for illicit sexual gratification rather than the complete surrender of erotic desire.[27]

By the time of the Renaissance, the north European tradition of wild man iconography had been modified in two important respects. In the first place, it had become closely connected with the classical pastoral tradition. In the work of some medieval writers there had been a confusion between the wild man and the satyrs and fauns of classical myth; now he was often compared to and identified with a range of classical figures, which included Pan and other satyr-like figures (Sylvanus, Silenus, Faunus) as well as Hercules and Actaeon.[28] Several of these figures had certain idealized associations. For example, as the Greek god of Arcadia and of shepherds, Pan had a certain connection with Diana; she is depicted with satyrs as well as nymphs in Clouet's 'Le Bain de Diane' (plate 7). Likewise, the figure of Hercules was much admired in the Renaissance as an example of the active life, while his *virtus* or force was often seen as the practical application of an occult knowledge which he shared with Pan and his satyrs.[29] At the same time, there had begun to circulate accounts of the inhabitants of the New World, living in an apparently idyllic environment which prompted comparison with the golden age.[30] The wild man consequently became associated in certain contexts with an incipient discourse of colonialism.[31] In other words, his medieval complexity was greatly enlarged in the Renaissance, and it is frequently difficult to know on which level to interpret the figure. This ambiguity certainly applied to his early appearances in the Elizabethan entertainment.

The wild man's challenge to the traditional pastoral pre-eminence of the shepherd in the Kenilworth entertainment was briefly reversed at Wanstead in 1578, by Sidney's *The Lady of May*. Subsequent to this, the shepherd was usually most notable by his absence from the Elizabethan pastime – this in spite of the fact that at Wanstead his lyric courtship had been preferred by Elizabeth. The predominantly poetic associations of this role may have had something to do with this. More popular as an alternative persona for the courtier (rather than the courtly poet or courtier–poets like Sidney or Ralegh, both of whom used the shepherd) was the figure of the hermit. While in his practice of contemplation the hermit resembled the shepherd–poet, like the wild man he had links with medieval chivalry, and so was presumably considered a more strictly courtly persona. The shepherd of pastoral was by inference implicated within a network of social relationships, to whose artifice his own poetic skills significantly contributed. But what is striking about both wild man and hermit as modes of aristocratic courtliness is that paradoxically they are both associated with a *rejection* of civilized society, rather than with the consummate mastery of its rules of etiquette. This foreshadows the ambiguous representation of Belphoebe in *The Faerie Queene*, who while she figures Elizabeth's chastity, the central element in her courtly cult, asserts that honour can only be found *away* from the court:

> Who so in pompe of proud estate (quoth she)
> Does swim, and bathes himselfe in courtly blis,
> Does waste his dayes in darke obscuritee,
> And in oblivion ever buried is:
> Where ease abounds, yt's eath to doe amis:
> But who his limbs with labours, and his mind
> Behaves with cares, cannot so easie mis,
> Abroad in armes, at home in studious kind
> Who seeks with painfull toile, shall honor soonest find.[32]

Like the wild man, the hermit was depicted as inhabiting a bleak wilderness environment far from civilized society: in fact the early Christian hermits (or desert fathers) were often depicted as wild men in late medieval and early Renaissance art.[33] In some conceptions the hermit was also characterized as mad: in other words, as in contact with instinctual or unconscious forces. But in medieval and Renaissance romances, although the mania, solitude, and extreme poverty common to wild man and hermit resulted in both being perceived in broadly ambiguous terms, as half human and half demonic, the wild man was typically seen in a far more threatening light than was the hermit, as a figure more sinister than benevolent. Sometimes it was a hermit who effected the transformation of a knight from a state of wildness or love madness back to mental equilibrium. And while the wild man might be said to represent the stage prior to the achievement of perfect chivalry, the hermit appears to signify a stage of knowledge beyond or succeeding knighthood. Thus Ramon Lull attributed his *Book of the Ordre of Chyvalrye* to a hermit who was once a knight.[34] Like the shepherd, the hermit had experienced civilized society before withdrawing from it: yet the hermit sought interior rather than aesthetic beauty in nature. Following the example of the Christian 'desert fathers' and their biblical predecessors (Christ himself, John the Baptist, Elijah, Moses), the hermit of chivalric romance was implied to have retreated to the wilderness in an attempt to regain Eden in his own person. In contrast, medieval and Renaissance literature usually depicted the wild man as never having experienced civilized society, and consequently having no knowledge of the Christian religion (even if he was sometimes seen as the possessor of a pagan or esoteric type of knowledge alongside his physical force). Yet while the wild man was often contrasted with the explicitly Christian hermit in medieval and Renaissance romances, the Elizabethan entertainment seems rather to associate these figures with different types of Christianity. The wild men of entertainments like those at Kenilworth and Wanstead appear to signify a militant Protestantism, and at Wanstead this is explicitly distinguished from the more Catholic religious associations of the hermit, whose withdrawal from the world for purposes of religious contemplation was inextricably connected with Catholic monasticism (the desert fathers had founded the first Christian monasteries).[35]

The use of wild man, shepherd, and hermit to explore models of courtiership, both in the courtly pastime and in several other Elizabethan literary texts, reveals to what extent the attempt to define Elizabeth's cult also involved a project of self-definition for her courtly servants. But it was the figure of the wild man who seems to have posed the greatest imaginative threat to Elizabeth's authority. Although this figure apparently deferred to Elizabeth's power, the courtly use of the persona was not necessarily connected with the theme of service, for in both the middle ages and the Renaissance it was often associated with kings.[36] Elizabeth's father, Henry VIII, had adopted a role related to that of the wild man, the forester, in some of his court revels.[37] In the specific context of the entertainments, the wild man claimed a relationship to wild nature which paralleled or equalled that associated with Elizabeth as a nature goddess, as another Diana or May queen; his relationship to the king of the May would have been obvious.[38] And while Elizabeth as May queen figures a saturnalian reversal of the patriarchal order of society, the wild man introduces the possibility of another saturnalia, with an implied challenge to royal authority (which simultaneously desires to reassert the rule of the male).

Indeed the encounters between queen and wild man which figured so prominently in Elizabethan entertainments (for example, at Kenilworth, Wanstead, Bisham, Cowdray, Elvetham) represented a less dramatic and comprehensive submission to the feminine than that implicit in the Diana–Actaeon myth. Although the appearance of the wild man in these courtly events could be interpreted within the terms of idealized love as a symptom of love mania, it conveniently defers the male courtier's civilizing metamorphosis which is supposed to follow this stage, either in sexual intercourse with his beloved, or in the sublimation of desire. Indeed it is a characteristic feature of literature connected with Elizabeth that the myth of Diana and Actaeon – which on one level could be interpreted in terms of a violent and tragic encounter between female sexual autonomy and male sexuality – is frequently gestured towards only to be displaced or altered. The sacrificial metamorphosis of Actaeon is either elided or deferred. And among the queen's male favourites, only sir Christopher Hatton appears to have deliberately represented his relationship with the queen in terms of Actaeon's transformation: he adopted a deer as his heraldic badge (the shepherd figure also seems evoked in the queen's nickname for him: 'sheep' or 'mutton'). Leicester's preference for a more assertive courtly role was consistent both with his heraldic badge (of bear and ragged staff) and with Elizabeth's nickname: Robin. Ironically, his wild man/May lord persona was somewhat at odds with his Protestant radicalism; the English Puritans were vehemently opposed to such folk traditions. Philip Stubbes, writing in the 1580s, equated the summer lord with Satan.[39] None the less, Leicester seems to have used the wild man to claim for himself a less constricted sphere of activity *outside* the court, in an attempt to retain a quality of masculine initiative and directness not fully compatible with the code of courtliness. What is proposed in these early events is not the subordination of male courtier to female monarch, but an *alliance* between a directed but still dynamic masculine energy and its feminine agent of control.

The Kenilworth entertainment of 1575

The Kenilworth entertainment was not the earl of Leicester's first involvement in the business of courtly revelry. Marie Axton has pointed out that he played an important part in an Inner Temple masque performed before Elizabeth in 1561/2, as prince Pallaphilos, defender of the Elizabeth state and its reformed religion (the temple of Pallas), and also provided a 'masque of Amazons' for the wedding of his brother, the earl of Warwick, in 1564.[40] The different emphases of these events, on militant activity *in defence of the feminine* in the Inner Temple masque, and *by the feminine* in the masque of Amazons, were to be combined at Kenilworth. Here a new acceptance of Elizabeth's unmarried state, as an emblem of the restored health of the English body politic, was given dynamic form by casting the queen herself as a militant defender of her state. In this conception, Diana as a goddess of chastity played an important part, in spite of the several references made in the event to Leicester's suit for Elizabeth's hand. The positive use of this figure in connection with the queen was a new departure.[41] But significantly, although the several meetings between the queen and a wild man figure point an obvious parallel with the Diana–Actaeon myth, there is no exact repetition of its conclusion.

Elizabeth arrived at Kenilworth on Saturday 9 July 1575. As she approached the castle, she was welcomed by a figure who identified herself as the Cumaean Sybil. Her verses of welcome promised peace to Elizabeth and her kingdom in terms which identified the queen with

Christ: 'You shal be called the Prince of peace. and peace shal be your shield./So that your eyes shall never see the broyls of bloody field.'[42] Yet the rest of the entertainment was to suggest that such an apocalyptic achievement would in fact require militant effort. and placed Elizabeth firmly in the role of a questing knight who must meet with and overcome various obstacles.[43] Thus at the castle's main gate. the queen was met by a porter identified with Hercules. holding a club and keys – the first adumbration of the wild man theme. At first he was reluctant to admit Elizabeth, but yielded the keys upon recognizing her. Then at the inner gate of the castle she was greeted by a figure from Arthurian romance, the Lady of the Lake: escorted by two nymphs, this figure floated to land upon a moveable island in the nearby lake. (This was the first occasion upon which the elaborate machinery of French and Italian water fêtes had been employed in England.) The Lady heralded Elizabeth as the descendant of Arthur. telling her: 'And as my love to Arthur did appeare./So shal't to you, in earnest and in sport. . . .'[44] But she also pointed out that since Leicester and his family were guardians both of the lake and of the castle beyond it. they too were in a sense Arthur's heirs.[45] On one level. this statement obviously claims an affinity between Elizabeth and Leicester, which of necessity compels them to be partners. Yet it could also be interpreted as raising some doubts as to who was the truer heir or custodian of the Arthurian chivalric tradition: fifteen years later. in Spenser's *The Faerie Queene*. the hero prince Arthur would seem to be associated with Leicester. while Elizabeth herself is displaced into the mythic realm of faerie which invisibly supports and inspires his chivalry. Then. as Elizabeth passed over the castle bridge. she found on its seven pairs of posts gifts purportedly left by seven Roman gods: Sylvanus. Pomona. Ceres. Bacchus. Neptune. Mars. and Phoebus. The gods themselves did not appear. but their gifts were explained by a boy dressed as a poet. This divine assembly was not a particularly conventional one (although it is notable that it was a figure related to the wild man, Sylvanus, whose gifts were placed first); however it was clearly intended to emphasize the queen's close relationship to the earth, its creatures, and its fruits, as the restorer of a lost paradise.

Sunday at the castle featured a fireworks display in the evening; on the Monday Elizabeth went hunting in the chase which Leicester had recently prepared for that purpose. and of which Robert Laneham wrote in his description of the Kenilworth visit: 'Diana her selfe might have deygned thear well enough too raunge for her pastime.'[46] Hunting was a key motif of the entertainment: Elizabeth hunted three times during her stay, and upon two of these outings the hunt was used as the occasion for some type of impromptu performance or diversion. Thus as she was returning to the castle after a successful hunt. the queen encountered a 'savage man', bearing an oaken branch and clad in moss and ivy. He presented himself as a wanderer, but stated:

> That continuing so long in these wilde wastes, whearin oft had he fared both far and neer, yet had he never to see so glorious an assemble afore: and now cast intoo great grief of mind, for that neyther by himself coold hee gess, nor knew whear else to bee taught, what they should be, or whoo bare estate. . . .[47]

Although he seemed menacing, once he had been told the identity of the figure before him, 'Hombre Salvagio' made a speech in praise of the queen which prophesied that her reign would be prosperous. His wandering suggests a connection with the 'masterless men' or vagrants, but his speech also hinted that his marginal social position was none the less invested with a indefinable authority. He revealed an especial knowledge of all the different levels of society, and constructed himself as a mediator between the estates and the monarch:

> hee reporteth the incredibl ioy that all estatez in the land have allweyz of her highness whear so ever it cums: endeth with presage and prayer of perpetuall felicitee, and with humbl subiection of him and hissen & all that they may do.[48]

Indeed, in the same phrase with which he promises the fealty 'of him and hissen', the wild man implies the existence of a realm within a realm, and so of a possible challenge to Elizabeth's monarchy. By inference, the success of her rule is vitally dependent upon his goodwill and collaboration.

The next major diversion was on the following Sunday, when the queen saw a variety of semi-dramatic episodes of both popular and courtly types; this seems to have been the only occasion in the short history of the Elizabethan entertainment that folk materials were presented in their original forms, rather than adapted to courtly ends. There was a burlesque of a folk marriage, with a mock bride and groom, which was followed by the courtly sport of running at the quintain. The men of Coventry presented a folk play to celebrate Hock Tuesday, which dramatized a battle between the English and the Danes in 1002. The theme of national defence was clearly articulated here, but in addition, since Hock Tuesday was associated in folk tradition with a time of sexual role reversal, there was especial emphasis upon the valiant action of the English women in this combat.[49] This theme of militant action by women was applied to the queen herself in an episode presented the next day.

On Monday evening, after another successful hunt, Elizabeth was approached by Triton, 'Neptune's trumpeter', who came across the lake outside the castle 'upon a swimming mermaid (that from top to tail was eighteen foot long)'. He entreated her to help the Lady of the Lake, who had just been imprisoned by a knight called Sir Bruse sans pitié 'in revenge of his cosen Merlyne the Prophet, whom, for his inordinate lust, she had inclosed in a rocke'.[50] The reference to lust indicates a further variation on the wild man motif, with which Merlin also had some association.[51] In this context, however, the wild man was connected with enemy forces rather than loyal subjects – an indication of the perplexing multivalency of the motif as used even within a single event. In what was probably a reference to the plight of the Netherlands Protestants fighting the Spanish across the channel, it was pointed out that Elizabeth should help the Lady, here compared to Diana, because she was also a 'maid' and opposed to the marriage goddess Juno who apparently encouraged Sir Bruse in his attempted rape:

> that yrefull knight Sir Bruce had hyr in chase;
> And sought by force her virgin's state full fowlie to deface.
> Yea, yet at hand about these bankes his bands be often seen:
> That neither can she come nor scape, but by your helpe, O queene:
> For though that Neptune has so fanst with floods her fortresse long,
> Yet Mars her foe must needs prevaile, his batteries are so strong.
> How then can Diane, Juno's force and sharp assaults abyde;
> When all the crue of cheefest gods is bent on Bruse his side?
>   . . . sure she cannot stand,
> Except a worthier maid than she her cause do take in hand.[52]

Elizabeth's mere presence was shortly announced to have effected the Lady's deliverance, a miracle which was celebrated by the poet Arion, who came riding across the lake on a dolphin. Realistic parallels to this imaginative assertion of the monarch's Christ-like transforming power had actually been offered earlier that day, when she had knighted five gentlemen and cured five people, presumably local inhabitants, 'of the peynefull and daungerous diseaz, called ye kings evill, for that only Kings & Queens of this realm, without other medsin (save only by handling a prayerz) only doo cure it . . .'.[53]

In the last week of the royal visit, bad weather made it necessary to cancel various other events. Marie Axton argues that among the most important of these omitted episodes was one which pressed Leicester's suit quite explicitly. This was the story of a nymph of Diana called Zabeta who, having accepted Juno's gift of sovereignty, is advised also to honour her as a goddess of marriage.[54] When Elizabeth left Kenilworth on the following Wednesday the author of this unperformed episode, the poet George Gascoigne, apparently followed her, dressed as Sylvanus. In what

Axton suggests was extemporizing from his unused verses, he begged her
to stay and to free 'deepe desire': 'O Queene commaunde againe/This
Castle and the Knight, which keepes the same for you . . . .'[55]
Gascoigne's disguise as a type of wild man, Sylvanus, points the
connection between earlier uses of this motif in the pastime and Leicester
himself. He asserted that Zabeta's rejection of 'deepe desire' has
transformed him into a holly bush. But while Diana's metamorphosis of
Actaeon had implied a sacrifice of phallic sexuality, the courtly lover as
holly bush signified a magnified (or multiplied) phallic desire:

> So is he now furnished on every side with sharpe pricking leaves, to
> prove the restlesse prickes of his privie thoughts. Mary there are two
> kinds of Holly, that is to say, He-Holly, and She-Holly. Now some will
> say, that She-Holly hath no prickes, but thereof I intermeddle not.[56]

Not only does this speech remind us that Elizabethan courtly discourse
could sometimes be sexually explicit, it effectively mocks Elizabeth's
assumption of a masculine authority along with her supposed freedom
from sexual desire, in a lewd and punning speculation on the question of
her prick-lessness. Leicester's statement of courtly devotion interweaves
an erotic challenge along with its ostensible subservience.

Marie Axton has interpreted this extemporized episode as proof that
the Kenilworth entertainment was intended as a furtherance of Leicester's
marriage suit, and a criticism of the queen's service of Diana (or choice of
chastity).[57] But that this adlibbing by Gascoigne from a cancelled event
should be read as a serious proposal of marriage seems doubtful. It was a
very different episode which formed the climax to the Kenilworth
entertainment, Elizabeth's freeing of the Lady of the Lake, and in that
episode the queen's identification with Diana was viewed most sym-
pathetically. Not only was Elizabeth's chivalrous release of the Lady of
the Lake obviously prepared for by her first encounter with this figure
upon her arrival at Kenilworth, it also had an integral relation to the
entertainment's use of chivalric motifs via the story of Arthur, and hence
to its theme of militant action against an enemy of virtue and pastoral
peace. What the episode does indicate, however, is that the mode of
courtiership which would soon become characteristic of Elizabeth's
courtly cult – a Petrarchan or Neoplatonic devotion to an unattainable
object of desire – had not yet been completely formulated. Courtly
compliment here consists of overt sexual innuendo rather than the elegant
literary displacement of erotic desire. At the same time, Gascoigne's
impromptu speech on Leicester's behalf also points to the presence of a
potential conflict which would appear in later entertainments, at
Wanstead and at Elvetham. There is an implied tension here between the
male courtier and the courtly poet, who translates his aristocratic patron's

aspirations into literary terms but threatens to usurp his role as a creator and interpreter of Elizabeth's courtly cult.

The Woodstock entertainment of 1575

Later in the same summer progress of 1575, the queen was entertained at Woodstock, home of Leicester's client, sir Henry Lee, and on this occasion we find the idea of Elizabeth as an object of sublimated desire articulated rather more clearly, although there is still not a fully Petrarchan or Neoplatonic conception of courtiership.[58] The desired military role of Leicester as her especial lover was still emphasized, but at Woodstock the hermit first entered the Elizabethan courtly pastime, replacing the wild man of Kenilworth as the figure who unified the different parts of the entertainment (a task he performed as narrator and guide). The first episode of the event began with a fight between two knights called Contarenus and Loricus, who appear to have represented Leicester and Lee. Their fight was interrupted by Hemetes the Hermit, who proceeded to explain to the queen the misunderstanding which had caused this fight.

The hermit's romance-like tale was of a fictional love affair implicitly based on Elizabeth's relationship with Leicester; explicitly, however, it accorded to the queen a transforming role as the ruler in whose country two noble lovers were finally reunited after a long separation. This dual role therefore establishes an interesting dialectic between Elizabeth's 'two bodies' of private person and ruler, for the true desire of her private self is suggested to be marriage and sexuality rather than chastity. In contrast to the view formulated in the 'two bodies' discourse of Elizabethan lawyers concerned with the succession (a view which was also implicit in *The Faerie Queene*, as I shall show in a later chapter), the decision to remain unmarried is here presented as the choice of the queen rather than the private woman: in other words, as a choice consistent with her embodying of the body politic. The hermit related that Gandina, only daughter and heir of the duke Occanon, loved and was loved by Contarenus, a knight inferior to her in rank, but her father found means to separate the lovers. A Sybil had advised Gandina to accept the assistance of the knight Loricus in her search for Contarenus, and prophesied that she would find her missing lover when they arrived at the best country in the world, and the one with the most just ruler. Unfortunately, when they finally found Contarenus he jealously attacked Loricus, but the hermit implied that Elizabeth's very presence had prevented tragedy and brought about a happy ending. And he declared that the queen had also restored his own sight, which he had forfeited long ago because of unfaithfulness in love. This was another proof of her miraculous Christ-like virtue. Then he led the queen to his hermitage in the forest:

> Here, most noble lady, have I now brought you to this most symple hermytage, wheare you shall see small cunnyng but of nature, and no cost but of good will. Myne hower approcheth for my orisons; which, according to my vows, I must never breake. I must here leave your Majesty, promysing to pray (as for my soule) that whosoever wishe you best, may never wishe in vayne.[59]

At this point a banqueting house was revealed nearby, where a lavish meal had been prepared for the queen and her retinue. At the end of this banquet, the fairy queen appeared (although this version of the May queen or nature goddess was not yet identified with Elizabeth herself). She expressed her sympathy for the lovers of the hermit's tale:

> Yet blame him not for mounting up so hie,
> She beares the blame for bending down so low,
> Whom fortune bids looke up, too blame were he
> if he should quaile, and worthy overthrow.
> And she too blame, of neere so high degree,
> not casting love where virtue doth agree. . . .[60]

Again, Leicester's especial courtly service is posed in terms of the desire for marriage. But that this was being used as a mode of courtly compliment rather than in a serious statement of intent was indicated on the second day of the entertainment, when it was revealed that Gandina and Contarenus had decided to separate, 'for reasons of state'. Gandina told Contarenus that she would always love him, and he set off on a quest, declaring: 'Yet this I am assur'de her Princely heart./Where she hath lov'd will never quite forget.'[61] The Woodstock entertainment accordingly made explicit the idea which had been less directly conveyed at Kenilworth: that the relationship between Elizabeth and Leicester was one in which a barred or obstructed desire was necessary, and that since his service could not be rewarded with marriage Leicester should be permitted to take the military initiatives abroad which he desired, as a 'questing knight'.

The Wanstead entertainment of 1578: Sidney's *The Lady of May*

The theme of Leicester's personal courtship of the queen was stressed in a courtly pastime for the last time in 1578, when Philip Sidney's pastoral play, *The Lady of May*, was performed before Elizabeth when she visited Leicester's house at Wanstead in the absence of its owner. Like the Woodstock entertainment, it used the theme of competition between two men, but in this context they were both seen as serious suitors for the hand of the Lady of May. Elizabeth was requested by the May Lady's mother to choose between these suitors. The event therefore focuses upon Elizabeth's association with the emerging energies of summer, and with natural growth leading to harvest: the theme which was implicit in all the entertainments. But as I mentioned earlier, the fertility of the May queen also had an erotic connotation. The queen was asked to choose between a shepherd, Epsilus, and a forester (or foster), Therion, upon the basis of their performance in a singing match. The close of the play makes it clear that the forester represents Leicester (not only was this figure associated with the wild man figure so prominent at Kenilworth, Therion was Greek for wild beast, and Leicester's heraldic badge was of the bear and the ragged staff). Many critics have pointed out that the queen's final choice, of the shepherd, does not seem to have been prepared for in the performance.[62] The victory song sung by Epsilus after the decision was declared would arguably have been more appropriate for Therion, since it refers to the triumph of Sylvanus, a figure related to the forester and wild man: '*Silvanus* long in love and long in vaine,/At length obtained the point of his desire. . . .'[63] In fact there were precedents for the connection of Silvanus with the poet; Sidney would probably have been aware that in spite of his wild man associations, this persona was adopted by Petrarch in his *Bucolicum Carmen*. And that the competition between shepherd and forester took the form of a singing match rather than a trial of arms could be read as according the shepherd an advantage from the start, given the associations of this figure with poetry.

Several critics have suggested that Elizabeth's choice of Epsilus implied a rejection of the foreign policy of the Leicester–Walsingham faction.[64] It has also been recognized that the conflict between action and contemplation figures prominently in the play.[65] But one is led to wonder which motive was foremost in the minds of the Leicester faction: the ideological commitment to Protestant militancy, or the need for a cause which could legitimate their absence from the woman-dominated, 'green' world of the Elizabethan court? In the Wanstead entertainment, conflict around religious values is almost inseparable from the implied debate about sexual roles. At the end of the play, a schoolmaster character called Rombus announced that the logical result of the queen's choice was that Leicester became a hermit, and declared that indeed the earl was already reported to be a 'huge Catholicam', murmuring first 'pater noster', then 'semper Elizabeth'. The play ended with Rombus solemnly presenting Elizabeth with what he asserted was Leicester's confiscated agate rosary. In the Woodstock entertainment, Lee had invested the hermit with positive associations, in his role as interpreter and supporter of a barred desire which was translated into chivalric action; three years later, the same figure had become a symbol of Catholicism, or of a Protestantism insufficiently purged of Catholic religious influences. Yet in spite of the criticism of the hermit at Wanstead, he would remain popular in Elizabethan literature, as a courtly persona which apparently had the queen's approval. Several later courtly pastimes depicted his association with retirement and contemplation in idealized terms: for example, the retirement tilt of sir Henry Lee as the queen's champion in 1590; the entertainment performed before Elizabeth when she visited lord Burghley's house at Theobalds; and Lee's entertainment of the queen at Ditchley in 1592. Significantly, the hermit was a figure closely associated (via his links with monasticism) with the celibate life.

In the entertainments of Kenilworth, Woodstock, and Wanstead, the major themes of the Elizabethan courtly pastime were elaborated. Although there would be no further entertainments until the 1590s, these themes were taken up and developed in the decade of the 1580s, in the context of the tilt or tournament. It is not clear exactly when the Elizabethan revival of tilting began in earnest; the practice had been discontinued in the latter years of Henry VIII's reign, and been frowned upon at the courts of both Edward VI and Mary as frivolous. In the first year of Elizabeth's reign, on 5 November 1559, lord Robert Dudley (the future earl of Leicester) and lord Hunsdon (the queen's cousin on the Boleyn side) jousted in honour of the new monarch, wearing scarves of white and black.[66] Apart from this occasion, we have no record of tilting at court until the 1580s. Sir William Segar asserted that the practice of celebrating 17 November, the queen's Accession Day, with tilting, was begun by sir Henry Lee at the very beginning of the reign, and La Motte Fenelon, the French ambassador, wrote in 1572 that a fête at court was customary upon Accession Day.[67] But it seems likely that the elaborately theatrical and highly ritualized tilts described by Frances Yates and Roy Strong only appeared after the entertainments of the 1570s had formulated the initial premises of Elizabeth's courtly cult.

'The Four Foster Children of Desire' (1581)

Both Yates and Strong laid especial emphasis upon Accession Day as affording the best examples of Elizabethan tilts organized around the idea of homage to the queen. Yet in fact the first Elizabethan tilt of which we have detailed knowledge was not performed on Accession Day, but at Whitsun in 1581, and was staged to honour the visit of ambassadors from France who had come to press the suit of the duc d'Alençon for the queen's hand. The radical Protestant courtiers opposed to the French marriage were, not surprisingly, closely identified with the Leicester–Walsingham faction; as Philip Sidney acted the part of one of the Foster Children it seems probable that he was also responsible, at least in part, for devising the tilt. While its message of Elizabeth's unavailability was obviously intended to address a specific political dilemma, it also provided the most coherent formulation of courtiership as sublimated desire that had yet been produced within the courtly pastime. But just as in earlier pastimes, that theme is still articulated in relation to the opposite stance, of instinctual masculine desires demanding expression. The subject of the action, which extended over two days, was the siege of the Castle of Perfect Beauty (signifying Elizabeth) by four knights calling themselves the Four Foster Children of Desire. In the Inner Temple Christmas revels of 1561–2, in which Leicester (then lord Robert Dudley) had played a prominent part, a masque of Desire and lady Beauty which seems seriously to have promoted Dudley's courtship had ended in marriage.[68] Interwoven with that masque had been the myth of Perseus' rescue of the maiden Andromeda; but the 1581 tilt presents a very similar defence of female chastity as incompatible with marriage. In 'The Four Foster Children', the supernatural and Christ-like powers attributed to the queen in the entertainments were combined with the sun imagery which had formerly been implicit in the representation of her as a May or summer queen. This produced a more Platonic conception of the royal beloved as necessarily out of reach. An angel asks the besieging knights:

> Will you subdue the sunne, who shall rest in the shadow where the weary take breath, the disquiet rest, and all comforte, wil ye bereave men of those glistering and gladsome beames, what shall then prosper in the shining . . . moste renowned and devine Beautie, whose beames shine like the Sun . . ., the same I call Beautie the lighte of the worlde, the marvel of men, the mirour of nature. . . .[69]

As at Kenilworth and Wanstead, the emphasis here upon the lover's need to curb his violent desires is connected with imagery related to the figure of the wild man; as Louis Montrose has pointed out, although the term 'foster-child' had been in use from the middle ages, it was also connected with the figure of the wild man as forester, a word often contracted to 'foster'.[70] The attack upon Beauty's castle by the four knights was also compared to the rebellion of the giants in classical antiquity, and the gigantism of the wild man was a frequent theme in medieval literature.[71] The proper use of this lustful force, however, was represented in the figure of a 'mossie knight'. He declared upon entering the tiltyard that he had long lived in hermit-like isolation in a cave by the sea, but had emerged from retirement to defend Beauty's castle:

> most excellent and devine Beawtie, devine it must needes be that worketh so heavenly, sith he is called from his solitarie Cave to your sumptuous Court, from bondage to liberty, from a living death to a never dying life, and all for the sake and service of Beawtie: vouchsafe his shielde, which is the ensigne of your fame to be the instrument of

his fortune. And for prostrating himselfe to your feete, he is here readie preste to adventure any adventures for your gracious favour.[72]

Plato's fable of the cave as a metaphoric representation of man's illusory bondage in the material world is used here to stress the transcendental significance of Elizabeth and her court. Like Plato's philosopher, the 'mossie knight' has used the mystical practice of contemplation to free himself from illusion, and can now see the true meaning behind earthly desires – Elizabeth as the *nous* or Platonic realm of Ideas. This proposes an interesting reversal of the priority given to the life of contemplative retirement by the queen's choice at Wanstead; it is only after he has attained the highest fruits of contemplation (a vision of the true meaning of that sign which is Elizabeth) that the knight abandons this seclusion for a life of active service of his monarch. The implication here appears to be that a Neoplatonic experience of conversion or *raptio* produced by contemplation, and followed by a mystical ascent or return to source, *remeatio*, should be the prelude to a descent or *emanatio* involving truly effective action in Elizabeth's service.[73]

The date originally planned for the tilt was 23 April, St George's Day, and it is probable that the mossie knight was intended to represent St George. Not only was the saint a key figure in Elizabethan chivalry; his famous defence of a maiden from a dragon closely paralleled the Perseus–Andromeda myth, used in the Inner Temple masque of Desire and lady Beauty to which this tilt seems partly indebted. St George was associated in English folk tradition with another male nature spirit, the green man (an idealized version of the wild man); his survival within the symbolism of the Elizabethan Protestant state has often been remarked upon.[74] An archetypal defender of threatened female virtue, St George's legend told how he had come to England by boat. Spenser made this figure the first of his emblematic knights in *The Faerie Queene*, and depicted his ascent of the Mount of Contemplation (whence he has a vision of the New Jerusalem) as the necessary prelude to the successful completion of his quest. And just as the mossie knight describes the lover's sight of Elizabeth to 'the eagle beholding the sunne', so Spenser tells us in book 1 of his epic of the hermit who lives on Contemplation's hill: 'wondrous quick and persant was his spright,/As Eagles eye, that can behold the Sunne'.[75] The speech of this knight, delivered near the close of the first day of tilting, prepared the audience for the Four Foster Children's admission of defeat on the next day:

They acknowledge Noble Desire shoulde have desired nothing so much, as the flourishing of that Fortresse, which was to be esteemed according to it selfes liking: They acknowledge the least determination of vertue (which stands for guard of this Fortresse) to be too strong for the strongest Desire, And therefore they do acknowledge themselves overcome, as to be slaves in this Fortresse for ever. . . .[76]

Jean Wilson, who has edited the text of 'The Four Foster Children' along with those of several other Elizabethan pastimes, interprets the tilt's message (that Elizabeth is unattainable) as proof that the radical Protestant pressure group which was opposed to the Alençon marriage had won its case.[77] It is difficult to determine the exact status of the tilt in this respect; it would not necessarily have been regarded as an official statement, and certainly this courtship dragged on for several years longer, until Alençon's death in 1584. None the less, it represents the first fully coherent celebration in the pastimes of Elizabeth's unmarried state in terms of a Petrarchan or Neoplatonic idealism, although concepts drawn from courtly love survive in the chivalric emphasis of the event. In later years, the tilt continued to follow similar formulae, whereby medieval romance themes were acted out with the embellishment of Renaissance devices, and with modernized interpretations. The figures used in the earlier entertainments (wild men, shepherds, hermits, even the fairy queen) appeared frequently in these events. Members of the Leicester–Walsingham faction, in particular sir Henry Lee and sir Philip Sidney (he was knighted in 1583), played important roles in the conception and performance of many of these tilts. It consequently seems probable that in the early 1580s at least the participants in such events saw them as a preparation, rather than as a substitute, for military activity.[78] But after Leicester finally obtained the queen's permission to lead a (largely unsuccessful) military expedition to the Netherlands in 1585, the issue of intervention in the Low Countries became less important; by that time the Catholic threat was nearer to home, in the shape of the impending Spanish Armada. And by the end of the decade, the radical Protestant and pro-war group at court had lost its leading protagonists: Sidney died in 1587, Leicester in 1588, Walsingham in 1590, and Lee retired as queen's champion in 1590.

Although the 1590s seems to have seen no decline in the desire of the Elizabethan aristocracy to prove themselves militarily (frustrated heroic ambitions were arguably one cause of the Essex Rebellion of 1601), such ambitions were no longer defined in terms of Puritan idealism, as they had been a decade earlier. During this period, spectacular tilts still continued to celebrate courtly service expressed in action; but in the entertainments of the 1590s, in spite of a continuing use of chivalric motifs, compliment to the monarch was no longer associated with emphasis upon the active role of the courtier. This can be related in part to the fact that several of these events were sponsored by courtiers such as the earl of Hertford at Elvetham in 1591 and lord Montague at Cowdray in 1592, who were using the event to restore themselves to the queen's favour rather than to make any coherent political statement. (Hertford had been exiled from court for marrying lady Catherine Grey, an heir to the throne, Montague was a Catholic.) None the less it is interesting to note that the figure of the hermit was privileged in two entertainments presented by men who were or had been leading courtiers, lord Burghley and sir Henry Lee. In 1591, at Burghley's house of Theobalds, Elizabeth was met by a hermit, apologizing to her for the absence of the lord of the house, whom he claimed had retired to a hermit's cell in grief over the loss of his wife and daughter. Lee had already compared himself to a hermit in his retirement tilt of 1590; at Ditchley in 1592 he repeated this identification.[79] To some extent their use of this figure can be attributed to the advanced age of these two courtiers; none the less this new emphasis contrasts strikingly both with the satiric presentation of the hermit role at Wanstead and also with the stress on emergence from contemplation into action adumbrated through the figure of the 'mossie knight' in 'The Four Foster Children of Desire'.

The Ditchley entertainment of 1592

At Ditchley, the theme of Elizabeth's miraculous transforming powers as an active female beloved (or knight errant) was reintroduced, in an echo of the Kenilworth and Woodstock entertainments, although the religious parallel to Christ was now more exaggerated. Significantly, however, this was no longer complemented by a parallel emphasis upon the military aspirations and sexual assertiveness of the male courtier. The miraculous deeds attributed to Elizabeth as a female saviour were here primarily on a spiritual rather than a political significance, while her implied comparison to Christ suggested that she had now successfully assimilated the polarity of the sexes within her own person. The entertainment covered two days: on the first day, Elizabeth passed through an enchanted grove where many knights and ladies were imprisoned, whom she released (a journey which obviously was intended to echo Christ's harrowing of Hell). On the second day, a chaplain told her the story of a retired knight, now a hermit:

> Vouchsafe, I beseeche you, from the matcheles height of your Royall graces, to loke downe on the humble dwelling of a reverend owlde Knight, now a new religious Hermite; as heretofore he professed the obedience of his youthe, by constant service of the worldes best Creature, so at this present presentethe the devotion of his yeares, by continuall serving of the worldes onlie Creator. . . . the two enimies of Prosperity, Envie and Age (the one greving at him, & the other growing on him,) cutt him off from following the Cowrte, not from goyng forwarde in his course. Thence, willingly unwilling, he retired

his tyred lymes into a corner of quiet repose, in this Countrie, where he lyved private in coelestiall contemplation manie winters together, and, as he once told me, seriouslie kept a verie courte in his owne bosome, making presence of her in his soule, who was absent from his sight.[80]

The figures of God and queen were implicitly fused in this speech, in that both were the subject of the old knight's meditations. This identification was made clearer in the last part of the episode, which presented the hermit–knight as being near death, and as having left all his worldly goods to Elizabeth. But it was shortly announced by a page that her presence had miraculously restored him to life:

> Where your Majestie hath don a miracle, & it can not be denied, I hope I may manifest, & it shall not be disliked: for miracles are no miracles unlesse they be confessed, & mirth is no mirth yf it be concealed. . . . Stellatus, his Chappelaine, besought him to blesse God onelie, for it was God's spirite who recovered his spirites. Truth (quoth he again) yet whoseover blesseth her, blesseth God in her: and ever blessed be God for her.[81]

In the Ditchley entertainment, the active and erotically challenging courtier figure who had figured so prominently in the initial courtly formulation of Elizabeth's cult was eclipsed. The emphasis of this event on spiritual rather than political metamorphosis also contrasted with the military and imperialist themes of a spectacular entertainment staged a year earlier, at Elvetham. But while Elvetham expanded the concern of earlier pastimes with foreign policy, it too had displaced the figure of courtier as hero. Yet in this entertainment, the persona chosen by the courtier–host was not that of the hermit, but the courtly poet.

The Elvetham entertainment of 1591

The central motif of the Elvetham entertainment recalled that of Kenilworth, in that events took place on and around a lake which had been especially created for the occasion. On it 'were divers boats prepared for musicke: but especially there was a pinnace, ful furnisht'. In the lake were three islands, termed a 'Ship Ile', a 'Fort Mount', and a 'Snail Mount' on which various scenes were staged, and the lake itself was shaped in the form of a crescent moon to honour Elizabeth as Cynthia (Diana's aspect of moon goddess and lady of the sea); by this time the moon had become the dominant planetary symbol in Elizabeth's cult. These images of sea and moon set the tone of the event, in spite of references to Elizabeth as a sun on her departure from Elvetham: 'how can Sommer stay, when Sunne departs?' It is sea-gods which have most prestige at Elvetham, while the wild men and satyrs which the pastime had typically associated with courtly service to Elizabeth are used as a comic diversion or type of anti-masque.[82] Of course the connection of the latter figures with sea-travel suggests an identification with the inhabitants of the New World; yet a more obvious association is with the Spanish nation, whose mastery of the sea was still being challenged by English ships in the wake of the Armada. The trickster-like ambiguity of the wild man in the pastimes, as a figure capable of supporting both positive and negative associations, has now been abandoned. Nereus, chief of the sea-gods at Elvetham, refers to 'Yon ugly monster creeping from the South/To spoyle these blessed fields of Albion'.[83] In the pinnace was a sea-nymph, Neaera: 'the old supposed love of Sylvanus, a God of the Woodes'. Yet a central episode of the entertainment demonstrated that this nymph did not reciprocate his love. After Sylvanus had sworn his fealty to Elizabeth, he asked Neaera to land: 'That, in compassion of old sufferance,/She may relent in sight of beauties Queene.'[84] But instead he was ducked by Nereus, and mocked by the other water gods:

> After that the sea-gods had sufficiently duckt Sylvanus, they suffered him to creep to land, where he no sooner set footing, but crying 'Revenge, Revenge.' he and his begunne a skirmish with those of the water. . . . At the last, Nereus parted the fray with a line or two, grounded on the excellence of her Majestyes presence, as being alwaies friend to Peace and ennemy to Warre. Then Sylvanus, being so ugly, and running toward the bower at the end of the Pound, affrighted a number of the country folk, that they ran from him for feare, and thereby moved great laughter. His followers retired to the woods. . . .[85]

A month before the Elvetham entertainment, sir Richard Grenville's ship *The Revenge* had been lost in the Azores (the only English ship taken in the Anglo–Spanish war); even if no explicit reference to the episode was intended here, nationalist feeling was undoubtedly high at this time.

Elizabeth's courtier–host at Elvetham, Thomas Seymour, earl of Hertford, was attempting by his lavish hospitality to restore himself to favour with the queen. But Hertford did not identify himself either with the wild man figure favoured by Leicester, or with the sea-gods of Elvetham, and there was no reference to the hermit persona used by Lee and Cecil. Instead, Hertford's chosen mouthpiece, the figure who was the implied author of the entertainment, and who unified events by his opening and closing speeches, was the poet. His speech of welcome to Elizabeth stressed that he claimed inspiration from Apollo rather than from Pan:

> While, at the fountaine of the sacred hill,
> Under Apollo's lute I sweetly slept,

Mongst prophets full possest with holy fury,
And with true vertue, void of all disdaine:
The Muses sung, and waked me with these wordes:
   Seest thou that English Nimph, in face and shape
Resembling some great Goddesse, and whose beames
Doe sprinkle Heaven with unacquainted light,
While she doth visit Semers fraudlesse house . . .?
See thou salute her with a humble voice. . . .
   Behold (Augusta) thy poore suppliant
Is here, at their desire, but thy desert.
O sweet Elisa, grace me with a looke,
Or from my browes this laurell wreath will fall,
And I, unhappy, die amidst my song.
Under my person Semer hides himselfe. . . .[86]

In spite of the poet's dissociation of himself from the god of the shepherd–poet, Pan, it is possible to discern a certain sexual innuendo in his reference to the hidden 'Semer'. Elizabeth's host was the nephew of the Thomas Seymour with whom she was reputed to have enjoyed a liaison when she was in her teens, although opinion has always been divided as to the extent of this affair. For whatever reason – whether he wished his concealment to be associated with supplication, or with the teasing memory of a more seductive encounter – the earl effaced himself behind the self-important poet. But in stressing his role as the inspired creator of Elvetham's idealized pastoral world, and simultaneously as the interpreter of that world to the queen, this *vates* (or visionary poet) was displacing the courtier – both as the chief purveyor of Elizabethan courtliness, and as the foremost initiate of its mysteries. In this respect, his pose paralleled that of Colin Clout in the April eclogue of Spenser's *The Shepheardes Calender*. At the same time, the Elvetham poet was effectively challenging an assumption central to Elizabeth's cult, that she was herself the creative source of the courtly pastoral experience. Although he begs Elizabeth to 'grace me with a looke', he does not affirm that she is the source of his inspiration (instead, he derives this from the Muses); nor does he compare his own creativity unfavourably to that of the queen, in the style of other poets of this period (including Spenser). This slight contradiction within the Elvetham entertainment points to the emergence of a problem which, while barely noticeable here, had already begun to feature more prominently in various other literary contributions to Elizabeth's cult: namely, the relationship of the self-conscious poet to the figure of the idealized female monarch whom he took as his poetic subject.[87] In the late 1580s and 1590s, this relationship between queen and poet often posed as many problems as had that between queen and courtier in the early Elizabethan pastimes.

Chapter five

Chastity and the power of interior spaces: Lyly's alternative view of Elizabethan courtiership

The debate articulated in the courtly pastimes, concerning the modes of courtiership appropriate to the servants of an unmarried queen, reveals that the discourse of Elizabethan courtliness was the site of a contest for sexual as well as political authority. But in a series of courtly comedies by John Lyly, written and performed during the decade of the 1580s, the grounds of this courtly conflict shifted. Lyly's plays reaffirmed the thesis which was promoted in entertainment and tilt, that Elizabeth's absolute power was founded in her unmarried situation. Yet the combination of his own aesthetic interests with the political and religious concerns of the Burghley faction (to which he was allied by ties of patronage) produced significant alterations in the original formulation of Elizabeth's courtly cult.

Lyly's version of Elizabethan courtiership was a mysticism of contemplation rather than of action: it was in these terms that he defined the roles of both female monarch and male courtier. And although this shift of emphasis (which paralleled but did not exactly resemble the formulation in Spenser's April eclogue) can be related to the views of certain courtiers, these plays rejected the pastimes' definition of the queen's chastity. She was no longer represented as either miming or passively acquiescing in the heroic fantasies of the Leicester–Walsingham faction. Lyly explored the private rather than the public meaning of Elizabeth's unmarried state, by relating it to a secluded and interior mode of courtliness. Like Spenser, he focused upon the space which the female monarch shared with other women, and from which the courtier who defined himself in terms of a phallic sexuality – as a wild man – was excluded. Thus in *Endimion: or the Man in the Moone*, the male courtly lover was called upon to imitate his queen, through a meditative withdrawal into the private, emotional and feminine sphere of experience symbolized by the moon – the planet which was now becoming the privileged emblem of her courtly cult. Yet while its superficial message is one of exaggerated courtly compliment, Lylyan drama is also marked by a distinct unease about the implications of this gynocentric definition of courtly service. Lyly attempted to purge Elizabeth's developing icono-graphic connection with Roman Diana of aggressive or military connotations. Still, his court plays reveal that the mythological association of Diana with a close-knit community of women, and so with a feminine mode of self-consciousness which was not necessarily devoid of sexuality, was equally if not more disconcerting.

In his two prose romances, *Euphues. The Anatomy of Wit* (1578) and *Euphues and his England* (1580), Lyly had already elaborated a literary style subsequently termed 'euphuistic'. This style deployed the number-less tropes or figures of speech listed in Renaissance handbooks of rhetoric (and derived from the Latin texts of writers such as Cicero and Quintilian) with considerable elegance. It was especially indebted to the ornamental language of Renaissance manuals of courtly conduct, and in particular to Baldessare Castiglione's *Il Cortegiano*, or *The Book of the Courtier*. (The English translation of this book, by sir Thomas Hoby, appeared in 1561, but did not achieve widespread acclaim until its second edition in 1577, when Lyly was composing *Euphues*.) Renaissance humanists asserted that beauty of language, the art of *bene dicendi*, should contribute to the moral impact of the spoken or written message; however as Daniel Javitch has pointed out, when humanist rhetorical skills were deployed within the framework of Renaissance courtly culture they were used not just to please and delight the mind with images of beauty, but in the service of the 'courtly' etiquette of indirection and subterfuge.[1] In Lyly's two prose romances, as in his drama later, the surface beauty created both by his language and by the highly symmetrical structure of his texts often obscures, rather than clarifies, his meaning. In view of the constraints imposed upon him by the need to cater to courtly tastes and courtly values, this was probably no accident. G.K. Hunter suggested that Lyly was a humanist turned courtier, forced to subordinate his humanist ideals of moral instruction to a courtly aesthetic; indeed, both his prose and his dramatic works sound an occasional note of scepticism about the courtly values which he appears superficially to be promulgating.[2] None the less, these barely discernible traces of anti-courtliness also reveal Lyly's mastery of the courtly 'style', which as codified by such as Castiglione facilitated and even encouraged dissimulation.

As a courtly dramatist, Lyly especially favoured the device of allegory or *allegoria*, described by George Puttenham in *The Arte of English Poesie* as the 'figure of *false semblant or dissimulation. . . .* which is when we speake one thing and mean another, and that our wordes and our meanings meet not'.[3] But Lyly's allegory functioned on a number of different levels. Critics have emphasized his use of *Neoplatonic* allegory, which flattered the queen by presenting her as an esoteric symbol decipherable only by a few. They have usually assumed that if his allegory functions on any other level, it is in terms of specific coded references to the events and personalities of the Elizabethan court. This has produced some fairly comical attempts to fit real names to characters in the different plays. My own view is that the connection of supporting characters with historical individuals is only rarely relevant, and that in general Lyly's political allegory is of a rather subtler order, dovetailing a commitment to factional court politics with a Neoplatonic emphasis upon Elizabeth as a contemplative figure. At the same time, certain features of his plays hint at the existence of another level of his allegory, in addition to the Neoplatonic and political, a level which was satiric rather than complimentary in implication.

In Lyly's first eulogistic description of queen Elizabeth, at the end of *Euphues and his England*, she was seen as uniting in her person intelligence and its practical worldly expression, contemplation and action. Lyly praised Elizabeth as 'a Glasse for all Princes', excellent for her skilful government as well as for 'hir sharpe wit, excellent wisedome, exquisite learning, and all other qualities of the mind, where-in she seemeth as farre to excell those that have bene accompted singular, as the learned have surpassed those, that have beene thought simple'.[4] But whereas Ficino had told Lorenzo de' Medici (presumably in consideration of the requirements of lineage, as well as of Lorenzo's temperament) that a prince should combine sexual pleasure or the *vita voluptaria* with the pursuit of wisdom and power, Lyly here attributed Elizabeth's success in government to her sacrifice of this third avenue of expression. Her most notable attribute as a ruler, he asserted, was her virginity, and in this resided her especial power:

> What greater mervaile hath happened since the beginning of the world, then for a young and tender Maiden, to govern strong and valiaunt menne, then for a Virgin to make the whole worlde, if not to stand in awe of hir, yet to honour hir, yea and to live in spight of all those that spight hir, with hir sword in the sheth, with hir armour in the Tower, with hir souldiers in their gownes. . . . This is the onelye myracle that virginitie ever wrought. . . .[5]

Yet this connection of Elizabeth's political authority with her 'virginity' differed in its emphasis from the formulation of the courtly pastime (at the same time as being truer to the political reality). The queen is represented as a virago who has disarmed her soldiers not in battle but by peace. The degree to which she has inverted a certain patriarchal order is indicated at the level of imagery, by her association with the images of sheath and Tower. In visual terms, these images have a phallic appearance; but their function in Lyly's passage is as receptacles – they serve as containers of the aggressivity normally deemed proper to a male monarch, imaged here by sword and armour. Lyly implies that this

113

concealment or relinquishment of military authority (which in any case her gender made it impossible for her to assume except in fantasy) has transformed her image as monarch. He defines it as a Christ-like gift: 'This is the blessing that Christ alwayes gave to his people, peace.' Thus in his very first literary reference to the queen, Lyly was interested in what he saw as her feminine style of government, a power from which the coercive attributes of patriarchal authority were (apparently) absent, yet which had none the less managed to disarm (and so, implicitly, to unman) the Elizabethan soldiery.

In his dramatic contributions to Elizabeth's courtly cult in the 1580s, Lyly developed this emphasis upon the feminine qualities of her rule. But he also accorded her public role of monarch progressively less importance, contracting her redemptive Christ-like power (described in the above passage as disseminated among the people) into the more limited and exclusive sphere of the court. The idea of the queen as a female knight errant favoured by the entertainments was replaced in *Sapho and Phao* and *Endimion* by more remote figures, whose involvement in the outer world (and in *Endimion*, in courtly affairs also) is extremely attenuated, and whose *political* power is subsumed into images of *emotional* and *spiritual* authority. It is difficult to decide how to interpret this new emphasis within the Elizabethan cult. By removing the disturbing figure of the female monarch from the arena of public politics, Lyly was in one sense merely reinforcing patriarchal stereotypes. In their apparent lack of traits designated masculine, such as activity and aggressiveness, his queen figures, Sapho and Cynthia, seem superficially less problematic than the figure of the woman warrior. Yet Lyly's exaggeration of Elizabeth's gender must have triggered other anxieties, since what could be termed his depoliticization of the queen's courtly image was accompanied by a redefinition of her relationship with her male courtiers. As in *Il Cortegiano*, their primary sphere of devotion was now the maternal or feminine domain of the court rather than the masculine space of the battlefield.

Lyly's dramatic focus both upon Elizabeth as a contemplative rather than active figure, one with predominantly feminine traits, and also upon the court in and for itself (rather than as an influence on the 'outside' world through the actions of various of its members), seems especially significant when one considers his long-term association with the Burghley faction at court. This group opposed the Puritan policies of the Leicester–Walsingham alliance, and favoured a foreign policy of non-intervention. Was it merely coincidental that *Endimion* took as its subject the story of the love of the moon goddess Cynthia for a shepherd: the courtly role which Leicester had rejected in favour of the forester or wild man? Patrick Collinson has described the Burghley faction as 'a looser constellation' than the Leicester–Walsingham group, which was united by the fairly specific ideology of militant Protestantism. It is noteworthy, however, that several members of this group were related to the queen on her mother's side. It comprised:

> the restless, disaffected and merely ornamental, including some scions of the older aristocratic houses, and some catholics and crypto-catholics. The connections here run from Burghley's unsatisfactory son-in-law, Edward de Vere, earl of Oxford, a secret convert, through his 'lewd' friends (Burghley's description) Lord Henry Howard and Charles Arundel, a likely candidate for the authorship of *Leycester's Commonwealth*, to Sir Edward Stafford, ambassador in France, and his powerful mother, and on to Howard's second cousin, the earl of Sussex; and more obscurely to Sir James Croft and [Sir Christopher] Hatton, both suspected of catholic sympathies. A common interest in the destruction of Leicester was perhaps the strongest force holding these elements together.[6]

Lyly had close ties with lord Burghley from 1574 (when he wrote to him requesting preferment at Cambridge) until the latter's death. It was probably Burghley who introduced Lyly to his former ward and son-in-law, the earl of Oxford. Lyly dedicated *Euphues and his England* to Oxford, and enjoyed the earl's patronage from around 1582 until 1588. There is no evidence that he shared his patron's Catholic religious views, although G.K. Hunter commented that in his romances Italy was idealized rather than treated as the kingdom of the wicked (as was common in Protestant anti-Catholic propaganda), and Lyly's uncle George had been secretary to Reginald Pole, Mary Tudor's archbishop of Canterbury.[7] But Lyly's opposition to Puritan radicalism was indicated by his involvement in the Martin Marprelate controversy of 1588–9, when together with Thomas Nashe he replied to the satiric attacks on the bishops made in the pamphlets of 'Martin'.

Although the Leicester–Walsingham faction had a majority of voices on her privy council, Elizabeth herself seems to have had most sympathy for the views of the Burghley group. It is therefore probable that in his altered conception of the roles of both monarch and courtier, Lyly was trying to please not just the Burghley faction, but also the queen. Oxford must have received a certain amount of personal credit for the work of his protégé, yet Lyly apparently hoped that he would himself receive some mark of especial royal favour; G.K. Hunter devoted several pages of his study of Lyly's career to a list of the numerous petitions which the dramatist sent to Elizabeth over a period of years.[8] It was wholly consistent with her general attitude towards patronage of the arts, however, that these many requests bore little fruit. After his association with Oxford ended, Lyly seems to have had some hope of being appointed to the court office of master of the revels; however these hopes were never realized, nor did he ever receive any other really substantial marks of royal favour, although he did enjoy various small but not very lucrative honours, such as a minor court appointment as esquire of the body, and four terms as a member of parliament.

It may have been due to the frustration of his hopes of courtly preferment that in his comedies after *Endimion* Lyly favoured satire rather than courtly compliment; but in any case he had inherited a divided attitude to women from both his humanist and his Neoplatonic sources. A tendency to satire as well as to misogyny is evident in his early prose works; the presence of similar elements in his courtly drama may also be attributable to his connection with a children's company of actors. A group of boy choristers performed Lyly's plays commercially in a small private theatre at Blackfriars both before and after they had appeared with them at court. This dual location of Lylyan comedy, in both court and private playhouse, enabled a private courtly experience, centring upon the idealization of Elizabeth, to be shared to some degree by a non-courtly (although still elite) audience. But since their emergence in the middle ages boy actors had often been connected with the drama of satire and burlesque, and with a licensed mocking of authority.[9] Perhaps the dual audience of his drama reinforced Lyly's double perspective, his ambivalence both towards courtly values and to their primary female referent – the queen. Whatever the determining factor, as Lyly's courtly image of Elizabeth became increasingly icon-like, and correspondingly remote from the real world, so a range of misogynistic attitudes began to intrude into these texts. Such references were either extremely indirect, or superficially dissociated from the queen, by their use in the satiric representation of a different female character. But alongside assertions that Elizabeth has overcome her sexual or corporeal 'nature' as a woman, there are innuendoes concerning lesbian sexuality, attacks on female lust, and satire of the woman who, instead of defeating time, has become its visible emblem, the crone. Perhaps most significant of all, in *Endimion* Lyly used his characteristic device of antithesis to set against the religious and supernatural powers attributed to Elizabeth as a goddess the more strictly contemporary and negative conception of the 'inspired' woman, the witch.

One of the most serious problems which Lyly faced in his attempt to produce dramatic compliments to an unmarried queen was the lack of historical or even mythological precedents for such a situation. It was presumably for this reason that his first play, *Campaspe*, which was performed at the Blackfriars theatre in 1580 and at court on New Year's Day 1582, looked at love and chastity from the perspective of a male ruler, Alexander. At the end of the play, Alexander afforded an illustrious example of princely continence by relinquishing his female captive Campaspe, with whom he had fallen in love, to the painter

Apelles. Yet unlike Lyly's later plays, which explored the links between sexuality and desire and the authority of a female figure (as ruler or deity), *Campaspe* presented the 'chastity' of Alexander not as incompatible with military activity, but rather as the necessary prerequisite to successful military action. The editor of Lyly's works, R. Warwick Bond, lists several possible sources for the play. What he does not note, however, is that the story of Alexander and Campaspe appears in a text which Lyly knew very well: Castiglione's *Il Cortegiano*: indeed, Alexander is mentioned several times in this text.[10] In other words, Lyly's chosen plot was already inscribed within a source text of Renaissance courtly discourse. The emphasis of his play, however, concerns the contradictions between an heroic or expansionist mode of masculine leadership and the idealized or courtly love of woman. The argument that Alexander's love for Campaspe is at odds with his career of peregrination as a conquering hero is voiced by his lifelong male companion, Hephestion. The lengthy sequence of antitheses in Hephestion's speech juxtaposes the 'safe' (because implicitly androcentric) terrain of potential military conquest – the world – against the far more threatening, interior space of love and courtly leisure. Woman's disarming of the male by love, in this other, gynocentric sphere of experience, is seen in negative rather than positive terms, as a humiliating unmanning, a transformation comparable to that of Hercules by the Amazon queen Omphale:

> What! is the sonne of *Phillip*, king of Macedon, become the subiect of *Campaspe*, the captive of Thebes? Is that minde, whose greatnes the world could not containe, drawn within the compasse of an idle alluring eie? Wil you handle the spindle with *Hercules*, when you should shake the speare with *Achilles*? Is the warlike sound of drum and trumpe turned to the soft noyse of lire and lute? the neighing of barbed steeds, whose loudnes filled the ayre with terrour, and whose breathes dimmed the sunne with smoak, converted to dilicate tunes and amorous glances? O *Alexander*, that soft and yeelding minde should not bee in him, whose hard and unconquering heart hath made so many yeelde.[11]

In contrast to the celebration of the king's metamorphosis through the feminine within French Renaissance absolutism, Hephestion warns against the loss of masculine sexual as well as political/military initiative which an idealized heterosexual desire may cause. As a result of the lover's courtly subordination to female emotional authority, a womanly or maternal phallus, the spindle, is substituted for a patriarchal power vested in the spear. But it is not clear that Alexander's is a choice between sexuality and continence. Implicit in Hephestion's sequence of oppositions is a further contrast, between the equal relationships of men and the degrading effects of heterosexual love. In spite of its emphasis upon chastity combined with action, the view expressed here derives from a strand within Neoplatonism rather than from courtly love: the bond between the two male companions, rather than the love of Alexander for Campaspe, is an inspiration to military action. It is in favour of this ideal of male friendship, which is here presented as compatible with deeds of valour – in other words, as supportive of an heroic or phallic masculine identity – that Alexander finally abandons his desire for Campaspe. (This affords an interesting contrast to the association of male homosexuality with effeminacy in Desportes' *Les Amours de Diane*.) At the end of the play, as he and Hephestion leave the stage together, ready for fresh martial endeavours, Alexander declares:

> But come, let us go. I wil try whether I can better beare my hand with my hart, then I could with mine eie. And good *Hephestion*, when al the world is wonne, and every countrey is thine and mine, either find me out an other to subdue, or of my word I wil fall in love.[12]

Hence in this, his first court play, Lyly implies that the 'chastity' of a ruler may not involve the sacrifice of all affective (and perhaps even sexual) ties.[13]

The central conflict of *Campaspe*, between two kinds of relationship, and between two modes of masculine self-definition, is consequently difficult to interpret in connection with Elizabeth. Are we to identify her with Alexander, who rejects (heterosexual) love? Or with the female object of this love, Campaspe, whose perfect beauty threatens to unman the male hero but inspires the painter Apelles? If the equal companionship of Hephestion and Alexander was intended to suggest the relationship which might be appropriate between monarch and courtier, then at this early stage in his career as courtly dramatist Lyly was presumably implying that some relation of near equality, expressed in action, was possible and even desirable, at least for a male monarch. But *Campaspe* also emphasized the difficulties inherent in another type of relationship: that between intellectual or artistic creativity and worldly power – in other words, between the *vita contemplativa* and the *vita activa*. In *Il Cortegiano*, Castiglione's frequent praise of Alexander apparently constructs him as a model of the perfect prince: the figure towards whom the would-be courtier's attentions were directed. For example, he refers to the philosopher Aristotle, who taught the young Alexander, as an ideal courtier.[14] Yet while Castiglione emphasized the harmonious relationship between Alexander and his 'courtiers' (Apelles, Aristotle), *Campaspe* explored the contradictions between an absolute political authority and the desire of artist and philosopher for a creative or intellectual autonomy. A conflict between wisdom and power is articulated through Alexander's exchange with the philosopher Diogenes. At one point in the play Alexander expresses a wish to make a school or philosophic centre of his court (an idea which is returned to in *Endimion*); but he never fulfils this in the course of the action.[15] The intellectual autonomy of the philosopher is asserted in Diogenes' dispute with Alexander; he refuses to come to court, but instead requires Alexander to visit him. He will not accommodate (and so subordinate) his wisdom to Alexander's princely rule. This encounter between philosopher and king challenges the absolutist claims of Renaissance monarchies:

Alex: Why then doest thou ow no reverence to kings? . . .
Diog: Because they be no gods.
Alex: They be Gods of the earth.
Diog: Yea, Gods of earth.[16]

At first sight, the hero's relationship with the painter Apelles seems more practical and less idealistic. When Alexander asks Apelles what he thinks of his (Alexander's) efforts in painting, the constrained (or courtly) nature of the relationship between the two men becomes apparent: Apelles resorts to the courtly tactic of indirection, being unable to say what he really thinks. Interestingly, however, Alexander is himself aware of the painter's feeling of constraint:

Alex: But how have I done?
Apel: Like a king.
Alex: I thinke so: but nothing more unlike a Painter.[17]

Again, one of the premises of absolutism is undermined by Alexander's modesty: admission of deficiency in a single skill contradicted the idea of the monarch's near-divine perfection (Lyly had himself asserted in *Euphues and his England* that Elizabeth excelled in all arts and languages). But while Apelles *appears* to accept a more limited intellectual or creative identity than the self-sufficient Diogenes, the play's conclusion suggests that the relationship between king and artist is actually more complex. It is to Apelles, after all, that Alexander surrenders Campaspe at the end of the play. The play seems to offer us contrasting perspectives on this conclusion. Viewed both from the misogynistic perspective of Hephestion, and also in terms of compliment to an unmarried monarch (even if she is female), we should consider the artist's choice of love as inferior to the chastity of the monarch. Alternatively, if we read the play in the light of Lyly's interest in the role of the creative intellectual or artist, we might conclude that what was an appropriate line of action for a king was not necessarily required of an artist, and even that Lyly's implication here was that the experience of this type of ideal beauty was properly the domain of the artist rather than the monarch.

Campaspe could be interpreted as complimentary to Elizabeth in so far as it endorsed her decision to remain unmarried. None the less, its consideration of the relationship of political power to intellectual and artistic creativity was not exactly flattering to the absolute monarch. When the play was performed at court in 1582, however, two years after its first performance at the Blackfriars theatre, it was followed by an especially written epilogue which asserted that as the play's primary spectator, who both interpreted and judged the play when it was performed before her, the queen was therefore its true creator:

> As yet we cannot tel what we should tearme our labours, yron or bullyon; only it belongeth to your Maiestie to make them fitte either for the forge, or the mint, currant by the stampe, or counterfeit by the Anvil. For as nothing is to be called whit, unles it had bin named white by the first creator, so can there be nothing thought good in the opinion of others, unlesse it be christened good by the judgement of yourselfe. For ourselves againe, we are those torches waxe, of which being in your highnesse hands, you may make Doves or Vultures, Roses or Nettles, Lawrell for a garland, or elder for a disgrace.[18]

Elizabeth is here not simply the play's implied subject and ideal spectator; she is also a type of transcendental sign, filling up the lack or deficiency in the artistic work. She is represented as the royal agent of a poetic mode of alchemy, which transforms the dross of text and performance to pure gold by stamping it with her image like a new-minted coin. Lyly states that he assumes recognition of her 'true' image in the play to be a prerequisite for the queen's seal of approval; like the face of the beloved in Petrarchism and Neoplatonism (in which the male lover seeks his own reflection), the play will prove acceptable only in so far as it does not disappoint a royal desire for resemblance. Yet while a quest for identity which the love discourses typically reserved for the male is here attributed to Elizabeth, she is simultaneously associated with the creative and transforming faculties of the female beloved. And interestingly, in the power of metaphoric selection or naming (christening) which this role attributes to her she does indeed combine opposites, since she can make of the play either 'lawrell for a garland, or elder for a disgrace'; only her favourable judgement can assure Lyly fame as a writer. The ruler, and not the artist, has here become the ultimate arbiter of meaning, invested with the creative properties of the Neoplatonic *nous* or *logos*; at the same time, she bestows concrete success in the material world (turning the plays into coins!). In this conception Elizabeth resembles the biblical Wisdom figure, who while close to deity could confer worldly power, and who signified the possibility of a spiritual transformation of material reality.

Lyly's next play, *Sapho and Phao*, which was performed at court a few months after *Campaspe*, retained this idea of the monarch as a creative figure comparable to the poet–dramatist. But the play's representation of the relationship between power, sexuality, and creativity was far from straightforward. By changing the sex of his amorous monarch to female, Lyly was able to make this figure the object as well as the subject of love. At the same time, he identified his play's female monarch with the historical figure of the greatest woman poet of classical antiquity, Sappho. By choosing this name for his queen figure, Lyly again suggested that (unlike the male ruler Alexander) the female monarch was herself a creator as well as a bearer of power. As in the court epilogue to *Campaspe*, she is seen both as having exceptional power over nature, and also as linking heaven and earth in the shape of an exotic tree: 'this is the court of Sapho, nature's miracle, which resembleth the tree salurus, whose roote is fastned upon knotted steele, & in whose top bud leaves of pure gold.'[19] A tree had been used to represent the state (*respublica*) in a pageant presented when Elizabeth entered the City of London in 1559, prior to her coronation.[20] But this phallic image may also be related to Elizabeth's identification with the May queen in aristocratic entertainments: traditionally, the maypole was the focus for the May festivities. Lyly's tree metaphor also parallels the arborescent description of Wisdom in Ecclesiasticus, and Petrarch's comparison of Laura to a laurel.

Lyly's recourse to the figure of the (female) poet in his search for metaphoric definitions of the authority of a female monarch preceded by several years the comparison proposed by George Puttenham in *The Arte of English Poesie*. Puttenham's manual of style was not published until 1589, although presumably it circulated in manuscript some years previously:

> But you (Madame) my most Honored and Gracious, if I should seeme to offer you this my devise for a discipline and not a delight. I might well be accounted of all others the most arrogant and iniurious, your selfe being alreadie, of any that I know in our time, the most excellent Poet; forsooth by your Princely purse, favours, and countenance, making in maner what ye list, the poore man rich, the lewd well learned, the coward couragious, and vile both noble and valiant: then for imitation no lesse, your person as a most cunning counterfaitor lively representing *Venus* in countenance, in life *Diana*, *Pallas* for government, and *Juno* in all honour and regall magnificence.[21]

By using the metaphor of poetry to describe Elizabeth's rulership, both these writers were of course simultaneously making ambitious claims for their own profession. But Puttenham's choice of the word 'counterfaitor' to describe the queen's skills of imitation suggests that he may have had some reservations about this use of the poetry trope to figure absolutist authority: as can be seen from Lyly's epilogue to *Campaspe*, the word could equally signify the falsification of an image. Indeed what is striking in both Puttenham's eulogy and Lyly's play is that while they attribute the poet's power over language to Elizabeth, the images which they provide of her powers of transformation and mimesis apparently bear no relation to language at all. None of the speeches which Lyly wrote for his queen and goddess characters was a notable example of that euphuistic style by which he signalled confidence in his own literary creativity.

In contrast to his emphasis in *Campaspe*, Lyly omitted the dimension of masculine conquest from this play in order to focus on the more feminine world of the court, where he represented Sapho as surrounded not by male courtiers bent on heroic activity, but by her ladies-in-waiting. In spite of its imagery of court as tree, *Sapho and Phao* differs from the Elizabethan entertainments by suggesting that the unconfined natural world beyond this domain is potentially hazardous for the equilibrium of the female monarch. It is on a journey out into the country that the goddess Venus, in an attempt to punish her pride, inspires the Sicilian queen Sapho with a passion for a young ferryman (thought by some critics to have been allegorically identified with the French duc d'Alençon, who was then courting Elizabeth). This inspires a love-sickness in which she dreams that a dove attempts unsuccessfully to nest in a tall cedar tree:

> scambling to catch hold to harbor in the house he had made, he sodenly fell from the bough where he stoode. And then pitifully casting up his eies, he cried in such tearmes (as I imagined) as might either condemne the nature of such a tree, or the daring of such a minde.[22]

Once again, an exotic tree is used as a phallic metaphor for Sapho's coupling of spiritual with political power: here the evergreen cedar from the Mediterranean. But this use of the tree reveals that Sapho's seeming conjunction of nature and culture is imperfect. The tree's height, which signifies the female beloved's ability to link different dimensions, also makes her branches too high for the ambitious dove, just as Sapho's rank puts her beyond the reach of the ferryman. It is noteworthy, however, that this figuration of the male lover's desire to use woman as a Platonic ladder between earth and heaven relates his ambition to the assumption of a maternal role: the dove seeks the shelter of the tree in which to build its nest. Yet not only does Sapho's dream attest to the impossibility of realizing her passion; it also reveals that the tree's trunk and leaves are infested. She goes on to relate how:

> Whilest he [the dove] lay quaking upon the ground, & I gazing one the Cæder, I might perceive Antes to breede in the rinde, coveting only to hoord, & caterpillers to cleave to the leaves, labouring only to suck,

which caused mo leaves to fall from the tree, then there did feathers before from the dove.[23]

This is obviously a reference to corruption at court; however it also reintroduces duality into an image of the female monarch which purports to link opposites. It hints too at a revulsion from or denial of the femaleness of the body which is metaphorically represented here (the rind?). Other aspects of the play certainly point to an underlying fear of female sexuality.

Sapho's triumph over her desire for Phao is emblematized by her capture of Cupid at the end of the play. She takes his bow and arrow, saying: 'Cupid, feare not. It is a toye made for ladies, and I will keepe it onely for ladies.'[24] In this visual resolution of the opposition between love and chastity, Lyly was employing the courtly tactic of *mediocrità*, by which the courtier sought always to reconcile extremes. At the same time, he was also identifying Sapho with a Neoplatonic image of *discordia concors*. But although in terms both of Neoplatonic allegory and of courtly tactic this device briefly aligns the opposing strands of Lyly's plot, it raises further questions. In allegorical terms, Sapho's triumph over Venus represents the conquest of chastity over love, signalled by her appropriation of Cupid's phallic weaponry for herself. Apparently she no longer needs to define herself in relation to the masculine, but has acquired (or restored) a Diana-like self-sufficency. It is unusual, however, to find the image of Diana appearing in a courtly rather than a natural setting. And when we remember that the primary allegiance of this goddess was to women, Sapho's words to Cupid could be interpreted as somewhat ambiguous.

Elizabeth had already been depicted among ladies-in-waiting rather than male courtiers in *The Shepheardes Calender*, and a female entourage would figure prominently in later literary references to her courtly cult, where she was frequently depicted as Diana surrounded by her nymphs. But in Lyly's play, emphasis on the queen's withdrawal into an exclusive feminine world as another Diana is invested with a certain innuendo by its conjunction with the name of Sapho. For a classical scholar, this was synonymous not just with great poetry but also with female homosexuality. It is difficult to overlook this inference alongside the near-explicit treatment of lesbianism in Lyly's next play *Gallathea*, as well as the reference to England as Lesbos in *Midas*.[25] The chief source for *Sapho and Phao* was one of the epistles of Ovid's *Heroides*, a collection of verse letters supposedly written by deserted women to their former lovers. In this case, the letter was attributed to the poet Sappho of Lesbos; although addressed to the youth Phaon whom she was reputed to have loved in her old age when she lived in Sicily, it was explicit about the supposed author's former lesbian passions:

> *Pyrino* is forgot,
> ne *Dryads* doe delite
> My fancie. *Lesbian* lasses eke
> are now forgotten quite.
> Not *Amython* I force,
> nor *Cydno* passing fine:
> Nor *Atthis* as she did of yore
> allures these eyes of mine.
> Ne yet a hundreth mo
> whome (shame ylaid aside)
> I fanside erst: thou all that love
> from them to thee hast wride.[26]

The text was well known in the Renaissance, and in 1567 had been translated into English by George Turberville. It was cited by Pierre de Bourdeilles, Seigneur de Brantôme, in a memoir of late sixteenth-century France, as proof that lesbians (whom he declared to have been quite numerous at the French Renaissance court) might occasionally abandon the pleasures of their own sex for men.[27]

In Lyly's next play, *Gallathea*, written around 1584 and performed at the St Paul's theatre in 1585, but probably not acted at court until either 1587 or 1588, the theme raised only by implication in *Sapho and Phao* was accorded rather more direct treatment. At the same time, the figure of the male lover was removed altogether (it was to be reintroduced in *Endimion*). Perhaps because of its somewhat ambiguous subject matter, *Gallathea* was the only one of Lyly's first five plays which did not focus on the figure of a monarch; none the less, the Diana imagery connected with Sapho, and the Diana persona of Cynthia used in *Endimion*, suggest a connection between Elizabeth and the goddess in this play also. Its plot juxtaposed a supernatural conflict between Diana and Venus, in which Cupid tries to inspire desire in Diana's nymphs, with what on one level could be read as a more direct treatment of the theme of love between women. By relating this topic to the Neoplatonic allegory of his play, Lyly associated an unconventional passion with the abstract idea of *discordia concors*, or the union of Venus and Diana. But as well as this Neoplatonic perspective the play explores a more practical or literal interpretation of the dialectic of love and chastity as personified by two female figures. The plot centres on two young women described as 'virgins', who are disguised as boys to protect them from sacrifice to a sea-monster in appeasement to Neptune. They fall in love, each supposing the other to be male, although as the action develops they become increasingly doubtful about this. The assumption is, however, that their love is impossible; when their identities are revealed, Neptune declares: 'An idle choyce, strange, and foolish, for one Virgine to doate on another: and to imagine a constant faith, where there can be no cause of affection.'[28] It is via this emphasis upon the necessary chastity involved in the love between two 'virgins' that Lyly associates their relationship with Diana; but at the end of the play, their supposed dilemma is resolved by Venus' promise to metamorphose one of the couple into a man: 'Never shall it be said that Nature or Fortune shall overthrowe Love and Fayth.'[29]

The allegory or concealed meaning that most critics find in *Gallathea* concerns the appropriate relationship both between chastity and love and between otherworldly and worldly dimensions: in Neoplatonic terms, the play is structured around the distinction between two Venuses or goddesses of love: one earthly (Venus), the other heavenly (Diana).[30] In the resolution of events on the human plane, it appears to be Venus who wins, as the balance is tipped in favour of (heterosexual) love and marriage by her act of metamorphosis. On the divine plane, Diana triumphs. She ends his attacks on her nymphs by capturing Cupid, just as Sapho had done in *Sapho and Phao*, and ransoms the boy to Venus in exchange for Neptune's agreement to end the sacrifice of virgins to the monster. In the love of the two 'virgins' the competing claims of the two goddesses are mysteriously reconciled; but this union of love with chastity appears to go beyond the merely emblematic. Indeed, the absence of any central male protagonist throws into especial relief the play's concern with female sexuality. What seems to be woman's fear of loss of identity in a surrender to masculine otherness (Neptune's sea-monster) is set against her desire for the maternal domain over which Diana presides, or for a relationship with herself. But in this case, what kind of resolution is afforded by Venus? Does her miraculous metamorphosis, which presumably involves the gift of a penis to a woman, assert the completeness and authority of the feminine, woman's possession of 'phallic' power? Or does it simply make a 'foolish' (because deviant) relationship conform to a heterosexual norm?

The fulfilment of some unspecified sexual fantasy is certainly implied by Lyly's choice of the name Gallathea for one of his nymphs, for Galatea was the name of the perfect woman made by the sculptor Pygmalion, whose statue the goddess Aphrodite vivified.[31] At the same time, reference to this myth enabled Lyly to introduce into this play also some implicit speculation on the supernatural or divine associations of artistic creativity, and hence perhaps to assert/insert his own invisible presence as male dramatist within the predominantly feminine world constructed by his play. We can see signs of a similar attempt in his next and best-known play, *Endimion*, where Lyly reinscribed the male courtier within the milieu of the court. While he defined the relationship of this figure to the female monarch in terms which were consistent with the policies of the Burghley faction, his emphasis upon true courtliness as contemplation rather than action implied that the best courtier was more of a poet than a knight.

The result was Lyly's most polished and exaggerated compliment to Elizabeth. It was also the first of his plays in which her identity as queen was explicitly compared to the goddess Diana (in her persona of the moon goddess Cynthia). There is no trace of any innuendo about lesbian sexuality in *Endimion*; however, its association of Elizabeth with Diana or Cynthia was shadowed by other inferences, in a dramaturgic repetition of the 'splitting' of the Petrarchan or Neoplatonic image of woman. This division or fragmentation of the feminine is left unresolved: there is no closing image of *discordia concors*. Lyly's plot reworked a Greek myth which related how the moon goddess found the shepherd Endimion asleep in a cave on Mount Latmus and kissed him, whereupon he fell into a different, deeper sleep from which he never awakened. Some versions of the myth asserted that the moon had fifty children by Endimion; but in the work of Renaissance writers the myth was usually seen as an allegory of a sublimated or Platonic passion.[32] This association of moon imagery with the queen, together with the name of Cynthia rather than Diana, suggests the influence of sir Walter Ralegh, thought to have written the greater part of his long narrative poem comparing Elizabeth to the moon, *The Ocean to Scinthia*, in the 1580s. But like the Elizabethan pastime, and like the work of visiting Neoplatonist Giordano Bruno (who in the middle of the decade was also developing his Neoplatonic idea of the queen with reference to Diana and the sea), Ralegh conceived of Elizabeth's power in imperialist terms; although the oceanic imagery which both he and Bruno used emphasized naval rather than military activity.[33] In *Endimion*, which was probably written between 1584 and 1585, and performed at court in 1586, Lyly's moon goddess (appropriately, for a wandering planet) is an extremely elusive figure; however, he does not associate this figure with imperialist politics but rather with a retreat both from history and from the world beyond the court.[34]

The pastoral environment of the Greek myth was replaced in *Endimion* by a courtly setting presided over by Cynthia as queen as well as goddess. The devotion which she inspires in one particular courtier, Endimion, arouses the jealousy of a female character called Tellus, whom Endimion had formerly loved, and she uses the assistance of a witch to enchant him into a perpetual sleep in which he ages dramatically. Cynthia's kiss finally awakens the enchanted Endimion, however, whereupon his courtly service to her is reaffirmed, and further rewarded by her miraculous restoration of his youth. This providential release from the powers of female erotic desire and female sorcery, as also from the ravages of time and mutability, apparently signals the completion of a vital stage in Endimion's development as both courtier and Neoplatonic lover, after which he is better able to apprehend the positive image of the feminine represented by Cynthia. But what is particularly striking about the definition of courtliness implicit here is the passivity which it attributes to the male lover and courtier. Like the heroine of the fairy tale Briar Rose or Sleeping Beauty, Endimion is awakened by a kiss, and he defines his Platonic love for Cynthia as an emotion which is best expressed in terms of eremitic contemplation rather than in action.[35] He describes himself as:

> that Endimion who, divorsing himself from the aimiableness of all ladies, the bravery of all courts, the company of all men, hath chosen in a solitary cell to live, only by feeding on thy favour, accounting in the world (but thyself) nothing excellent, nothing immortal.[36]

This introspection is paralleled by the insular nature of Cynthia's court as a whole, from which there are no excursions into the outer world, and upon which (in contrast to the Alexander–Diogenes conflict in *Campaspe*) the intellectual as well as the male courtier is now presented as being wholly dependent. At the end of the play, Cynthia tells the philosophers whom she had summoned to attempt to end Endimion's trance to stay with her, rather than return to their homes in Greece and Egypt. She instructs them to 'content yourselves in our court, to fall from vain follies of Phylosophers to such vertues as are here practised'. When she has persuaded him and his companion to stay, Pythagoras asserts: 'I had rather in Cynthia's court spend tenne years, then in Greece one houre.'[37]

In *Endimion*, desire for Elizabeth as a symbol of an eternal, rather than historical, dimension is presented as the basis of her authority. While the pastimes pretended to a unity of *political* interest between courtier and monarch, which they suggested required active military expression, this play stressed the *mystical* or interior link between these figures, but subordinated courtier to queen. Yet although Cynthia's powers are contrasted with the relative powerlessness of her male courtier, she does not display the dynamic creativity attributed to Elizabeth in the pastimes, and even (implicitly) in the tree simile of *Sapho and Phao*. Lyly's use of the lunar image connects his Neoplatonic conception of Cynthia as a female beloved with the world soul rather with the higher principle of *nous* (usually associated with Christ as well as with the sun).[38] Yet while in the Neoplatonic conception the world soul had both passive and active functions, combining the contemplation of *nous* with the active (and implicitly creative) supervision of the material world, the exercise of this latter role seems an exceptional occurrence in *Endimion*; the only creative intervention of Cynthia (which itself is limited to the affairs of her court) occurs at the climax of the play, and is depicted in miraculous terms. Moreover, the principle which she embodies is chang*elessness*, a defiance of the processes of mutability. It is a conservative rather than a revolutionary force, which maintains the status quo instead of establishing a new order. (As a courtly audience would have known, the queen's conservative motto was *semper eadem* or 'always the same'.) Even the diversity produced by Cynthia's heavenly progress (as the moon) through successive lunar phases is depicted simply as a pleasing variety, which is ultimately contained within a single overriding image of unity. Endimion's speeches raise this trope of a constant inconstancy to the level of a mystical truth:

> O fayre Cynthia, why doe others terme thee unconstant, whom I have ever founde unmoveable? Iniurious tyme, corrupt manners, unkind men, who finding a constancy not to be matched in my sweete Mistris, hath christned her with the name of wavering, waxing, and waning. Is shee inconstant that keepeth a setled course, which since her first creation altereth not one minute in her moving? . . . What thing (my Mistris excepted) being in the pride of her beauty, & latter minute of her age, that waxeth young againe? . . . Such is my sweete *Cynthia*, whom tyme cannot touch, because she is divine, nor will offend because she is delicate. O *Cynthia*, if thou shouldest alwaies continue at thy fulnes, both Gods and men woulde conspire to ravish thee. But thou, to abate the pride of our affections, dost detract from thy perfections, thinking it sufficient, if once in a month we enioy a glympse of thy maiestie, and then, to encrease our greefes, thou dost decrease thy glemes, comming out of thy royall robes, wherewith thou dazelist our eyes, downe into thy swath clowtes, beguiling our eyes.[39]

The comparison of Cynthia's rare revelation of her true self to the incarnation of Christ, which ends this panegyric, echoes the compliments of the pastimes and once again connects the female monarch with the Wisdom figure. Endimion suggests that a traumatic experience of wounding or loss is the necessary prelude to this event: it is when the moon is eclipsed in darkness (conventionally the least idealized phase of the lunar cycle), that the mysterious conjunction of spirit with matter occurs, via the mediation of the lunar principle of soul. Yet his analogy also throws into relief the highly exclusive character of Cynthia's inspiration. Far from appearing in 'swath clowtes' in a stable, she is secluded both from the outer world and from nature, within the confined and artificial sphere of her court. And even there, her powers are only occasionally manifested in full.

1584, the year in which Lyly probably wrote his play, was a time of heated debate on the Elizabethan privy council concerning England's policy towards the intensifying Catholic–Protestant conflict in the Netherlands. The leading Protestant prince, William of Orange, was assassinated in the middle of that year, and it was also a time when the Spanish duke of Parma was gaining military initiative in the region. The strictly limited role which Lyly's play accords to the male courtier may thus be related to political divisions between the council's two factions. Its unprecedented stress on the passive and meditative role of the male courtier seems to correspond in imaginative terms to the preference both of the queen and of the Burghley faction for isolationism, in opposition to the militant and interventionist policies of the Leicester–Walsingham group.[40] But the play's distancing of Elizabeth not just from nature and the outside world, but also from the affairs of her court, now involved a splitting of the female beloved into good and bad, asexual and sexual. In terms of political allegory, this duality is related to the conflict between two queens: Elizabeth and her captive cousin, Mary queen of Scots (as Tellus), who had recently been the focus of the abortive Throckmorton plot.

In order to define Tellus as an alternative, 'bad' object of erotic and courtly desire, *Endimion* introduces the theme of witchcraft. Although the legal and religious discourse concerning witchcraft was overdetermined by the needs of the Elizabethan state, it had a specifically popular focus, in that it was concerned with identifying and punishing what was perceived as a certain type of subversive behaviour by members of the peasant class, who were usually (elderly) women. The plot of *Endimion* hinges on a (somewhat tenuous) distinction between different modes of enchantment by or subjugation to the feminine. While Cynthia's power over Endimion, described at one point as 'bewitching', is accepted and idealized (though not without some reservations being expressed by his friend Eumenides at the beginning of the play), this power is only fully established after Cynthia frees Endimion from the spell commissioned by Tellus and woven by the witch Dipsas. But Lyly's use of witchcraft as a central element in his plot should have reminded anyone versed in classical mythography of the connections between Cynthia or Diana and witchcraft. In the numerous classical dictionaries and mythographies available at this time, Hecate, Roman goddess of witchcraft, death and the underworld, was identified as the third, waning face of the moon: that is, of triple or 'triformis' Diana. As Natale Conti wrote in his best-selling *Mythologiae*: 'the moon, Hecate, and Diana are the same'.[41]

In representing Elizabeth as the moon, Lyly evidently wished to stress her saint-like transcendence, not just of the material processes of history, but also of that cycle of feminine mutability which the moon was held to rule. But even a saint (and of course such figures were accorded no *official* recognition anyway in Protestant England, in spite of the implicit continuation of a cult of St George and so on) was held to defeat the corruption of the physical body only very rarely, and then *after* death. More significant, perhaps, is the fact that this extraordinary assertion that she could defeat time's power over herself as well as over her lovers, which would become commonplace in the literature and art produced in the rest of her reign, was being made of a woman who had been 50 in 1583, and who had therefore entered the phase of the female life cycle connected in classical myth and folk tradition with the waning moon and the crone.[42] Was it merely coincidental that the courtly conception of Elizabeth, which deliberately effaced her ageing bodily reality, yet simultaneously attributed to her exceptional (even supernatural) powers as the immortal body politic of the state, coincided with a scale of popular anxiety and legal debate about witchcraft which had never occurred in England before? This development is generally dated from around 1580; a major witchcraft trial occurred at Chelmsford in Essex in 1582, where eighteen women were condemned and hanged.[43] It seems to have been the widespread hysteria connected with this famous trial that prompted Reginald Scot to write his *Discoverie of Witchcraft*, which was published in 1584, the year in which Lyly probably composed *Endimion*. Scot did not believe that witchcraft existed; however, he was interested in the social phenomenon of belief in witches (and the apparent belief of many accused as witches in their own powers). His treatise mentioned the long-established theme of Christian demonology, reiterated in all manuals on the subject, that the pagan goddess Diana had an especially close connection with witchcraft:

> certain wicked women following Sathan's provocations, being seduced by the illusion of divels, beleeve and professe, that in the night time they ride abroad with Diana, the goddesse, or else with Herodias, with an innumerable multitude, upon certaine beasts, and passe over manie countries and nations, in the silence of the night, and doo whatsoever those faires or ladies command.[44]

And he also asserted that:

> The most of such as are said to be witches, are women which be commonly old, lame, blear-eyed, pale, fowle, and full of wrinkles. . . . They are learne, and deformed, shewing melancholie in their faces, to the horror of all that see them. They are doting, scolds, mad, divelish . . .[45]

Viewed from the perspective of this almost exactly contemporary yet superficially unrelated Elizabethan discourse around witchcraft, *Endimion* takes on a new meaning. On the one hand, the figure of Cynthia is opposed to those of the old witch Dipsas and her client, the lustful Tellus. As a Neoplatonic or Petrarchan beloved, Cynthia's spiritual or super-natural powers are linked with her transcendence of her female nature, while Dipsas and Tellus are each presented as under the influence of their bodies in different ways. Tellus is the victim of an insatiable physical desire; Dipsas is the victim of her age, and at one point in the play is the object of a satiric parody of Petrarchan courtship which stresses her age and unattractiveness:

> O what a fine thin hayre hath Dipsas! What a prettie low forehead! What a tall & statelie nose! What little hollowe eyes! What great & goodly lypes! How harmlesse shee is being toothlesse! . . . In how sweete a proportion her cheekes hang down to her brests like duges, and her pappes to her waste like bagges! . . . How thrifty must she be in whom there is no waste! How vertuous is shee like to be, over whom no man can be ielous![46]

But perhaps these misogynistic representations also contaminate by their proximity the icon of Elizabeth. It certainly seems significant that *Endimion* was Lyly's last play which took the material of the cult for its primary subject matter. By this time, according to G.K. Hunter, he had become disillusioned by the lack of concrete remuneration from the queen.[47] In his later drama, the predominance of satire and burlesque as well as romance plots leading to marriage suggests that he was now catering more for the tastes of his private theatre audiences than for the court. Only in two of these plays did Lyly make any reference to the cult of Elizabeth: in *Midas* (performed at court in 1589) and *The Woman in the Moone* (performed there sometime between 1593 and 1595). But in both plays, the queen's figure is decentred, along with the gynocentric domain with which it had formerly been associated by Lyly.

The ostensible occasion and inspiration of *Midas* was the defeat of the Armada in 1588. Yet significantly, Lyly chose not to eulogize Elizabeth as an Amazonian victor, but rather to satirize her defeated opponent, Philip II of Spain, who is here identified with Midas. This was consistent with his emphasis upon the monarch as a predominantly passive and contemplative figure in *Endimion*; none the less, in his satire of a defeated ruler Lyly did not simply reject once again the imperialist and expansionist conception of monarchy promoted in the Elizabethan pastime. He also returned to the thorny question of the creativity and even attributed divinity of the absolute monarch. The play interweaves the classical myth of Midas' desire for gold (intended as a reference to Spain's ransacking of the Americas for gold and silver) with an invented account of his attempt to invade the kingdom of Lesbos (which symbolizes England). At the same time, Lyly uses the additional mythical episode of a celestial contest between Apollo and Pan for sovereignty in music, and erroneously judged by Midas, to emphasize that the king has abused his royal power in his desire for absolute sovereignty on earth. Midas' choice of Pan as winner elicits the favour of Pan: 'Blessed by *Midas*, worthie to be a God.' But Apollo's reaction is very different: 'Wretched, unworthie to bee a King, thou shalt know what it is to displease Apollo.'[48] The rejected god's revenge, by endowing the king with ass's ears, reminds the audience forcibly of Midas' humanity, rather than his divinity.

On one level, Midas' punishment can be read simply in terms of nationalism, of anti-Hispanic and anti-Catholic sentiment (with the competing music of the two gods interpreted as the ideological conflict between Protestantism and Catholicism). Possibly Elizabeth may be considered the absent centre of the play, as Sappho, ruler of Lesbos (a comparison which of course carries the ambiguity I mentioned earlier). But in contrast to *Gallathea* and *Endimion*, she is distinguished from (rather than identified with) the presiding deity of the play. This divinity is not female but male, not Diana or Cynthia as moon goddess, but her brother Apollo, the sun god. Given the play's exploration of the links between monarchy and poetic inspiration, and in the light of Lyly's (by this time desperate) need for patronage, it might also be read as an appeal to Elizabeth: to remember that creative affinity to writers with which both Lyly and (by 1589) Puttenham had credited her (albeit reservedly), and to fulfil her responsibilities of artistic patronage. Midas' final abandonment of his invasion and deferral to Apollo, following the god's promise to remove his ass's ears, relates the security of Lesbos to the victory of a god whom, while he might *signify* Protestantism, in his classical guise was also a patron of the arts:

> Come my Lords, let us repaire to our palace, in which *Apollo* shall have a stately statue erected: each month will we solemnize there a feast, and here every yere a sacrifice. Phrygia shal be governed by Gods, not men, leaste the Gods make beasts of men. . . . So blessed be *Apollo*, quiet be Lesbos, happie be *Mydas*: and to begin this solemnitie, let us sing to *Apollo*, for so much as Musick, nothing can content *Apollo*.[49]

In Lyly's last court play, *The Woman in the Moone*, there was a similar displacement of the figure of Elizabeth. But this time the decentring was part of the dramatic action. It was also satiric in its insinuation, as Lyly's former idealized representation of the queen in Petrarchan and Neoplatonic terms, as the moon goddess Cynthia, was superseded by a very different image of the moon and its association with women. The play tells the story of Pandora, the approximate equivalent to Eve in Greek myth, whose feminine mutability is attributed by Lyly to the influence of Cynthia or the moon. She claims: 'Cynthia made me idle, mutable,/Forgetfull, foolish, fickle, franticke, madde:/These be the humours that content me best./And therefore will I stay with Cynthia.'[50] Finally, Nature places Pandora in the moon in Cynthia's stead. In terms of Neoplatonic allegory, the play could be read as suggesting the eclipse of the transcendent ideal which Elizabeth had represented by a baser image of human (and specifically womanly) nature, like Donne's lament for the departure of the world soul from the earth in *The First Anniversary*:

> She whom wise nature had invented then
> When she observ'd that every sort of men
> Did in their voyage in this worlds Sea stray,
> And needed a new compasse for their way:. . .
> Shee, shee is dead, shee's dead:[51]

Yet Lyly emphasizes that Pandora is as she is *because* of the moon, whose influence he now defines in the (predominantly negative) terms proposed by medieval and Renaissance astrology rather than as a Neoplatonic symbol.[52] It is certainly striking that at the same time that Elizabeth's image is definitively eclipsed (never to appear in his drama again), Lyly's court prologue to this play placed unprecedented emphasis upon his own professional identity as a poet–dramatist, and presented this figure as inspired with Platonic *furor*. He claims to have privileged access to the same sources of inspiration which he had formerly attributed to the queen. In the past, of course, he had virtually credited her with the creation of his plays, in her (non-mythological) triple role of theatrical subject, spectator, and interpreter. In fact in the court prologue to *Sapho and Phao* he had actually described his play as the stuff of Elizabeth's very own private fantasy-world:

> I on knee for all, entreate, that your Highnesse imagine yourself to be in a deepe dreame, that staying the conclusion, in your rising your Maiestie vouchsafe but to saye, *And so you awakte.*[53]

In the prologue to *The Woman in the Moone*, the privilege of dreaming has been reclaimed by the artist: 'Remember all is but a Poet's dreame/The first he had in *Phoebus* holy bowre'.[54] On this, the last occasion when Elizabeth formed part of the subject matter of his drama, the 'dream'-image which Lyly presented apparently corresponded to his own fantasy, rather than to that of the queen.

Chapter six

Rewriting chastity: representations of the unmarried queen by Chapman, Shakespeare, Ralegh, and Spenser

Flesh and blood or ideal form? Some versions of woman in literature of the 1590s

Although he may have favoured a 'courtly' style, the intervention of the professional poet or dramatist in the Elizabethan cult transformed an exclusive aristocratic experience into a literary commodity, challenging the claim of the male courtier to a privileged view of Elizabeth. Literary representations of Elizabeth as a Petrarchan or Neoplatonic beloved were widely disseminated outside courtly circles during the decade of the 1590s.[1] Both in published poetry and in drama performed outside the court, there were numerous references to Elizabeth as another Diana or Cynthia, a figure who, remote from historical reality, inhabited instead a secluded otherworldly dimension, often depicted in pastoral terms:

> It was a valley gaudy green
> Where Dian at the fount was seen;
> > Green it was,
> > And did pass
> All other of Diana's bowers
> In the pride of Flora's flowers. . . .[2]

The lunar image privileged in Lyly's *Endimion* (as well as in Ralegh's unpublished verse of the 1580s) appeared frequently in such descriptions. At the same time, following the formulation of Spenser's *The Shepheardes Calender* as well as of Lylyan drama, they often placed additional emphasis upon the predominantly feminine attributes of this Elizabethan *temenos* or sacred space, by reference to Diana's accompanying cohorts of nymphs.

In Neoplatonic terms, while a comparison to the sun implicitly connected the object of desire with the category of *nous* or Mind, which was associated with the realm of pure Forms or Ideas, lunar imagery suggested a parallel with the world soul and the individual souls derived from it, which as a mediating term between earth and heaven was an altogether more ambiguous concept. As *l'oro* (gold) Petrarch's Laura was connected with the sun rather than the moon, and in the early Elizabethan entertainment the same comparison had been implied by Elizabeth's representation as a summer queen or nature goddess whose life-giving effect upon the natural world paralleled that of the sun. In the Elizabethan tilt, an association between the queen and the sun was common: she was described in these terms in the 'Four Foster Children of Desire' tilt of 1581, and the armour of sir Henry Lee, her champion at court tilts from 1580 until 1590, was decorated with suns.[3] The sun was also accorded prominence in several state portraits, such as the Ditchley and Rainbow portraits, and was a central motif in sir John Davies' *Hymnes of Astraea*, a sequence of acrostic poems dedicated 'To that cleere maiestie, which in the North,/Doth like another Sunne in glory rise'.[4] As a signifier of Elizabeth's 'body politic', of her public role as ruler, the solar image appears to have been unproblematic; it did not focus attention upon the gender of the monarch. But by the end of Elizabeth's reign it was the moon which was most closely associated with the queen as embodying the *corpus mysticum* of the state. The moon had been accorded a similar significance in literary and artistic representations of French Renaissance absolutism; but what is exceptional about the use of this image within Elizabethan absolutism is that it highlights an unusual conjunction of gender: between the monarch's female 'body natural' and the immortal 'body politic' of the state (or *respublica*), which was itself gendered feminine.

Lyly's initial use of the lunar symbol appears to have been intended to elide the problematic fact of a woman's possession of 'masculine' political power. But her connection with this changeable planet (whose difference from the sun was further accentuated in the post-Copernican world view, where both moon and earth were distinguished from the sun as moving rather than fixed planetary bodies) also exaggerated the queen's wandering or deviation from the passive role of the Petrarchan and Neoplatonic beloved, together with her femaleness. Abraham Fraunce wrote in *Amintas Dale*, published in 1592: 'Diana is so called, as if a man would say *Deviana*, a stragler or wanderer: for, the Moone strayeth from the Eclipticall line. . . . Her garment is changeable; the moone hath diverse phases and apparitions.'[5] In another (pseudo-)scientific discourse this planetary sign had a long-established connection with a theory of woman's temperament as overdetermined by her body. The cold and moist qualities (equated with the watery or phlegmatic humour) which medieval Galenic psychology attributed to woman were held to be caused by the influence of the moon.[6]

Not only was the increasing use of lunar imagery in connection with the queen potentially problematic; her representation in Platonic terms was now at odds with the general trend of late sixteenth-century literary culture. The 1590s was a time of serious economic and political unrest in England; while in cultural terms it was a highly productive decade, this productivity was in itself symptomatic of a time of major epistemological transition, when many early Renaissance assumptions were being subjected to intense scrutiny.[7] In these years, although the mystical idealism associated with Platonic and Neoplatonic philosophy did not disappear altogether, it was significantly qualified by a more secular world view, as the new scientific philosophy began to secure its ideological hegemony. Ideas drawn from the Renaissance discourses of love were widely disseminated within Elizabethan literature in the early 1590s, which was marked by a flood of 'sonneteering'. Yet certain intellectual reactions against these attitudes (reactions which had only gradually developed in Europe) were also influential at this time, and had their impact compounded by a variety of local factors. As a result, a sophisticated grasp of Renaissance concepts of sublimated desire coexists within many Elizabethan literary texts with other, contradictory attitudes towards love and sexuality, as well as towards the figure of woman which was privileged in the love discourses.

Especially significant in its implications for Elizabeth's cult of chastity was the increasing ideological emphasis upon marriage in the literature of these years. This theme is usually attributed exclusively to the influence of Protestant doctrine, whose rejection of monastic celibacy led to the formulation of a more positive attitude to marriage, publicized in England chiefly by the means of domestic conduct books addressed to a predominantly middle-class readership.[8] But late sixteenth-century English culture also assimilated a newly idealized conception of marriage from a (post-Counter-Reformation) Catholic source, which consisted of Italian and French conduct books aimed at an aristocratic and courtly readership, such as Stefano Guazzo's *Civile Conversation* (translated 1581), and Pierre de la Primaudaye's *The French Academye* (translated 1586).[9] Such works appear to have been directly or indirectly influenced by a second wave of Italian Neoplatonism, whose exponents (in particular Benedetto Varchi and Flaminio Nobili) defined married love with reference to that intermediate concept of *amore humano* or humane love with which Ficino had attempted to reconcile his binary opposition between an heavenly and earthly desire.[10]

At the same time, although the first few years of the 1590s saw the publication of many sonnet sequences, we find idealized conceptions of love being treated with some reserve even in these texts. These English sequences appeared not at the beginning but at the end of a literary tradition, and in many of them can be found attitudes often called anti-Petrarchan. These often encompassed, not only a critique of the mannered and formulaic Petrarchan style, and an emphasis upon sexuality and the body which implicitly criticized the Platonic separation of spirit from matter, but also (in a development of a representational strand already present in the *Rime Sparse*) a growing anxiety concerning those imaginative powers which Petrarchism had attributed to the female beloved. In two of the most radical of these sequences, Spenser's *Amoretti* (1595) and Shakespeare's *Sonnets* (probably composed around mid-decade), interest in her (licit or illicit) sexuality is closely related to woman's loss of her formerly privileged position within Petrarchan discourse. She is gradually subordinated to the poet as spouse in Spenser's sequence, and contrasted with a more idealized (though not completely asexual) object of desire, the figure of a male beloved/patron, in that of Shakespeare.

Anti-Petrarchan and anti-Platonic themes were given more explicit expression in another mode of poetic discourse which was also popular in the early 1590s: that of the epyllion or erotic narrative poem, which offered modern reworkings of certain classical myths. These poems are marked by a new, more realistic interest in classical literary culture, a changed perspective which early sixteenth-century humanist scholarship had facilitated. Most epyllion poets ignored the reductionist interpretations of Platonic allegory; instead, they looked to the text as a literary model, and to the erotic and highly self-conscious poetry of Ovid in particular.[11] Ovid's compendium of classical myth, the *Metamorphoses*, was now available without the cumbersome addition of moralized commentaries, but the epyllion writers also imitated his *Amores* and *Ars Amatoria* in their poetic explorations of sexual passion.[12] The Petrarchan poet's metonymic displacement of his mistress' body by means of various stylized conceits, like the Renaissance vogue for emblems or 'speaking pictures', assumed a Neoplatonic theory of representation, in which correct response to these images was held to depend upon the eye as a spiritual rather than physical organ (in the Platonic tradition, sight was usually considered the highest of the senses, and so the least contaminated by man's animal nature).[13] In the epyllion, however, there was an erotic yet simultaneously comic emphasis upon the physical expression of love and upon the sensuous aspects of reality, which appealed rather to the eye as an organ of pleasure, and hence implicitly rejected its Neoplatonic status. But in spite of its erotic imagery, the epyllion's ambiguity and even hostility towards woman challenges the modern critical assumption that the carnivalesque necessarily implies a complete rejection of patriarchal convention.[14] While it gestures towards the possibility, indeed the potency of female desire, its comic treatment of this topic reinforces traditional 'feminine' behaviour.

This positioning of the reader of the epyllion as a sinful observer or scopophiliac initially suggests a parallel with one of the most famous classical accounts of illicit viewing, Ovid's description of Actaeon's discovery of Diana as she bathed. Yet while the epyllia linked voyeurism with reading, they did not in fact enact poetic repetitions of Actaeon's transgression. Although his emphasis upon erotic pleasures challenged many of the attitudes of Petrarchism and Neoplatonism, the epyllion poet never extended this challenge by inscribing that most tabooed object – the female body – at the centre of his poetic discourse. Instead, he substituted for the real female body its imitation. In Marston's *The Metamorphosis of Pygmalion's Image* this substitute took the form of a vivified female statue. More typical, however, was a further gesture of carnivalesque inversion (which was none the less in another sense an act of evasion), whereby in a reversal of conventional sexual roles a feminized version of the male body was represented as the primary poetic object of erotic desire: 'At this Adonis smiles as in disdain,/That in each cheek appears a pretty dimple:/Love made those hollows, if himself were slain,/He might be buried in a tomb so simple.'[15] To this significant absence of any representation of the female body can be related the epyllion's more explicit, but viciously satiric treatment of another topic absent from the love discourses: female erotic desire. Its pastoral landscapes are peopled not only by reticent, effeminately beautiful men – Shakespeare's Adonis in *Venus and Adonis*, Drayton's Endimion in *Endimion and Phoebe*, Marlowe's Leander in *Hero and Leander* – but also by aggressive female wooers such as Shakespeare's Venus, Lodge's Scilla in *Scillaes Metamorphosis*, Drayton's Phoebe. At times, the reader of these poems is constructed as a male homosexual voyeur, as at the end of Marlowe's tantalizing description of Leander: 'The barbarous *Thratian* soldier moov'd with nought,/Was moov'd with him, and for his favour sought./Some swore he was a maid in man's attire,/For in his looks were all that men desire.'[16] But the emphasis of the epyllion upon woman as lover rather than beloved also implies appeal to the erotic desires of a female readership – at the same time, paradoxically, as it uses satire to censure female fantasies of sexual dominance.[17]

A further striking feature of the epyllion which seems to have an indirect relationship to the courtly cult of Elizabeth is its frequent connection of the aggressive female wooer's desire for dominance with her possession of a spiritual authority, as a priestess (Hero) or goddess (Venus, Phoebe). The reaction against Platonic attitudes to love in much literature of this period points to an increasing anxiety concerning the love discourses' capacity to control and limit woman's access to meaning, especially when these systems were assimilated by the cult of a female monarch. Could they continue to define the female object of desire as a disposable mirror and signifier, as merely the passive mediatrix of the *logos*? Or was sexual difference beginning to contaminate the masculine purity of that vital philosophical category?[18] Significantly, in the play in which Lyly made the most ambitious claims for Elizabeth's spiritual power as a female *logos*, *Endimion*, the theme of witchcraft had also entered his drama. The philosophical and religious implications of Elizabeth's cult were pushed to their logical conclusion in an obscure narrative poem by George Chapman, entitled *The Shadow of Night*. The extreme view of the cult proposed in this text, which was published in 1594, seems closely related to the author's sense of the intellectual challenge currently being posed by the rise of the new philosophy.

Chapman's poem is broadly Platonic in that it is organized around a dualist conception of the relation between spirit and matter, within which an immaterial spiritual reality is privileged. Yet his assimilation of ideas derived from the pre-Socratic philosophical system of Orphism revealed the extent to which the courtly idea of the queen was now at odds with the Platonic emphasis upon masculine identity and sameness.[19] As Chapman describes her, Elizabeth closely resembles the creative figure of Wisdom or Sophia as 'mother of all things in the universe', but with the important difference that she is not subordinated to the supervising authority of a father–God. Instead, she emerges from the pre-existent matrix of the 'Great Goddesse', Night, like a daughter from her mother's womb. At the same time, by drawing on highly complex and often contradictory mythological material from various Renaissance mythographies (especially the *Mythologiae* of Conti), Chapman produced a many-faceted image of Cynthia or Diana which was no longer divided or split: her idealized associations were now indistinguishable from the darker and explicitly pagan aspects of the classical myth. She is: 'Nature's bright eye-sight, and the Night's faire soule./That with thy triple forehead dost controule/Earth, seas, and hell.'[20]

In the first of the poem's two parts, 'Hymnus in Noctem', or the Hymn to Night, Chapman presents himself as a priest conducting a pagan rite or sacrifice, of which the first stage is an invocation to Night. This was the first principle of the Orphics, equivalent to the state of chaos and unformed matter which preceded creation. Chapman invokes her as:

> Sorrowes deare sovereigne, and the queene of rest,
> That when unlightsome, vast, and indigest
> The formelesse matter of this world did lye,
> Fildst every place with thy Divinitie,
> Why didst thy absolute and endlesse sway,
> License heavens torch, the scepter of the Day,
> Distinguisht intercession to thy throne,
> That long before, all matchlesse rulde alone?
> Why letst thou order, orderlesse disperse,
> The fighting parents of this universe?
> When earth, the ayre, and sea, in fire remaind,
> When fire, the sea, and earth, the ayre containd,
> When ayre, the earth, and fire, the sea, enclosde

When sea, fire, ayre, in earth were indisposde,
Nothing, as now, remainde so out of kinde,
All things in grosse, were finer than refinde,
Substance was sound within, and had no being,
Now forme gives being; all our essence seeming,
Chaos had soule without a bodie then,
Now bodies live without the soules of men,
Lumps being digested; monsters, in our pride.[21]

This pre-existent rule of Night or Chaos has, according to Chapman, been replaced by a different and wholly inferior chaos, a 'blindnesse of the minde' which is paradoxically signified by the sunny light of day. The inference is that man's retreat into an increasingly secular world under the growing influence of the new scientific and rationalist philosophy has made him monstrous rather than godlike. Chapman asserts that only Cynthia or the moon, as the 'soule' or the purest part of Night, can re-establish a golden age on the 'infectious dunghill of this Round', restoring an esoteric or spiritual mode of knowledge in which what seems 'blindnesse' will paradoxically lead to clearer vision. But when, at the end of this first part of his poem, Chapman introduces his female saviour, he does so in terms which Elizabeth's cult had always studiously avoided. For she is no longer seen as a passive emblem of spiritual power, but as its active manipulator. Chapman's description of Cynthia's supernatural progress not only contrasts with the more worldly pageantry of contemporary royal processions; it also throws into vivid relief the fact that western culture had no positive image of active female spirituality, or of what he terms Cynthia's 'Magick authoritie'. She appears:

Enchantresse-like, deckt in disparent lawne,
Circkled with charmes, and incantations,
That ride huge spirits, and outragious passions. . . .
This traine, with meteors, comets, lightenings,
The dreadfull presence of our Empresse sings. . . .[22]

In Chapman's conception, Elizabeth as Cynthia or Diana still represents the heights of mystical contemplation, equivalent to the Platonic *nous* or *logos* as 'the forces of the mind'.[23] Like Orpheus, revered by Renaissance Neoplatonists as a custodian of secret knowledge, he presents himself as an inspired poet who is uniquely able to invoke or conjure the goddess' emergence from the maternal womb of Night.[24] Now, however, this task apparently needs extraordinary strength and courage. Chapman's description of his poetic role in the dedicatory letter to the poem as an 'Herculean labour' reintroduces the figure of the Herculean hero or wild man as a male counterpart to the queen as a source of mystical power. But while this reference stresses the mythic courage required of the masculine subject who wishes to plumb the deepest mysteries of woman as *logos*. Chapman's poem attributes the militant activity of a Hercules – his phallic power – to the female beloved alone. Instead of defining Cynthia's role of redeemer (as a Christ or Wisdom figure) in passive terms, he stresses that it must be accompanied or preceded by the enactment of an apocalyptic vengeance. In the Christian tradition, such behaviour was usually attributed to the unforgiving father-God of the Old Testament, whose justice Christ tempered with mercy in the New Testament. Aided by hitherto unavailable accounts of the barbarous practices associated with Diana and Hecate in antiquity (taken from the *Mythologiae* of Conti). Chapman represents his goddess as an 'All-ill-purging puritie', a supernatural portent of disaster for all who have rejected her. The second part of the poem, 'Hymnus in Cynthiam', uses imagery which evokes the gloomy fatalism of medieval art, or the macabre fantasies of Hieronymus Bosch, rather than a Renaissance humanist concern with self-determination. Cynthia's huntress role is transposed from its usual pastoral setting to scenes which resemble the last judgement. Those who do not acknowledge her authority are condemned to perpetual torment:

> In this vast thicket, (whose descriptions task
> The penns of furies, and of feends would aske:
> So more than humane thoughted horrible)
> The soules of such as liv'd implausible,
> In happie Empire of this Goddesse glories.
> And scorned to crowne hir Phanes with sacrifice
> And [*sic*] ceaseless walk: exspiring fearefull grones,
> Curses, and threats, for their confusions.
> Her darts, and arrowes, some of them had slaine.
> Others hir doggs eate, panting hir disdaine,
> After she had transformed them into beasts:
> Others her monsters carried to their nests,
> Rent them in pieces, and their spirits sent
> To this blind shade, to waile their banishment.[25]

In this passage, the individual fate of Actaeon, so often elided or evaded in Renaissance texts influenced by the discourses of love, is not only described in full: it has become a collective experience. For the capacity for masculine self-definition which the Renaissance lover had sought through the female beloved is substituted an endlessly repeated process of the fragmentation and destruction of identity.

The most disturbing metamorphosis of the Cynthia figure occurs at the end of the poem, where she assumes the aspect of Hecate, goddess of death and witchcraft. In Greek myth, Hecate was described as a Titan, one of the gigantic pre-Olympian gods deposed by Zeus and imprisoned in the underworld. Unlike her fellow Titans, however, she had been assimilated by the later pantheon of gods, although as a goddess of the underworld.[26] Gradually she became identified with the moon and with Artemis (the Greek precursor of Diana). Yet while she had won the favour of the new father-God, Zeus, Hecate's mythology retained visible traces of her affinity with a pre-patriarchal cosmology, and this is clear from Chapman's description. Cynthia is presented here as prototype of both the magician and the witch, the practised executor of occult ritual as well as an expert in the lore of deadly herbs. Her return to her gigantic size 'of halfe a furlong' reveals the grotesque female body not as an object of satire, but as intensely threatening, forcing the reader to reassume the dwarfed perspective of the child in relation to the mother's body. Her numerous serpentine attributes, which were associated in antiquity with the fearful Gorgon Medusa, but were often found in representations of the all-powerful mother goddesses of the pre-classical epoch, signify her possession of a phallic authority usually reserved for the male; they also challenge the stasis and uniformity of patriarchal definitions both of power and of sexuality.[27] The possible translation of this power from the domain of myth to the material and historical realm is represented in cataclysmic terms: Chapman suggests that a revolution in the natural or earthly order would necessarily be accompanied by similar events in the cosmos. In view of his hostility to the sun as a symbol of the new philosophy, this rearrangement of the order of the heavens probably corresponds to a rejection of a heliocentric or Copernican astronomy and its implications:

> Then in thy cleare, and Isie Pentacle,
> Now execute a Magicke miracle:
> Slip everie sort of poisond herbes, and plants,
> And bring thy rabid mastiffs to these hants.
> Look with thy fierce aspect, be terror-strong;
> Assume thy wondrous shape of halfe a furlong:
> Put on the feete of Serpents, viperous hayres,
> And act the fearfulst part of thy affaires:
> Convert the violent courses of thy floods,
> Remove whole fields of corne, and hughest woods,
> Cast hills into the sea, and make the starrs,
> Drop out of heaven, and lose thy Mariners.
> So shall the wonders of thy power be seene,
> And thou for ever live the Planets Queene.[28]

The detailed exploration of the 'other' face of the Petrarchan and Neoplatonic beloved articulated in *The Shadow of Night* seems ostensibly to have been intended as an exaggerated compliment to the queen, however embarrassing its implications might have been.[29] Yet at times one glimpses a thread of political satire; for example, in the use of the myth of the Calydonian boar as a metaphor for the extent of religious oppression in the distinctly imperfect contemporary society. This beast had been sent by Diana to punish the unfortunate house of Cadmus:

> Religious curbe, that managed men in bounds,
> Of publique welfare; lothing private grounds,
> (Now cast away, by selfe-lovs paramores)
> Are all transformd to Calydonian bores,
> That kill our bleeding vines, displow our fields,
> Rend groves in peeces; all things nature yeelds
> Supplanting. . . .[30]

Thus while Chapman calls upon Elizabeth as Cynthia to reform the current state of disorder by drastic measures, this passage implies that he also accords her some blame for the current deterioration. His poem certainly asserts, in contrast with most other literary compliments to the queen as Diana or Cynthia, that as yet she has not fully manifested that 'Magick authoritie' which can restore the golden age. Indeed, by comparing Elizabeth with the waning phase of the moon, Chapman implies that failure to establish a new order will cause her eternal form to experience a damaging and perhaps fatal eclipse within the mutable time of history, 'in that sable day/When interposed earth takes thee away'.[31]

Whatever its political message, by uncovering the 'other' side of the queen's courtly cult, Chapman's poem provides us with an interesting insight into its ambiguous status in the 1590s. Its emphasis upon the occult dimension of Elizabeth's courtly image, and its focus on the bizarre and menacing figure of Hecate, has some significant parallels with that version of the cult found in *A Midsummer Night's Dream*, thought to have been written a year or two later. But while Chapman stressed the spiritual autonomy and even supremacy of his Cynthia, Shakespeare's whole endeavour in his play was to restore her to the control of the patriarchy.[32] The fairy queen of *A Midsummer Night's Dream*, Titania, shares her title with Elizabeth, and her name is an appellation of Diana as moon goddess; it also stresses Diana's connection with the Titaness Hecate.[33] Through the metonymic associations of the 'little western flower' whose juice enchants her, Titania is simultaneously linked with and distinguished from the historical queen, for on this flower had fallen the dart Cupid aimed at the 'imperial votaress'. The play's grotesque coupling of spirit and matter, of Titania and the ass-headed Bottom, may be an image of misrule, but it uses a critique of Platonic dualism to enforce patriarchal norms of behaviour. By this sexual humiliation, Oberon brings a free-wheeling image of female divinity comically and cruelly down to earth. But *A Midsummer Night's Dream* does not only challenge the Platonism of Elizabeth's cult by its emphasis upon female heterosexuality and the subordination of woman in marriage. Its use of lunar imagery also points to an anxiety about the love discourses' attribution of an imaginative or spiritual authority, together with the task of mirroring an idealized masculine identity, to the enigmatic and unstable figure of woman.

All its critics point out that the ruling symbol of *A Midsummer Night's Dream* is the moon, for whose new crescent Theseus and Hippolyta are waiting to celebrate their wedding. The play's events consequently occur in the dark phase of the moon, the phase associated with that aspect of Diana or Cynthia as a lunar deity which was most difficult to idealize – Hecate, goddess of witchcraft, death, and the underworld. Puck tells us that the faeries 'run/By the triple Hecate's team/From the presence of the sun./Following darkness like a dream'.[34] The play records a male–female conflict over control of these lunar powers, which as attributes of faerie are associated here both with imagination and fantasy and also with the energies of nature. Since their dissension over the changeling boy, Titania's 'moonlight revels' have always been disturbed by Oberon, and she asserts that as a result the cycles of nature have been disordered:

> Therefore the moon, the governess of floods,
> Pale in her anger, washes all the air,
> That rheumatic diseases do abound,
> And thorough this distemperature we see
> The seasons alter:[35]

This theme of natural disorder as a manifestation of feminine anger through the agency of the moon echoes the closing lines of Chapman's *The Shadow of Night*. But the order which is established at the end of the play, with the coming of the new moon, is characterized by an altered relationship between male and female. The woman-centred or matri-archal character of Titania's power at the beginning of the play was indicated by her desire to keep the changeling boy in memory of her former intimate relationship with his mother, her 'votaress'. By the end of the play, this loyalty to the ties of female friendship has been replaced by a submission to masculine or patriarchal authority. At the same time, the imaginative faculty which the love discourses connected with the mediating role of woman has been appropriated by the male.

In the Neoplatonic conception, it was the soul or world soul's image-making faculty which enabled it to mediate between matter and spirit (or intellect). George Puttenham, writing at the end of the 1580s, described the imagination as a

> representer of the best, most comely and bewtifull images or appearances of things to the soul and according to their very truth.

This is the imagination in action, yet the contemplation of this very truth is the operation of the intellect.[36]

But its intermediary role also meant that the imaginative faculty partook of the same ambiguity which characterized soul, as well as the lunar image often connected with soul. *A Midsummer Night's Dream* begins by presenting Titania as a governess of the imagination in her role of faerie queen and moon goddess. When she first appears, her speeches are full of images of wind and airy movement which suggest the rapid motions of the imagination. Apparently she and her faeries 'wander everywhere'. In the course of the play this lunar mutability is eclipsed by a more earthly, masculine use of fantasy, which appeals primarily to the material desires of the body, and ignores the restlessness of the spirit.

For it is by means of heterosexual fantasy, as contrived and directed by Oberon and Puck, that Titania is ensnared and defeated. With his ass's head, Bottom not only symbolizes phallic sexuality and lust, he also represents the animal which Apuleius in *The Golden Ass* (translated into English in 1566) had asserted was most hated by the moon goddess. The 'little western flower', whose white colour has turned 'purple with love's wound', and whose 'juice' bewitches the faerie queen as well as the mortal lovers, offers a metaphoric representation of female sexual experience and sexual pleasure; none the less, it also indicates that the watery or fluid character attributed to woman can be directed and controlled by the male through the enchantments of a genital heterosexuality. This achievement of control, both over female mutability and over the imaginative faculty which the love discourses had connected with woman as a chaste object of desire, is implicitly linked with the establishment of a new masculine control over the natural world, and over what were formerly seen as the operations of fate. The irresistible power of fate leads to tragedy in the play of Pyramus and Thisbe performed by Bottom and his fellow artisans; by contrast, in the fairy epilogue Oberon asserts control over these very forces: 'So shall all the couples three/Ever true in loving be;/And the blots of Nature's hand/Shall not in their issue stand.'[37] Viewed in relation to the play's concern to fix or redirect a mutable quality formerly attributed to woman, Theseus' oft-quoted speech about the imagination acquires a new significance. For whilst he attacks the dangerous deceptions of this unstable faculty, his description of the imaginative activity of the poet stresses the need to impose boundaries upon the potentially limitless substance of the imagination. The poet's ability to localize and ground this faculty suggests a literary parallel to the success with which both Theseus and Oberon have restricted the wanderings of their queens:

> The poet's eye, in a fine frenzy rolling,
> Doth glance from heaven to earth, from earth to heaven;
> And as imagination bodies forth
> The forms of things unknown, the poet's pen
> Turns them to shapes, and gives to airy nothing
> A local habitation and a name.[38]

In challenging the powers which the love discourses attributed to a female beloved, *A Midsummer Night's Dream* drew on both the eroticism of the epyllion and the emergent ideology of married love. The play also seems to be in dialogue both with Chapman's provocatively esoteric version of the cult of Elizabeth and with the idea of the 'faerie queene' popularized by Spenser. It is unlikely that Shakespeare had read sir Walter Ralegh's *The 11th: and last booke of the Ocean to Scinthia*, for it was unpublished in Ralegh's lifetime. Yet there are some striking parallels between Shakespeare's play and Ralegh's highly personal statement of disillusionment with Elizabethan courtiership. Ralegh's increasing unease with the lunar persona of Elizabeth which he had helped to popularize is also an anxiety about the imagination and its powers. But unlike Oberon and Theseus, he is unable to control the female figure whom he identifies with these qualities. His poetic fragment reveals the extent to which, by refusing to elide the feminine gender of the monarch, the courtly idea of Elizabeth now subverted the focus of Renaissance love discourses upon masculine subjectivity.

Mis-ruler of the ocean: Ralegh's rewriting of his Cynthian poetics

The career of sir Walter Ralegh, like that of sir Christopher Hatton (another adept of the arts of Elizabethan courtiership), illustrates how far it was possible for a mere member of the gentry to rise at Elizabeth's court, if he courted the queen with skill. Ralegh's personal debt, as a successful courtier, to Petrarchan poetics is clear from his commendatory sonnet written for the publication of the first three books of Spenser's *The Faerie Queene*: 'Methought I saw the grave where Laura lay.' In this poem he asserts that Elizabeth has completely eclipsed Laura as an object of Petrarchan devotion:

> All suddenly I saw the Faery Queene:
> At whose approach the soule of *Petrarke* wept,
> And from thenceforth those graces were not seene.
> For they this Queene attended, in whose steed
> Oblivion laid him downe on *Lauras* herse.[39]

Yet Ralegh's life as well as his surviving poetry poignantly reveals the gap between the imagined and the real experience of the Elizabethan courtier as Petrarchan or Neoplatonic lover.[40] In its emphasis upon the active and quasi-military role of the male courtier, Ralegh's poetic representation of Elizabeth closely resembled that initially proposed by the Leicester–Walsingham faction (although he did not share their passionate Protestant convictions). But the 11th book of Ralegh's *The Ocean to Scinthia* appears to have been written at a time of crisis in his courtly career. In 1592 he was sent to the Tower of London because of his secret marriage to one of the queen's ladies-in-waiting, Elizabeth Throckmorton. Ironically, this poetic fragment is the only complete sequence that survives of Ralegh's long narrative poem to Elizabeth as Cynthia, whose earlier sections had been composed during the 1580s, in the years of his rise to power.

This sole surviving book of Ralegh's poem was found among Robert Cecil's papers at Hatfield House. It describes the frustration of his attempt to use her cult to manipulate Elizabeth as monarch, and his painful recognition of the concrete political authority wielded by his female object of desire. By failing in his role of a Petrarchan or Neoplatonic lover, Ralegh has apparently lost the power to determine his own destiny which he had sought to achieve through or across compliments to Elizabeth as an object of sublimated desire. Now the queen no longer mirrors him in the image of his own fantasy: 'Thos streames seem standing puddells which, before./Wee saw our bewties in, so weare they cleere.'[41] Her figure has escaped from his rhetorical control, like the moon passing behind clouds: 'Bellphebes course is now observde no more/that faire resemblance weareth out of date.'[42] And in consequence his idealized self-image has been irreparably 'wounded'. Fear of a similar metamorphosis of the beloved, leading to emasculation of the male lover's narcissistic identity, had haunted both the Petrarchan and Neoplatonic systems. But Ralegh's poem indicates how much more difficult it was for the courtier–lover to achieve the control over fate which these discourses sought. Sir Robert Naunton commented of Ralegh that he

> was one that it seems fortune had pickt out of purpose, of whom to make an example . . . for she tossed him up [out] of nothing, and to and fro to greatnesse, and from thence down to little more than to that wherein she found him [,] a bare Gentleman.[43]

Unlike her father, Henry VIII, Elizabeth was not noted as a tennis-player. For most of Ralegh's career as courtier, however, it was her changing moods which represented the operations of 'fortune' in his life. During the 1580s, Elizabeth's whims tossed him 'to and fro' from the West Country to the court; and from the court to the sea, to Ireland and America; but in 1592, less pleasantly, into the Tower. It consequently seems highly appropriate that the moon was chosen as her dominant persona in Ralegh's courtly poetry to his queen; Valeriano, in his *Hieroglyphica*, actually compared the moon goddess to *Tyche* or Fortuna: 'Luna is *Tyche* because she is guardian of bodies, which are swayed by alterations of fortune.'[44]

None the less, in describing Elizabeth as Cynthia, moon goddess and ruler of the sea, Ralegh appears initially to have believed that he could turn this mutable and fickle image to both personal and political advantage. At the same time as being a leading proponent of Elizabethan naval power, he was also an enthusiastic advocate of English colonialism; he played a major role in the establishment of colonies in Ireland and America.[45] The early Elizabethan entertainments had accorded the queen the persona of a Diana-like huntress or Amazonian female knight in the hope of furthering the militant foreign policy of the Leicester–Walsingham faction. In the same way, by choosing for his poetic persona the ocean or the shepherd of the ocean over which Cynthia ruled as moon (a choice presumably inspired by the queen's nickname for him, 'Water'), Ralegh urged Elizabeth to identify with this aspect of her mythic image, to commit herself to an imperialist policy of expansion overseas. Such a policy, of course, would affirm his own fantasized self-image as an explorer and charter of hitherto unknown territories: a heroic seaman and colonizer. Territorial expansion would also forge a new definition of Elizabeth as the English 'body politic', by making her the 'Empress' of foreign colonies.

In a sense Ralegh's choice of poetic persona paralleled Petrarch's poetic appropriation of attributes he accorded to Laura. But unlike that of Petrarch, Ralegh's imagery of self was protean in its significance, characterized by a fluidity which was conventionally associated with the feminine rather than by the solid, fixed (and so more masculine?) significations of the laurel and the gold which Petrarch associated with Laura. He used his Cynthian poetics to articulate an idea of himself which, although it required a sphere of active expression, was not defined primarily in terms of the worldly success which so preoccupied Petrarch. As the link between two continents, the ocean bridged the known and the unknown rather as did the female beloved of Petrarchism and Neoplatonism. Indeed in Plato's *Symposium*, the myth of Venus' birth from the sea, as daughter of Uranus, was used by Pausanias to describe that sublimated desire which could lead the lover to mystical heights. This image certainly appears to have signified for Ralegh a literal pathway to the future, a means of personal expansion beyond the restrictive limits imposed by English (and especially courtly) society. In fact, the desire for English territories in North and South America seems to have corresponded more closely to Ralegh's dreams than to those of Elizabeth herself; but as early as 1584, by naming the first English colony in America Virginia, he attempted to assert the identity of the English

queen and the New World through which he hoped to define himself.
Thus while as the moon, ruler of the seas he wished to cross, Elizabeth
apparently signified the *means* of his explorations, he did not present
himself as bypassing her assistance entirely once his oceanic transition
had been accomplished. Instead he suggested that she was also his
ultimate destination; that he expected to re-encounter her in a brighter
and less obscure aspect, as the earthly paradise of the New World.

Like so much absolutist ideology of the Renaissance, Ralegh's appeal
to Elizabeth to make an imperialist intervention in contemporary history
is paradoxically justified through the imagery of a golden age; he suggests
that possession of these territories would signify not only a historical
achievement but also an end to the fluctuations and aberrations of the
historical process, in a symbolic return to Eden and the timeless
dimension of myth: 'She as the valley of Perue/Whose summer ever
lastethe./Time conquering, all she mastr'eth/By beinge alwaye new.'[46] In
one respect, Ralegh's aim of discovering or revealing to his English
contemporaries a supposedly paradisal land, which he identified with his
monarch, can be read as a desire to achieve a metaphoric political control
over Elizabeth, as 'Lord and Governor of Virginia' for example (the title
he was granted in 1585). Alternatively, it could simply confirm that even
his desired self-image as New World explorer and colonizer was
overdetermined by the absent but still constraining authority of
Elizabeth. What it does indicate is that, for the male courtier seeking self-
definition through Petrarchan or Neoplatonic courtship of a female
monarch, there could be no genuine escape from this figure's sphere of
influence, only a changing perception of their role in relation to the
masculine subject. The only order that Ralegh could present himself as
imposing upon the alien territories of America was the image of
Elizabeth.

But in *The 11th: and last booke of the Ocean to Scinthia*, the earthly
paradise which Ralegh had hoped to arrive at both metaphorically and
literally through his courtship of the queen has been transformed into a
post-lapsarian world by the male lover's fall into sexual activity. The
natural environment which the poem describes is characterized not by
fruitfulness but sterility. The harvest of goods and favours he had
formerly enjoyed at Elizabeth's hands has been blighted:

> from frutfull trees I gather withred leves
> and glean the broken eares with misers hands,
> who sumetyme did inioy the waighty sheves
> I seeke faire floures amidd the brinish sand.[47]

Ralegh's poetic landscape is no longer unified by a passively nurturing
female presence. Instead, its violent mutability appears to offer an
anatomy of a different, highly sexual idea of femininity, which has been

revealed by the act of coition responsible for his downfall:

> as the eayre in deip caves under ground
> Is strongly drawne when violent heat hath rent
> Great clefts therin, till moysture do abound,
> And then the same imprisoned, and uppent,
> Breakes out in yearthquakes teringe all asunder.[48]

By this analogy, Ralegh effectively displaces responsibility for his own error on to the activity of woman. The female body has not been entered, but has rather opened or revealed itself. Moreover, the image paradoxically fuses the figures of the monarch as political and courtly mistress and the maid of honour as sexual mistress. Indeed, even in Ralegh's initial admission of sexual error the courtly idea of Elizabeth as above sexuality and the body appears to be qualified by a punning reference to the bodily pleasure which that same error had afforded the other Elizabeth: 'yow that then died when first my fancy erred'.[49] The shadowy presence of this other, actively sexual Elizabeth in his poetic landscape is thus implicitly connected with her lover's simultaneous experience of his queen's buried sexuality, as expressed in her violent anger.

Ralegh presents himself as having lost control over both the solar and lunar attributes of the queen. The collapse of his courtly identity is sometimes related in the poem to extremes of shade or scorching sunlight. These translate into visual terms his loss of equilibrium, or the courtly quality of *mediocrità*, in relation to Elizabeth: 'all in the shade yeven in the faire soon dayes/under those healthless trees I sytt a lone'.[50] This imbalance is also closely related to his now distorted relationship to that element of water with which he had formerly identified, and which is ruled by Elizabeth as the moon. The idealized meanings which her cult had initially attributed to this image, as a sign of Elizabeth's transcendence of both body and gender through her choice of chastity, have been eclipsed by its negative aspect; erratic movements of water mimic the ebbs and flows of what Ralegh now perceives as a disconcertingly mutable and active femininity. The diversion of the course of water which the poem describes implies not simply Cynthia's disfavour, but more specifically the loss of Ralegh's privileged position as the queen's courtier–lover, her 'Water'. He can no longer control the element with which he had identified, and experiences it in terms of extreme states which relate to excesses of solar or lunar power. Either he is parched with a thirst for her personal favour which Elizabeth now refuses to satisfy: 'To seeke for moysture in th'arabien sande/is butt a loss of labor, and of rest.'[51] Or alternatively, the boundless power of water becomes a flood: 'With suddayne stremes the vallies oveflow'.[52]

This terrifying manifestation of feminine rage is perceived in terms of woman's escape from certain boundaries or restrictions (presumably imposed upon her by patriarchy) and reversion to her 'auncient channells' or patterns of behaviour, to a path which is also 'nature's course':

And as a streame by stronge hand bounded in
from natures course wher it did sumetyme runn
by some small rent or loose part douth beginn
to find escape, till it a way hath woone

douth then all unawares in sunder teare
the forsed bounds and raginge, runn att large
in th'auncient channells as they wounted weare
such is of weemens love the carefull charge

helde, and mayntaynde wuth multitude of woes
of longe arections such the suddayne fall
onn houre deverts, onn instant overthrowes.[53]

The stream which has torn apart 'the forsed bounds and raginge, runn att large' signifies both the sexual jealousy of the queen and the passionate eroticism which Ralegh apparently encountered in her namesake. The male courtier's position of privilege, established over a long period, has been destroyed along with that physical boundary of the female hymen which had enclosed the bodily honour of Elizabeth's lady-in-waiting. The 'suddayne fall' of his 'longe arections' which followed this defloration (he also speaks of 'the broken monuments of my great desires') implies that his former capacity to control the queen's mutable feminine 'nature' had itself depended on his erotic appeal to her as a woman, through the constantly deferred promise of sexual gratification.[54] Now the political authority achieved and maintained by the lure of the apparently ever-erect phallus has been destroyed by his overwhelming experience of female sexual desire. Unable any longer to defer his own phallic pleasure in the interests of courtly success, Ralegh allowed himself to be distracted from courtly meditation upon Elizabeth the queen as 'my fancies adamande'. As a result, his higher faculty of mind, to which a rejection of fleshly fantasies was supposed to grant access, has been fatally 'wounded', subjected to error and mutability along with his body. It is now as 'dround', 'wasted', and 'withered' as was his penis in the forbidden act of coition.

Like the absence of sunlight to which the poem frequently refers, this theme of a mental error rooted in sexuality indicates that Ralegh can no longer hope to define the Elizabethan body politic by courting the queen as private woman. It also signals the end of a mimetic mother–son relationship, in which his representation of Elizabeth as a fleshly but pure vessel of the *logos* or *nous*, as a female Christ or Wisdom figure, had been mimed on a smaller scale by his own courtly role of a 'shepherd' of the ocean. A slight decline in favour had seemingly preceded his fall, when he was: 'Mich like the gentell Lamm', which, 'though lately waynde./Playes with the dug though finds no cumfort ther'.[55] But now he is 'as a body violently slayne' which 'Retayneath warmth although the spirrit be gonn/And by a poure in nature moves agayne/Till it be layd below the fatall stone'.[56] The juxtaposition of these images not only suggests the violent (albeit metaphoric) sacrifice of Ralegh's lamb-like or Christ-like identity, and a consequent severing of body from spirit; it also connects the enactment of adult erotic desire with the body as the site of state punishment. The male courtier is now the victim, rather than the manipulator, of Elizabeth's body politic as monarch: 'a Queen shee was to mee, no more Belphebe/a Lion then, no more a milke white Dove,/A prissoner in her brest I could not bee/Shee did untye the gentell chaynes of love.'[57]

This painful transition from the secure domain of the mother to a space of violent paternal coercion and punishment (from the court to the Tower) is emphasized by a further layer in the poem's palimpsest of textual connotations. Not only does it combine Platonic with erotic imagery; it also gestures towards biblical accounts of the avenging wrath of the Jewish and Christian father-God, who ruthlessly punishes those who oppose him, and even causes those who do not to learn through suffering. The promised land which Ralegh has lost is briefly compared to Israel: 'Seeke not the soonn in cloudes, when it is sett. . . ./On highest mountaynes wher thos Sedars grew/Agaynst whose bancks, the trobled ocean bett'.[58] And in the flood of Elizabeth's anger can be traced echoes of the biblical flood, as well as of the return of the Red Sea to its natural path (thereby drowning the Egyptians) once the Israelites had passed through. At the same time, Ralegh's structuring of his situation in terms of extremes of climate suggests the story of Jonah, who as a reluctant prophet of Yahweh was first exposed to the tempestuous wrath of the sea, then to the raging heat of the sun.

But disconcertingly, at the point at which Elizabeth is revealed as the possessor of a coercive or phallic power conventionally attributed to the father, her feminine gender is more obvious than ever before:

> Yet have these wounders want which want compassion,
> yet hath her minde sume markes of humayne race
> yet will shee bee a wooman for a fashion
> So douth shee pleas her vertues to deface
>
> and like as that immortall pour doth seat
> an element of waters to allay
> the fiery soonn beames that on yearth do beate
> and temper by cold night the heat of day

So hath perfection which begatt her minde
added therto a change of fantasye
and left her the affections of her kynde
yet free from evry yevill but cruelty. . . .[59]

In so far as the queen no longer seems distinguished from the generality
of her sex, or from the other Elizabeth, Ralegh can imply that the error
inherent in *her* femaleness, which she has inherited from Eve, has
preceded and overdetermined his own misdirection of fantasy to erotic
ends. If he has broken the perfect circle of his Platonic search for
resemblance (through the female monarch) along with the hymen of his
mistress, none the less he suggests that this deviation was already
prefigured in the erratic orbit of Elizabeth's courtly persona of the moon,
for 'fancy seildume ends wher it begunn'.[60]

A speaking absence: the textual and historical exile of Spenser's faerie queen

It was Edmund Spenser who had first codified the image of Elizabeth as
the self-absorbed inhabitant of a predominantly feminine world, in his
description in the April eclogue of his *Shepheardes Calender* of 'Eliza' as
a queen of shepherds who was paradoxically surrounded solely by her
nymphs. But the epic poem which Spenser published a decade later (yet
never finished) was informed by a more complex view of Elizabeth's
courtly cult. *The Faerie Queene* accorded Elizabeth as a female beloved
greater imaginative or spiritual powers than ever before. Simultaneously,
it restricted the exercise of these powers in the world of human affairs, by
distinguishing between two different spheres of existence, the mythic and
the historical, which paralleled the Platonic division between an ideal and
a real world. The fairy queen herself is 'enfolded' within her mythic and
seemingly woman-dominated domain of faery, as all-embracing but
enigmatic a figure as the hermaphrodite Venus described in book IV of
Spenser's epic:

The cause why she was covered with a vele,
　　Was hard to know, for that her Priests the same
　　From peoples knowledge labour'd to concele.
　　But sooth it was not sure for womanish shame,
　　Nor any blemish, which the worke mote blame;
　　But for, they say, she hath both kinds in one,
　　Both male and female, both under one name:
　　She syre and mother is her selfe alone,
Begets and ekes conceives, ne needeth other none.[61]

Spenser's epic structure offers an extended parallel to this disturbing passage. Just as the hermaphrodite Venus' mystical union of spirit and nature, emblematized by her bodily completeness, is asserted but never imaged, so his poem only gestures towards the fairy queen who supposedly contains within herself all meanings: the hymeneal boundary or 'covert vele' of allegory obscures her within her otherworldly dimension.[62] Although Spenser presents his scene as set in fairyland, the world through which his protagonists move is one where access to the Platonic dimension which Gloriana is held to embody has been obstructed by the fall. In consequence, the epic's narrative focus is primarily on the sphere of historical and worldly action which had been emphasized by humanist philosophy. This fallen 'real' world intersects with and is creatively influenced by the ideal forms still existing in the world of myth or faery; but it cannot operate according to the same laws, since the organs of spiritual perception (especially the sight) have been distorted by the fall. The exercise of power in this historical dimension, where no sign is free of ambiguity and mutability, is defined by Spenser in patriarchal rather than matriarchal terms. Petrarchan or Neoplatonic attitudes to women are now interpreted as potentially destructive for the masculine subject who is limited both by bodily and by historical necessity. And the figure of the woman whose chastity signifies a bodily and psychological self-sufficiency in the synchronic world of myth is an unsettling and inappropriate figure within the 'real' or diachronic space of history.

As Spenser first conceived of the epic, his theme of chivalric action in a fallen and historical world implied sympathy for the desire of male courtiers such as Ralegh to use the queen's cult for self-affirmation. In the figures of its questing knights, *The Faerie Queene* reintroduced into Elizabethan courtliness the radical Protestant doctrine which had informed it when promoted by the Leicester–Walsingham faction. Although they did not share his religious radicalism, Spenser's association of courtiership with activity also flattered the expansionist impulses of a new generation of courtiers, which included Ralegh and the earl of Essex. (He had enjoyed Leicester's patronage along with that of his nephew Sidney in the 1570s, and Ralegh was his neighbour in Ireland during the late 1580s and early 1590s as well as an acknowledged poetic influence.) But while Spenser's epic narrative began by giving pre-eminence to the male courtier, as a questing subject motivated but not physically caged by love, he seems to have become increasingly uneasy about the limitations imposed upon this figure's historical effectiveness by his dependence upon an idea of woman. And as his poem progressed, Spenser's exploration of the inappropriateness of Petrarchan or Neo-platonic attitudes in a fallen and mutable world also affected the status of the courtier–knight in his narrative. In fact, from the beginning of his epic, the proems (or sets of prefatory verses) to the individual books had traced a different and more personal search for masculine self-affirmation from that of the courtier. Recent Renaissance criticism has defined this alternative masculine mode of identity as that of the self-conscious poet.[63] But when, in book VI, Spenser finally places himself within his narrative proper (in his persona of Colin Clout), it becomes apparent that his growth of poetic self-consciousness depends on a new relationship to woman, one which rejects courtly attitudes.[64] For Elizabeth the queen he substitutes Elizabeth his wife, as both object of desire and source of poetic inspiration. Ralegh's sexual enactment of his desire for the queen with her mere namesake undid his courtly identity. But Spenser's poetic imitation of this process is a repetition with a difference: it secures his bourgeois self-image as both poet and husband, and decentres the male courtly subject along with his female monarch.

In his initial narrative emphasis upon the male courtier Spenser implied that Gloriana's power could only be manifested in the fallen world of history through a masculine intermediary. The poem's title leads the reader to expect that Elizabeth, in her persona of the faery queen, is both the poem's chief protagonist and its principal theme; indeed, in the proems to each of the six books of *The Faerie Queene*, Spenser told Elizabeth that she 'in this faire mirrhour maist behold thy face'.[65] This statement is difficult to reconcile, however, with the critical perspective offered in an explanatory letter addressed to sir Walter Ralegh, which Spenser annexed to its first three books when they were published in 1590. Here he declared that his poetic purpose was 'to fashion a gentleman or noble person in vertuous and gentle discipline'. Note the significant transition in this sentence from a definite and masculine-gendered subject to one of indefinite gender (but perhaps by inference feminine), as a result of the substitution of 'noble person' as a synonym for 'gentleman'. Just as the address of his explanation to Ralegh leaves us uncertain of the identity of Spenser's ideal reader (female monarch or male courtier), so the poet was also apparently in some doubt as to whether his epic was concerned with the representation of a masculine or feminine courtly subject. Although both his title and the proems pointed to Elizabeth as 'the argument of mine afflicted stile', an emphasis on masculine self-fashioning was implied by Spenser's statement later in his letter that the mythic English hero Arthur was the prototype of his perfected 'gentleman or noble person'.[66]

In Spenser's poetic conception, Arthur contained within himself the twelve Aristotelian moral virtues which were to be the themes of his epic's twelve books.[67] Arthur was presumably intended to appear in every book, but Spenser explained that each of these virtues would also be explored in turn, through the quests of a series of knights. Both Arthur and these knights link the dimension of chronological time with an eternal otherworld: the golden-walled city of Cleopolis at the centre of faerieland where Gloriana resides. She is the 'true glorious type' of all of these various virtues, their feminine receptacle or source.[68] Yet it is Arthur and the other questing knights who are her earthly imitators or surrogates, miming and concretely applying her individual and composite qualities – and in this way dissecting a feminine figure into an assembly of masculine parts. Providing for poetic *occasio* or pretext only a representational lacuna which the poet fills with a multiplicity of other signs, Elizabeth–Gloriana is expelled to the mythic margins or boundaries of his epic. As Elizabeth, she inhabits the proems which preface the different instalments of its narrative. As Gloriana, she is concealed behind the golden walls of Cleopolis. This failure of representation is justified by Spenser in Platonic terms; the ideal form that is Elizabeth cannot adequately be imitated:

> But living art may not least part expresse,
>   Nor life-resembling pencill it can paint,
>   All were it *Zeuxis* or *Praxiteles*:
>   His daedale hand would faile, and greatly faint,
>   And her perfections with his error taint:
>   Ne Poets wit, that passeth Painter farre
>   In picturing the parts of beautie daint,
>   So hard a workmanship adventure darre,
> For fear through want of words her excellence to marre.[69]

Spenser's allegory also legitimates this displacement in religious terms. by its use of the apocalyptic imagery of Revelation. All of the knights are in a sense Gloriana's lovers. But the direction of those who represent the different virtues is centrifugal: their quests take them away from Gloriana and the heart of faery, and so parallel the Neoplatonic concept of soul's progressive emanation or separation from deity, *emanatio*. In contrast, Arthur's direction is centripetal: in the movement of return to spiritual source called by Neoplatonism *remeatio*, his quest leads him not away from but towards the faery queen, to whose court he does not belong and whom he has seen only in a dream.[70] On the level of political allegory, the meeting and marriage between Arthur and Gloriana with which Spenser presumably intended to end his poem would seemingly have represented Arthur's initiation into kingship as ruler of the immortal body politic of England (signified by Gloriana). This restoration of a masculine political authority by marriage to the powerful female beloved is foreshadowed in the epic by the story of Britomart and Arthegall. From the perspective of religious allegory, Arthur's quest appears to imitate an event Christianity defined as historical – Christ's resurrection and ascension following his incarnation or descent into matter. Gloriana's enthronement within Cleopolis – a mythic equivalent to the New Jerusalem – connects her not only with the unmanifest Wisdom of God, which will inform a restored paradise, but also with the hidden glory of

God as 'father' (while simultaneously raising doubts about the stability of the *unmoved mover*'s gender). And according to Revelations, the New Jerusalem will not be revealed to the elect until the day of judgement. Her hidden figure therefore represents a future potentiality rather than a past event, a resolution which Spenser's narrative must perpetually defer. Arthur's arrival at Cleopolis, the city of history, would in biblical terms signal history's end: the union of Christ with his spouse, the New Jerusalem, in a post-apocalyptic world. As an image whose time had not yet come, the faery queen could therefore be conveniently placed beyond representation until the moment of her subordination in marriage.

None the less, while the faery queen herself is absent from Spenser's text, a moment of ecstatic surrender to the advances of her dream-image is described by Arthur in the first book of the epic:

> For-wearied with my sports, I did alight
>> From loftie steed, and downe to sleepe me layd;
>> The verdant gras my couch did goodly dight,
>> And pillow was my helmet faire displayd:
>> While every sence the humour sweet embayd,
>> And slombring soft my hart did steale away,
>> Me seemed, by my side a royall Mayd
>> Her daintie limbes full softly down did lay:
> So faire a creature yet saw never sunny day.

> Most goodly glee and lovely blandishment
>> She to me made, and bad me love her deare,
>> For dearely sure her love was to me bent,
>> As when iust time expired should appeare.
>> But whether dreames delude, or true it were,
>> Was never hart so ravisht with delight,
>> Ne living man like words did ever heare,
>> As she to me delivered all that night;
> And at her parting said, she Queene of Faeries hight.[71]

This apparent gesture of physical intimacy by the 'royall Mayd', in lying down beside the sleeping knight, is in fact presented by Spenser as the prelude to an act of spiritual rather than sexual intercourse (we are told that Arthur's senses are 'embayd' or shut up in sleep). In this otherworldly mode of eroticism, the dream-woman is the active partner; apparently she 'ravisht' Arthur's heart with delight. This role-reversal parallels that of the relationship between Cynthia and Endimion in Lyly's play. Moreover she uses her power over language as an integral part of this love-making. Such a combination of assertiveness and eloquence contrasts strikingly with the silent and passive women idealized by the love discourses. But later in his epic, when he represented waking encounters with another otherworldly mistress, Belphoebe, Spenser defined the relationship between fairy woman and knight (and so between myth and history) less positively.

Spenser's letter to Ralegh suggests that while Gloriana figured the public body of Elizabeth as monarch and embodiment of the body politic, Belphoebe represented her body natural:

> considering she beareth two persons, the one of a most royall Queene or Empresse, the other of a most vertuous and beautifull Lady, this latter part in some places I doe express in Belphoebe, fashioning her name according to your owne excellent conceipt of Cynthia (Phoebe and Cynthia being both names of Diana).

Although Spenser here associates Belphoebe alone with Diana, Gloriana herself, as a fairy queen, was by inference linked with the same goddess, as is indicated by Shakespeare's use of the name Titania in *A Midsummer Night's Dream*. In the proem to book III, the poet emphasized that Belphoebe was an image of Elizabeth's own chastity:

> Ne let his fairest *Cynthia* refuse,
> In mirrours more than one her selfe to see,
> But either *Gloriana* let her chuse,
> Or in *Belphoebe* fashioned to bee:
> In th'one her rule, in th'other her rare chastitee.[72]

This suggested that Belphoebe was to be book III's chief protagonist; but significantly, this role was accorded to another female figure, the woman warrior Britomart. While the fairy Belphoebe only played a minor part in the events of the book, Spenser used the quasi-historical heroine Britomart to articulate a definition of chastity which evidently in his view was more suited to the historical needs of the patriarchy than the version privileged by Elizabeth's cult.

Belphoebe's various appearances in the epic indicate that her androgynous chastity is a sign which historical man cannot hope to decipher correctly. Significantly, in none of the three books in which she figures does she encounter its knight-protagonist; in other words, she is not presented as contributing to the human application of the different virtues which the books explore – temperance, chastity, friendship. Although not a human figure, Belphoebe is represented by Spenser as combining spiritual and sensual qualities in a most unsettling way. We first see this 'goodly Ladie clad in hunters weed' in book II, where she is described in the imagery of the Song of Solomon. The explicit eroticism of this text was interpreted by Christian commentators as an allegory of the union of Christ with either the church or the individual soul. But by interpellating a scopophiliac or lustful viewer within his description, the vain and cowardly knight Braggadocchio, Spenser emphasizes Belphoebe's disturbing combination of sexual with spiritual power, of Venus with Diana:

> And in her cheekes the vermeill red did shew
> Like roses in a bed of lillies shed,
> The which ambrosiall odours from them threw,
> And gazers sense with double pleasure fed,
> Hable to heale the sicke, and to revive the ded.[73]

The passage reveals the problems attendant upon constructing a female figure as an earthly incarnation of the *logos*. Christ-like powers of healing the sick and reviving the dead are ascribed to Belphoebe's pleasing 'odours' and erotic appeal to the 'gazers sense' (hence the reference to resurrection probably carries a sexual pun).[74] This ambiguity is subsequently compounded by the description of the huntress' clothing. While she is identified by her name with Cynthia or Diana as moon goddess, Belphoebe's golden and bejewelled trappings accord her solar attributes. In Platonic terms, these figure her interior or spiritual perfection. They also bring to mind the ornamental excess of an Elizabethan state portrait. Spenser tells us that she

> . . . was yclad, for heat of scorching aire,
> All in a silken Camus lylly whight,
> Purfled upon with many a folded plight,
> Which all above besprinckled was throughout
> With golden aygulets, that glistred bright,
> Like twinckling starres, and all the skirt about
> Was hemd with golden fringe.

> Below her ham her weed did somewhat traine,
> And her streight legs most bravely were embayld
> In gilden buskins of costly Cordwaine,
> Allbard with golden bendes, which were entayld
> With curious antickes, and full faire aumayld:
> Before they fastned were under her knee
> In a rich Iewell, and therein entrayld
> The ends of all their knots, that none might see,
> How they within their fouldings close enwrapped bee.

> Like two faire marble pillours they were seene,
> Which doe the temple of the Gods support. . . .[75]

Supposedly an image of Elizabeth's 'body natural', Belphoebe also bears the marks of sovereignty. The reader is reminded that Elizabeth's Christ-like role has a political as well as religious significance, that she is the bodily incarnation of the *corpus mysticum* of the English state. But the passage also hints at Belphoebe's auto-erotic delight in her own body.

Its visual perspective moves from her golden attire to a highly sexualized yet curiously self-referential body. The sexual appeal of Belphoebe's bare legs to the observing male voyeur (Braggadocchio) is juxtaposed with the multiple fastenings, knots, and foldings of her costume: hymen-like boundaries which emblematize her refusal of any phallic attempt at the unravelling and decoding of her body.[76] At the same time, these features of her clothing also hint at an alternative, many-faceted eroticism, whereby the female body is 'close enwrapped' within itself. This theme is reinforced by Spenser's borrowings from his source text, for he accorded Belphoebe the attributes of both lover *and* beloved in the Song of Solomon. As huntress of 'the bleeding hind', she imitates the desiring female of the biblical text who longs for the roe or hart who is her male partner. But she is also identified with the male beloved which it describes: her cheeks too are full of spices, her legs too are 'faire marble pillours', and so on.

Although a fairy rather than a human, the figure of Belphoebe problematically combines the attributes of myth with those of history, for she incarnates religious as well as political authority within a body that insists both on its femaleness and on its self-sufficient autonomy. Not surprisingly, Spenser's description of Belphoebe ends with the juxta-position of two analogies which hint at the inappropriateness of any intrusion by this mythic figure within a historical frame of reference. She is compared to Diana as she wanders 'by the sandie shore/Of swift *Eurotas*, or on *Cynthus* grene'; but also to 'that famous Queene/Of *Amazons*, whom *Pyrrhus* did destroy'.[77] Diana is an idealized figure, described as ranging widely in her pastoral domain; but the Amazon queen Penthesilea, her historical imitator, is not allowed such textual latitude. She is the object rather than the subject of the accompanying verb, which images her death – in contrast to Diana's all-powerful immortality.

The effect that the contradictory figure of Belphoebe has upon Arthur's squire Timias, whose idealized love for her is related in books III and IV, is to jeopardize rather than assist his aspiration to knighthood, and eventually to disorder his reason. At the level of historical allegory, this narrative strand clearly referred to Ralegh's courtship of Elizabeth and his subsequent fall from favour; indeed Ralegh's changed perception of the queen's courtly cult (as related in *The 11th: and last booke of the Ocean to Scinthia*) probably contributed to Spenser's own developing critique of its use of the love discourses. As soon as he meets Belphoebe, Timias forgets his service to Arthur and retreats into eremitic solitude in the forest in order to be near his mistress. When he falls from her favour, he loses all powers of speech and communication, changing from a hermit figure into a type of wild man. In this context, however, the squire's 'salvage' attributes signify not an instinctual sexuality expressed through or across a male body, but the dangers inherent in sacrificing sexual desire to the service of a Petrarchan or Neoplatonic beloved. Arthur finds his former squire

> Spending his daies in dolour and despaire,
> And through long fasting woxen pale and wan,
> All overgrowen with rude and rugged haire;
> . . . to his speach he aunswered no whit,
> But stood still mute, as if he had beene dum,
> Ne signe of sence did shew, ne common wit,
> As one with griefe and anguishe overcum,
> And unto every thing did aunswere mum.[78]

In its way, Timias' condition seems to be just as bad as that of the knights reduced to beasts by the sexual enchantment of Acrasia in book II, or those feminized by the Amazon Radigund in book V. Although his experience was ostensibly with the representative of Elizabeth's body natural, it none the less introduces a shade of ambiguity into the definition of Arthur's chivalric quest as an extended courtship of her other self, her body politic or Gloriana.

The female protagonist of the book of chastity, Britomart, contrasts with Belphoebe in several important respects. Indeed it was primarily through this figure that Spenser articulated his critique of those Petrarchan and Neoplatonic attitudes to woman which the fairy huntress personified. This involved a redefinition of Belphoebe's most important attributes: her chastity and her androgyny. Instead of Belphoebe's startling combination of masculine and feminine attributes, Britomart uses masculine armour to *conceal* her femininity, a device which enables her to range widely across Spenser's text in a way Belphoebe cannot. This masking or denial of her feminine attributes can be attributed to her parentage: unlike Belphoebe, who with her twin sister Amoret was conceived without a father, Britomart has no visible mother. She serves the interests of the father by not allowing her femininity to disturb the patriarchal power balance, and by defining her 'chastity' according to historical necessity: the same vision which prompts her to become a warrior also emphasizes her destined place in a patrilineal sequence, as the genetrix of a line of kings.[79] Thus even her future motherhood is defined by the needs of a male political hierarchy. Inevitably, Britomart's maternal destiny would have reminded an Elizabethan reader that the reigning monarch had defined her chastity very differently. By refusing to subordinate her private body to the needs of the state, Elizabeth had *ended* a dynasty of kings, not secured its long survival.

Of course Spenser could not bring the figure of Britomart into open conflict with that of Belphoebe, and so directly insult the monarch to whom the huntress had been compared. None the less, his fear of the powers accorded woman in myth being transferred to the historical scene is dramatized in the encounter between Britomart and the Amazon Radigund in book V, which follows the latter's capture and feminization of Britomart's betrothed, sir Arthegall, the knight of justice. Radigund's appearance resembles that of Belphoebe in certain important respects, for 'on her legs she painted buskins wore,/Basted with bends of gold on every side,/And mailes betweene, and laced close afore'. But her more earth-bound and less idealized feminine nature is emphasized by the fact that the full moon is her dominant attribute: 'and on her shoulder hung her shield . . . that shined wide,/As the faire Moone in her most full aspect'.[80] Arthegall is defeated not by Radigund's superior arms, but by her beauty; Britomart, however, experiences no such attraction, and summarily decapitates the Amazon queen after she has defeated her. She then overturns the matriarchal structure of the Amazon state. In terms of political allegory, this episode refers to Elizabeth's execution of her cousin Mary queen of Scots in order to end the many Catholic plots against her which Mary had inspired. But this episode does not only criticize Radigund's combination (like the historical Mary) of sexuality and political power; Britomart's dismantling of the Amazonarchy is also used to make a less direct attack on Catholic monasticism, which had formerly offered an alternative to women seeking to avoid the married state. The historical Radegund was a sixth-century saint, who combined scholarship with religious devotion, and was especially interested in medicine. She became a nun on leaving the brutal Merovingian king she had been married to against her will, and later founded a famous monastery for women near Poitiers.[81]

The androgyny of Belphoebe and Radigund, which privileged feminine over masculine attributes, closely resembled that of Diana, who kept the company of women. It also imitated the sexual and political order pertaining in the world of myth. We are told of Venus' relationship with Adonis: 'she her self, when ever that she will,/Possesseth him, and of his sweetness takes her fill.'[82] Britomart's vision in Isis' church is likewise of Isis 'on top', her mercy firmly controlling the justice of Osiris.[83] But her own androgyny privileges the masculine half of this *discordia concors*, and ensures the continuity of the father's name and identity in an unbroken chain of political patriliny. Her mythological connection is not with Diana, but with the Greek and Roman goddesses Athene and Minerva, both of whom enjoyed an especially close relationship with the father, and had an important connection with patriarchal society and government.[84] We are told of Britomart's destruction of the Amazon state that she 'them restoring/To mens subiection, did True Iustice deale:/That all they as a Goddesse her adoring,/Her wisedome did admire, and harkened to her loring.'[85] Against a female political authority based on sexuality, Spenser sets up a patriarchally defined image of woman's power. Britomart is a heroine who does not unsettle by combining deeds of arms with feminine attraction. Instead, her military force is linked with an ungendered mode of 'wisdom'. This 'wisdom' involves a dissociation from her body and her gender – a symbolic repetition of the beheading of the mother, as well as of the female cousin. But it is a vital prerequisite for Britomart's union with Arthegall.[86] And while Britomart's denial of her ties to other women culminates in a displacement of her sexual power, Arthegall is a Herculean hero who only temporarily sacrifices the phallic attributes of the wild man, during his captivity to Radigund.[87]

The story of Britomart implies a serious criticism of the Elizabethan cult, which had exalted a private image (of the queen as woman) to the level of a public icon. Rather than being placed in the service of the state and her royal lineage. Elizabeth's gender had become an image of political authority in and for itself, and had seriously restricted the potential of her male courtiers for action. It is significant that the apotheosis of Britomart as a goddess of wisdom was followed later in book V by the meeting of sir Arthegall and prince Arthur with Mercilla, the embodiment of regal justice: the visual impact of this queen depended not at all upon the attractions of female beauty.[88] Yet at around the same time Sir John Davies could write of Elizabeth, in a hymn 'Of her Justice', 'By Love she rules more than by Law.'[89] By this stage in his narrative Spenser's epic had certainly reached a point of serious contradiction with the assumptions upon which Elizabeth's cult was based. It was in the following and last book that he inserted himself within his text, as a visionary poet looking for inspiration to his wife (whom he could control) rather than to his queen (whom of course he could not). Once again, female chastity is defined in relation to marriage. Indeed, Spenser's wife Elizabeth has other 'soveraine' attributes formerly identified with Elizabeth the queen:

> Another Grace she well deserves to be,
>   In whom so many Graces gathered are,
>   Excelling much the meane of her degree;
>   Divine resemblaunce, beauty soveraine rare,
>   Firme Chastity, that spight ne blemish dare:
>   All which she with such courtesie doth grace,
>   That all her peres cannot with her compare,
>   But quite are dimmed, when she is in place.
> She made me often pipe and now to pipe apace.[90]

The scene echoes that in the April eclogue of *The Shepheardes Calender*, written some fifteen years earlier. The difference is, however, that by replacing queen with wife, as the feminine receptacle of numerous virtues, Spenser has the right to enter the circle of graces which also figures the body of his beloved. Now his 'piping' affirms, not his surrender of the powers of the phallus, but rather his phallic control of the female body, as both poet and lover. In this relationship, the male calls the tune.

Spenser died in 1599, leaving his epic unfinished, although its changing assumptions must have already made completion seem unlikely. But his two *Cantos of Mutability* offer an interesting appendix or coda to *The Faerie Queene*. Not only do they describe the same process of metamorphosis that had afflicted the development of Spenser's epic, they also seek in some degree to account for its displacement of the courtly version of the Elizabethan cult, along with its privileged mythic figure of Diana. In the first of the two cantos, Diana is forced to retreat from the pastoral world of Arlo Hill because lust has entered her sacred enclosure or *temenos*, in the person of the satyr Faunus. Faunus is a type of the wild man, but most importantly he resembles Actaeon. The false knight Braggadocchio had mistakenly interpreted Belphoebe's appearance as inviting sexual advances when he spied on her in her 'hunters weeds'. Faunus, however, goes further, observing Diana naked while she bathes. Yet he escapes Actaeon's punishment: 'But he more speedy, from them fled more fast/Than any deere: so sore him dred aghast.'[91] It seems that Diana is now powerless to protect her feminine space from violation by the male, and in disgust, she leaves her place of residence and her nymphs, in a scene which recalls Astraea's departure from earth at the end of the golden age.[92] This canto suggests that man can no longer tolerate the enigma posed by a female chastity or autonomy. Faunus is prompted to unveil the mystery which Diana signifies out of a desire for sexual knowledge, and the power he expects this to confer. Significantly, he does not pay the penalty of Actaeon for his taboo-breaking; none the less, the result of his action is loss rather than wholeness. In this version of the biblical fall, it is man who is the transgressor.

But while Diana leaves the earth, it seems that her figure has not been dethroned altogether, merely expelled to the periphery of human experience. For in the second of these two cantos, an attempt by Mutability to dethrone Cynthia and the other gods from their planetary spheres is unsuccessful. The final judgement upon Mutability's plea is made not by a father but a mother figure, by Nature. Like the faerie queen, Nature combines femaleness with spiritual authority. And like the hermaphrodite Venus, while referred to as 'she' her actual gender is claimed to be an enigma: 'whether she man or woman inly were,/That could not any creature well descry:/For, with a veile that wimpled every where,/Her head and face was hid, that mote to none appeare.'[93] In other words, Nature's veil is a device which enables Spenser to conceal or elide yet again the disturbing conjunction of feminine gender and power. The goddess concedes that 'all things stedfastnes do hate/And changed be': the stable order of the golden age no longer pertains, myth has been replaced by history.[94] None the less, she asserts that human submission to the law of change will not last for ever: 'But time shall come that all shall changed bee./And from thenceforth, none no more change shall see.'[95] The apocalyptic ending of history towards which Spenser's allegory had moved has been postponed, but apparently it has not been cancelled altogether. His deferral of poetic as well as historical closure had confirmed the decentring of Spenser's queenly subject, Elizabeth. But in these closing lines, the possibility of such a resolution is once again associated with an indecipherable feminine figure.

Notes

Introduction

1 I am indebted for this formulation to Luce Irigaray's *Speculum of the Other Woman*, trans. Gillian C. Gill (Ithaca: Cornell University Press, 1986). See especially pp. 103, 135.

2 This transition has been analysed most interestingly in recent critical studies of the *Essais* of Michel de Montaigne, which were published in 1580 and 1595. See in particular Jean Starobinski, *Montaigne in Motion*, trans. Arthur Goldhammer (Chicago: University of Chicago Press, 1985), especially pp. 1–14; and Richard L. Regosin, *The Matter of My Book: Montaigne's Essais as the Book of the Self* (Berkeley: University of California Press, 1977).

3 For two rather different accounts of the implications of this contrast between medieval and Renaissance attitudes to nature, see H. Paul Santmire, *The Travail of Nature: the Ambiguous Ecological Promise of Christian Theology* (Philadelphia: Fortress Press, 1985); and Keith Thomas, *Man and the Natural World: Changing Attitudes in England 1500–1800* (London: Allen Lane, 1983).

4 The implications of this philosophical decentring of God and spirit in René Descartes' *Discourse on Method* have been explored from a new historicist perspective by Francis Barker in *The Tremulous Private Body: Essays on Subjection* (London: Methuen, 1984), pp. 94–103.

5 Frances A. Yates, *Astraea: the Imperial Theme in the Sixteenth Century* (London: Routledge & Kegan Paul, 1975).

6 Leonard Tennenhouse, *Power on Display: the Politics of Shakespeare's Genres* (London: Methuen, 1986), p. 30.

7 Especially influential in this respect has been Daniel Javitch's *Poetry and Courtliness in Renaissance England* (Princeton: Princeton University Press, 1976). See also Ann Rosalind Jones and Peter Stallybrass, 'The politics of Astrophel and Stella', *Studies in English Literature*, 24, i (Winter 1984), pp. 54–68, and Louis Adrian Montrose, 'Celebration and insinuation: Sir Philip Sidney and the motives of Elizabethan courtship', *Renaissance Drama*, n.s. VIII (1977), pp. 3–35.

8 Jonathan Dollimore, 'Shakespeare, cultural materialism and the new historicism', in *Political Shakespeare: New Essays in Cultural Materialism*, eds Jonathan Dollimore and Alan Sinfield (Manchester: Manchester University Press, 1985), pp. 2–17.

9 Stephen Greenblatt, *Renaissance Self-Fashioning: From More to Shakespeare* (Chicago: University of Chicago Press, 1980).

10 Frank Lentricchia, *Criticism and Social Change* (Chicago: University of Chicago Press, 1983), p. 15.

11 See John Lechte, *Julia Kristeva* (London: Routledge, 1990), pp. 127–32, for a detailed explanation of the use of the term '*chora*' in Kristeva's conception of the 'semiotic'. In the Freudian and post-Freudian versions of the pre-Oedipal stage, the child is still dependent upon the body of the mother, a figure termed as 'phallic' in some accounts because she is perceived by the child as wielding an all-embracing power. Kristeva, for example, writes of 'the Mother who is presumed to exist at the place where (social and biological) identity recedes'. 'Motherhood according to Giovanni Bellini', *Desire in Language: a Semiotic Approach to Literature*, ed Leon S. Roudiez, trans. Thomas Gora, Alice Jardine, Leon S. Roudiez (Oxford: Basil Blackwell, 1980), p. 242. But the mother figure who presides over the pre-Oedipal phase is also held to play an important mirroring role in her child's ego formation. See Melanie Klein, 'Early stages of the Oedipus conflict', in *The Selected Melanie Klein*, ed Juliet Mitchell (Harmondsworth: Penguin, 1986), pp. 69–83.

12 Irigaray, *Speculum*, p. 54.

13 Although my reading of the implied narcissism of the female beloved is not specifically Freudian, I was interested to find some similar emphases to my own in Sarah Kofman's stimulating essay on Freud's early interest in this topic in *The Enigma of Woman: Woman in Freud's Writings*, trans. Catherine Porter (Ithaca: Cornell University Press, 1985).

1 Mirrors of masculinity

1 For example, Frances Yates in *Astraea: the Imperial Theme in the Sixteenth Century* (London: Routledge & Kegan Paul, 1975), and Roy Strong, in *The Cult of Elizabeth* (London: Thames & Hudson, 1977), both suggest that representations of Elizabeth I in these terms implicitly identified her with the Virgin Mary. In *The Origin and Meaning of Courtly Love: a Critical Study of European Scholarship* (Manchester: Manchester University Press, 1977), Roger Boase outlines the case made by critics who have interpreted courtly love in terms of Mariology, along with other critical perspectives upon the phenomenon.

2 There is a discussion of the Wisdom figure in Marina Warner's admirable and compendious study, *Monuments and Maidens: the Allegory of the Female Form* (London: Weidenfeld & Nicolson, 1985), chapter 9. Peter Dronke hints at a connection between this figure and the beloved of courtly love, in *Medieval Latin and the Rise of the European Love-Lyric*, 2 vols (Oxford: Clarendon Press, 1965), I, pp. 87–97.

3 Diana's connection with Wisdom can be seen in Mantegna's 'Triumph of Wisdom over Vice', now in the Louvre, where with Minerva she defeats Venus as mother of all the Vices.

4 Marina Warner discusses what in my view was only a partial assimilation of the attributes of Wisdom by the figure of the Virgin Mary in *Alone of All her Sex: the Myth and the Cult of the Virgin Mary* (London: Weidenfeld & Nicolson, 1976), pp. 247–8. Louis Bouyer in *Le Trône de la sagesse*, trans. Fr. A. Littledale as *Woman and Man with God* (London: Darton, Longman & Todd, 1960), pp. 193–6, points out that there was no link between the two figures in the New Testament, where it was the figure of Christ who 'borrowed' Wisdom's creative attributes; the continuation of this identification in much patristic thought is discussed by Harry Austryn Wolfson, *The Philosophy of the Church Fathers*, 2nd edn (Cambridge, Mass.: Harvard

University Press, 1964) vol. 1, *passim*. That this identification was popular as well as scholarly by the middle ages is evidenced by the fact that in several mystery and morality plays Christ was identified with Wisdom or Sapientia. Wisdom's occasional identification with the Holy Spirit in the middle ages is discussed by Joseph B. Collins, *Christian Mysticism in the Elizabethan Age, with its Background in Mystical Methodology* (Baltimore: Johns Hopkins University Press, 1940).

5 Proverbs 3: 13–18. (References are to the King James Bible unless otherwise specified.) James Wood, in *Wisdom Literature: an Introduction* (London: Duckworth, 1967), sees the Wisdom figure not as a personification but as a hypostasis. This view is not shared by all theologians: John Dunn, in *Christology in the Making* (London: SCM Press, 1980) recently argued that Wisdom was no more than a personification of certain divine attributes (p. 210).

6 Proverbs 8: 22–30.

7 The Wisdom of Solomon 7: 22. All references to apocryphal texts are from *The Apocrypha*, revised edn (Oxford: Oxford University Press, 1898).

8 Wisdom of Solomon 8: 2.

9 Ecclesiasticus 24: 13–22.

10 Wisdom of Solomon 7; Proverbs 31: 10.

11 Warner, *Monuments and Maidens*, p. 179.

12 See William Gray, 'Wisdom Christology in the New Testament', *Theology*, LXXXIX, no. 732 (November 1986), pp. 448–59, and James Wood, *Wisdom Literature*, p. 106.

13 Philo, *Quod Deterius Potiori insidiari soleat*, 115–16, cited and translated in John Dillon, *The Middle Platonists* (London: Duckworth, 1977), p. 164.

14 Philo, *De Fuga et Inventione*, 52, cited and translated in Richard A. Horseley, 'Spiritual marriage with Sophia', *Vigiliae Christianae*, 33, i (March 1979), pp. 30–54.

15 See Wolfson, *The Philosophy of the Church Fathers*; Gray, 'Wisdom Christology'; and F. Schillebeeckx, *Jesus* (London: Collins, 1974), p. 429.

16 See for example Philo, *Legum Allegoriarum*, in *Philo*, 10 vols (London: Heinemann, 1924), I, 65.

17 *De Fuga et Inventione*, in *Philo*, V 109. For the early Church fathers' debt to Platonism, see Robert M. Berchman, *From Philo to Origen: Middle Platonism in Transition* (Chico, California: Scholars Press, 1984); John Dillon, *The Middle Platonists*; C. Bigg, *The Christian Platonists of Alexandria* (Oxford: Clarendon Press, 1886); S.R.C. Lilla, *Clement of Alexandria: a Study in Christian Platonism and Gnosticism* (Oxford: Oxford University Press, 1971), p. 199. For the prominence accorded to Sophia (a female Wisdom figure) in Gnostic thought, see Elaine Pagels, *The Gnostic Gospels* (New York: Random House, 1979); *The Nag Hammadi Library*, trans. members of the Coptic Gnostic Library Project of the Insitutute for Antiquity and Christianity, directed by James M. Robinson (Leiden: E.J. Brill, 1977); and Rose Horman Arthur, *The Wisdom Goddess: Feminine Motifs in Eight Nag Hammadi Documents* (New York: United Press of America, 1984).

18 Bertrand Russell, *A History of Western Philosophy* (London: Allen & Unwin, 1946), pp. 256–7.

19 J.M. Rist, *Plotinus: the Road to Reality* (Cambridge: Cambridge University Press, 1967), p. 10.

20 Plotinus, 'On the Intellectual Beauty', *The Enneads*, trans. Stephen MacKenna, 3rd edn (London: Faber & Faber, 1962), V vii.

21 ibid., VI ix.

22 Hildegarde of Bingen, *Liber Divinorum Operum*, I i, trans. Kent Kraft in *Medieval Women Writers*, ed Katharina M. Wilson (Manchester: Manchester University Press, 1984), pp. 109–30.
23 Eugene F. Rice Jr, *The Renaissance Idea of Wisdom* (Cambridge, Mass.: Harvard University Press, 1958).
24 Georges Duby, *The Chivalrous Society*, trans. Cynthia Postan (London: Edward Arnold, 1977). Meg Bogin, in *The Women Troubadours* (London: Paddington Press, 1976), also explores the complexities of social relations implicit in courtly love, and asks if the male poets of courtly love were really courting women to reach their men (p. 59).
25 A generalized but most interesting account of this process in terms of its long-term historical development is to be found in Norbert Elias, *The Civilizing Process: the History of Manners*, trans. Edmund Jephcott (Oxford: Basil Blackwell, 1982).
26 Georges Duby argues that courtly love was manipulated by the married elder sons of the aristocracy, or 'senors', in order to control and manipulate the younger sons of the class, the bachelors or 'iovens', who were not permitted to marry. See *Medieval Marriage: Two Models from Twelfth-Century France*, trans. Elborg Forster (Baltimore: Johns Hopkins University Press, 1978), and *The Chivalrous Society*, op. cit.
27 For Wisdom's importance in thirteenth-century 'mirrors of princes', see Nicolai Rubinstein, 'Political ideas in Sienese art: the frescoes by Ambrogio Lorenzetti and Taddeo di Bartolo in the Palazzo Pubblico', *Journal of the Warburg and Courtauld Institutes*, XXI (1958), pp. 179–207. 'Sapience' is the subject of several chapters in Guillaume Budé's *De l'institution du prince* (Paris: Nicole Paris, 1547).
28 Marcabru, 'Cortesamen vuoill comenssar', trans. Alan R. Press in *Anthology of Troubadour Lyric Poetry* (Edinburgh: Edinburgh University Press, 1971), pp. 59–61.
29 Peire d'Alvernhe, 'La fuelhs e.l flors' (ll. 57–8), cited in L.T. Topsfield, *Troubadours and Love* (Cambridge: Cambridge University Press, 1975), pp. 163–4. Peire Vidal, 'Ab l'alen tir vas me l'aire', trans. Anthony Bonner in *Songs of the Troubadours* (London: Allen & Unwin, 1973), pp. 169–70.
30 Dante's achievement was built upon the work of two earlier poets of the 'dolce stil nuovo' group, Guido Cavalcanti and Guido Guinzelli, who had begun the process of etherealization of the lady which Dante completed.
31 Dante Alighieri, *Il Convito*, trans. Katherine Hillard (London: Routledge & Kegan Paul, 1889), XV, p. 218.
32 See for example *Divine Comedy: 3 Paradiso*, trans. John D. Sinclair (Oxford: Oxford University Press, 1971), XXXI. 128–9, which echoes Ecclesiasticus xxiv: 21.
33 Dante Alighieri, *Divine Comedy: 3 Paradiso*, XXXI. 70–93.
34 ibid., XXXI. 85.
35 ibid., XXXIII. 112–14.
36 ibid., XXXIII. 126–32.
37 ibid., XXXIII. 106–8.
38 Perry Anderson, *Lineages of the Absolutist State* (London: New Left Books, 1974), p. 148.
39 John Freccero, 'The fig tree and the laurel: Petrarch's poetics', *Diacritics* 5 (Spring 1975), pp. 34–40.
40 Francesco Petrarch, *Rime Sparse* 9, ll. 12–14. Both the Italian text and the English translations of Petrarch's *Rime Sparse* or *Canzoniere* are from *Petrarch's Lyric Poems: the 'Rime Sparse' and Other Lyrics*, ed and trans.

Robert M. Durling (Cambridge, Mass.: Harvard University Press, 1976).

41 ibid., 193, ll. 1–2.

42 ibid., 4, ll. 9–14.

43 ibid., 3, ll. 5–6.

44 ibid., 36, ll. 5–6.

45 In *John Donne Undone* (London: Methuen, 1987), Thomas Docherty has related a similar concern with error and wandering in the poetry of Donne to the traumas of post-Copernican man. Yet of course Petrarch's metaphysical deviation anticipates rather than succeeds Copernicus' scientific revolution.

46 For a discussion of metaphor and symbol in terms of the contrasting philosophies of Aristotelianism and Platonism, see E.H. Gombrich, 'Icones symbolicae', in *Symbolic Images: Studies in the Art of the Renaissance* (London: Phaidon, 1972), pp. 123–99. See also Brian Vickers, 'Analogy versus identity: the rejection of occult symbolism, 1580–1680', in *Occult and Scientific Mentalities in the Renaissance*, ed Brian Vickers (Cambridge: Cambridge University Press, 1984), pp. 95–163.

47 Petrarch, *Rime Sparse*, 321 and 185.

48 ibid., 135.

49 For discussions of this aspect of Petrarch's collection, see the introduction by Durling to *Petrarch's Lyric Poems*, pp. 26–33; and Freccero, 'The fig tree and the laurel: Petrarch's poetics'. I am also indebted to Jennifer Stone, who in an unpublished paper, 'Rewriting Petrarch: the codification of bourgeois love ideology' (1978) explored the transformation of Laura into a commodity.

50 Petrarch, *Rime Sparse* 23, ll. 38–40.

51 ibid., 266, ll. 9–14.

52 ibid., 128, ll. 1–6.

53 Charles Trinkaus, *The Poet as Philosopher: Petrarch and the Formation of Renaissance Consciousness* (New Haven: Yale University Press, 1979), describes how Petrarch searched for 'wholeness and integrity of self' in his Latin prose works, especially the *Secretum*, the *De remediis utriusque fortune*, and the *De vita solitaria*.

54 *Rime Sparse* 71, ll. 52–3.

55 Dante, *Divine Comedy: 2 Purgatorio*, trans. John D. Sinclair (Oxford: Oxford University Press, 1971), XXX. 31–3.

56 See Julia Kristeva, 'Giotto's Joy', in *Desire in Language*, ed Leon S. Roudiez (Oxford: Basil Blackwell, 1980), pp. 210–36.

57 In her important essay, 'Diana described: scattered woman and scattered rhyme', in *Writing and Sexual Difference*, ed Elizabeth Abel (Brighton: Harvester, 1982), pp. 95–110, Nancy J. Vickers has analysed the motif of fragmentation in the *Rime Sparse* as this applies to both lover and beloved.

58 Petrarch, *Rime Sparse* 23, ll. 147–60. In the fourteenth-century *Ovide Moralisé*, this myth was held to be an allegory of the incarnation of Jesus Christ (Diana was equated with the Trinity, Actaeon with the human Christ).

59 ibid., 366, ll. 111–12. Freud's essay on 'Medusa's head', which linked this motif with castration fears, has recently been analysed by Sarah Kofman in *The Enigma of Woman* (Ithaca: Cornell University Press, 1985). She cites Freud's comment that: 'This symbol of horror is worn upon her dress by the virgin goddess Athene. And rightly so, for thus she becomes a woman who is unapproachable and repels all sexual desires – since she displays the terrifying genitals of the mother' (p. 83).

60 Marsilio Ficino, *Commentary on Plato's Symposium*, trans. Sears Jayne, 2nd edn (Dallas: Spring Publications, 1985), Or. II, ch. vi, p. 52.

61 Cited in Paul Oskar Kristeller, *The Philosophy of Marsilio Ficino*, trans.

Virginia Conant (New York: Columbia University Press, 1943), p. 375.
62 ibid., p. 401.
63 See D.P. Walker, *Spiritual and Demonic Magic: from Ficino to Campanella* (London: Warburg Institute, 1958).
64 Marsilio Ficino, *Letters*, trans. London School of Economics, vol. 1 (London: Shepheard–Walwyn Ltd, 1975), p. 94.
65 Cited in Kristeller, *The Philosophy of Marsilio Ficino*, p. 268.
66 Paul Oskar Kristeller, *Renaissance Thought and its Sources* (New York: Columbia University Press, 1979), pp. 71, 140. The reference is to Pico's *De hominis dignitate*, ed E. Garin (Florence: Valecchi, 1942).
67 There is an interesting analysis of Giordano Bruno's post-Copernican reworking of Renaissance Neoplatonism in John C. Nelson, *Renaissance Theory of Love: the Context of Giordano Bruno's Eroici Furori* (New York: Columbia University Press, 1958), although in my view Nelson lays insufficient emphasis upon the radical implications of Bruno's rejection of the Platonic dualism of spirit and matter.
68 Ficino, *Opera Omnia* (Basle: n.p., 1561), pp. 919f.
69 Ficino, *Platonic Theology*, XIII, 3, trans. Josephine L. Burroughs, *Journal of the History of Ideas*, 5 (1944), pp. 227–39.
70 Ficino, *Commentary*, II, viii, p. 57.
71 ibid., II, vii, pp. 53–4.
72 ibid., VI, viii, pp. 118–20.
73 Plato, *The Symposium*, trans. Walter Hamilton (Harmondsworth: Penguin, 1951), p. 19.
74 Ficino, *Commentary*, VI, i, p. 108.
75 Pietro Bembo, *Gli Asolani*, trans. Rudolph B. Gottfried (Bloomington: Indiana University Press, 1954), pp. 104–5.

2 A curious conjunction

1 See Ralph E. Giesey, *The Juristic Basis of Dynastic Right to the French Throne* (Philadelphia: American Philosophical Society, 1961), pp. 1–5.
2 Giesey, ibid., comments on the declining status of the ritual of consecration in France from 1270, when the king's succession had to be divorced from the act of consecration for reasons of state (p. 6).
3 Frances A. Yates, *Astraea: the Imperial Theme in the Sixteenth Century* (London: Routledge & Kegan Paul, 1975).
4 K. Kerényi, *The Religion of the Greeks and Romans*, trans. Christopher Holme (London: Thames & Hudson, 1962), p. 106.
5 Virgil, *Works* (2 vols) ed and trans. H. Rushton Fairclough (London: Heinemann, 1912), I, 'Eclogues', iv, 4–10.
6 *Catullus, Tibullus, and Pervigilium Veneris*, trans. F.W. Cornish (London: Heinemann, 1916–18), xxxiv, pp. 39–41.
7 W. Warde Fowler, *The Religious Experience of the Roman People from the Earliest Times to the Age of Augustus* (London: Macmillan, 1911), p. 147.
8 The association of Diana with witches in many medieval and Renaissance treatises on demonology and witchcraft derives from a reference in a text called the *Canon Episcopi*. This was supposedly issued by the church council at Ancyra in AD 314, but the first reported copy of it dates from the ninth century. See Julio Caro Baroja, *The World of the Witches*, trans. Nigel Glendinning (London: Weidenfeld & Nicolson, 1964), pp. 60–1.
9 Horace, 'Carmen Saeculare', *Odes and Epodes of Horace*, trans. C.E. Bennett

(London: Heinemann, 1914), II, 104, ll. 13–20, p. 35.

10 See R.A.G. Carson, *Principal Coins of the Romans, II: The Principate* (London: British Museum, 1980); Harold Mattingly, *Coins of the Roman Empire in the British Museum* (London: British Museum, 1923–40), vols I and IV; Laura Breglia, *Roman Imperial Coins*, trans. Peter Green (London: Thames & Hudson, 1968).

11 In *Studies on the Iconography of Cosmic Kingship in the Ancient World* (Oslo: T. Aschehons & Co., 1953), H.P. L'Orange states that, while the Roman emperor was especially associated with the sun, 'the emperors of late antiquity are represented between the Sun and Moon, as is the case, for example, on the Roman arch of Constantine. These sun–moon symbols, originally distinguishing the Eastern king, make the emperor appear a *particeps siderum, frater Solis et Lunae . . .*' (p. 36). Frances Yates, however, argued that during the Renaissance, while the moon was a symbol of empire, the sun was associated with the papacy, *Astraea*, p. 37.

12 Michael Grant, *The Roman Emperors* (London: Weidenfeld & Nicolson, 1985), p. 13.

13 For the medieval theory of the king's identification with the immortal body of the state, see Ernst Kantorowicz, *The King's Two Bodies: a Study in Medieval Political Theology* (Princeton: Princeton University Press, 1957). Ralph E. Giesey, *The Royal Funeral Ceremony in Renaissance France* (Geneva: Droz, 1960), notes that the concept of the king's two bodies appears in French law from the 1530s.

14 Lodovick Lloyd, *The Triplicitie of Triumphes* (London: Richard Jones, 1591), sig. F2v.

15 I owe this term to Matthew Fox.

16 Some modern historians take the view that French absolutism was not properly established until the seventeenth century, such as A. Lublinskaya, *French Absolutism: The Crucial Phase 1620–1629* (Cambridge: Cambridge University Press, 1968), and Perry Anderson, *Lineages of the Absolutist State* (London: New Left Books, 1974), pp. 85–112. Others have argued that it was already well established in the early sixteenth century: see for example R.J. Knecht, *Francis I* (Cambridge: Cambridge University Press, 1982) and J.H. Shennan, *The Origins of the Modern European State 1450–1725* (London: Hutchinson, 1974), pp. 44–51. An idiosyncratic view was proposed by J. Russell Major in 'The French Renaissance monarchy and the Estates General', *Studies in the Renaissance*, IX (1962), pp. 113–25. He argued that the basis of the French Renaissance monarch's power lay in the support he could win from the people, not in those conventional attributes of 'absolute' monarchy, a standing army or bureaucracy.

17 Claude de Seyssel's *La Monarchie de France*, published in 1515, and Guillaume Budé's *De l'Institution du Prince*, published in 1547 (seven years after Budé's death and some three decades after its composition), represented the two tendencies in absolutist theory at the beginning of the century. Budé argued that the king alone had the right to govern, while de Seyssel argued for collaboration between the king and the sovereign courts. But the idea of divine right was not elaborated until half a century later, in Jean Bodin's *Six Livres de la République* (1576) and Pierre de Belloy's *De l'Authorité du Roi* (1587).

18 See Helen W. Henderson, *Dianne de Poytiers* (London: Methuen, 1928), p. 140. Claude Paradin, in *Devises héroiques* (Lyons: 1557), associated Henri's crescent moon device with the Holy Catholic Church (pp. 20–1).

19 Marc–René Jung, *Hercule dans la littérature française du XVIe siècle* (Geneva: Droz, 1960).

20 Timothy Husband (ed.), *The Wild Man: Medieval Myth and Symbolism*, exhibition catalogue (New York: Metropolitan Museum of Modern Art, 1980), p. 10.

21 Jung, *Hercule*, p. 131.

22 Baldessare Castiglione, *The Book of the Courtier*, trans. sir Thomas Hoby (London: 1561), sig. XX, iv. In 'Francis I and the courtiers of Castiglione's *Courtier*', *European Studies*, 8 (1978) pp. 23–70, Cecil H. Clough discusses not just the impact of Castiglione's book upon the French court, but also the possible significance for readings of *The Book of the Courtier* of the meeting between François and Castiglione which took place in 1515.

23 *Pierre Gringore's Pageants for the Entry of Mary Tudor into Paris*, ed Charles Read Baskervill (Chicago: University of Chicago Press, 1934), p. 12.

24 Josephe Chartrou, *Les Entrées solennelles et triomphales à la Renaissance (1485–1551)* (Paris: Presses Universitaires de France, 1928), p. 53.

25 Louis Dimier, *French Painting in the Sixteenth Century* (London: Duckworth & Co., 1904), p. 87.

26 Jean Festugière, *La Philosophie de l'amour de Marsile Ficin et son influence sur la littérature française au XVIe siècle* (Paris: Vrin, 1941).

27 In 'The mistress in the masterpiece', printed in *The Poetics of Gender*, ed Nancy K. Miller (New York: Columbia University Press, 1986), pp. 19–41, Nancy J. Vickers has argued that François I was himself represented in Cellini's 'Nymph of Fontainebleau' – as the stag's head.

28 This was the interpretation given in three of the best-known allegorized Ovids: the *Ovide moralisé*; Pierre Bersuire's *Metamorphosis Ovidiana*; and *La bible des poètes*.

29 *Giordano Bruno's The Heroic Frenzies*, trans. Paul Eugene Memmo Jr (Chapel Hill: University of North Carolina Press, 1964), II, iv, pp. 124–5.

30 ibid., II, i, p. 205.

31 See Dimier, *French Painting*, pp. 150–7.

32 In 'Graces, Muses, and arts: the urns of Henri II and Francis I', *Journal of the Warburg and Courtauld Institutes*, XXIX (1966), pp. 200–18, Victoria L. Goldberg points out that Apollo and the Muses were represented in the eight cartouches upon François I's funeral urn, and speculates that a similar theme might underlie the design for Henri II's urn, where three figures usually thought to be Graces (but which she argues may be Muses) hold up the urn.

33 Françoise Bardon, *Diane de Poitiers et le mythe de Diane* (Paris: n.p., 1963), *passim*.

34 Edouard Bourciez, *Les Moeurs polies et la littérature de cour sous Henri II* (Paris: Hachette, 1886), p. 97.

35 Clement Marot, 'Etrenne XI', in *Oeuvres Diverses*, ed C.A. Mayer (London: University of London, Athlone Press, 1966), p. 246.

36 Marot, 'Églogue IV', *Oeuvres Lyriques*, ed C.A. Mayer (London: University of London, Athlone Press, 1964), pp. 354–9, ll. 11–24.

37 See for example a late fifteenth-century collection by the Italian poet Benedetto Gareth, 'Libro di Sonetti et Canzoni di Chariteo intitulato Endimione', in *Opera di Chariteo* (n.p., n.d.), sigs aa iiir–dd iiiv.

38 It was this device which led a verse in the prophecies of Michel de Notredame, or Nostradamus, to be interpreted as a prognostication of the king's death a few years later in a jousting accident: 'Le Lyon jeune le vieux surmontera,/En champ bellique par singulier duelle' ('The young lion will defeat the old, on the tournament ground in single combat'). *Les Vrayes Centuries et propheties* (Avignon: 1556), I, 35.

39 *L'Entrée de Henri II à Rouen, 1550*, a facsimile with introduction by Margaret McGowan (Amsterdam: Theatrum Orbis Terrarum, 1974).

40 Etienne Jodelle, *Le Recueil des inscriptions* (Paris: André Wechel, 1558), figs 28–30.
41 In *Ideal Forms in the Age of Ronsard* (Berkeley: University of California Press, 1985), Margaret McGowan says that Henri's moon device was usually shown in triple form to indicate his claim not just to the throne of France, but also to the thrones of England and Scotland (p. 26).
42 Joachim Du Bellay, *Oeuvres Poétiques*, ed Henri Chamard, 6 vols (Paris: Edouard Cornely, 1931), II, clix, pp. 179–80.
43 Anthony Blunt, *Philibert de L'Orme* (London: A. Zwemmer, 1956).
44 *Les Illustres Observations Antiques du Seigneur Gabriel Symeon Florentin, en son dernier voyage d'Italie l'an 1557* (Lyons: Jean de Tournes, 1558), p. 99.
45 Pierre de Ronsard, 'A Madame la Duchesse de Valentinois', *Oeuvres Complètes*, ed Paul Laumonier, 2nd edn, 8 vols (Paris: Alphonse Lemerre, 1914–19), VI, p. 339, ll. 1–6.
46 Ronsard, 'Elégie: Au Roy (Henri III)', *Oeuvres*, IV, p. 6, l. 1. For the poet's extensive use of this image see two essays by Terence Cave: 'Ronsard's mythological universe', in *Ronsard the Poet*, ed T. Cave (London: Methuen, 1973), pp. 159–208; 'Ronsard as Apollo: myth, poetry and experience in a Renaissance sonnet cycle', *Yale French Studies 47: Image and Symbol in the Renaissance* (1972), pp. 76–89.
47 Ronsard, 'Au Roy Henri II', *Oeuvres Complètes*, II, pp. 181–4.
48 Du Bellay, 'A Madame Diane de Poictiers', *Oeuvres Poétiques*, V, pp. 367–75, ll. 187–92.
49 See *L'Ecole de Fontainebleau*, eds Sylvie Béguin, Bertrand Jestaz, and Jacques Thirion (Paris: Editions des Musées Nationaux, 1972), no 164.
50 Scève's Délie is thought to have been the Lyonnaise poetess, Pernette du Guillet, who probably replied to him with verses of her own.
51 Maurice Scève, *Délie*, ed I.D. Macfarlane (Cambridge: Cambridge University Press, 1966), dizain 193, p. 224.
52 Jodelle, 'Sonnet', *Oeuvres Complètes*, ed Enea Balmas, 2 vols (Paris: Editions Gallimard, 1965), I, pp. 393–4.
53 Marot, *Les Epigrammes*, ed C.A. Mayer (London: University of London, Athlone Press, 1970), LVI, p. 142.
54 Jacques Cellard and Alain Rey, *Dictionnaire du Français non conventionnel* (Paris: Masson, 1981), p. 34.
55 Salomon Reinach, 'Diane de Poitiers et Gabrielle d'Estrées', *Gazette des Beaux Arts*, 12, ser. 2 (1920), pp. 157–80.
56 For the use of the sun imagery in connection with Henri III, see Yates, *Astraea*, pp. 163–4. For late sixteenth-century theories of divine right see note 16 above.
57 There are numerous biographies of Henri III which treat this subject. See for example Georges Brezol, *Henri III et ses mignons* (Paris: Editions des Bibliophiles, 1912).
58 Christopher Marlowe, *Edward II*, I. i. 62.
59 An interesting visual example of the interest of French absolutism in feminizing its image of the monarch in the earlier part of the century can be seen in a painting of François I as an androgyne in the Bibliothèque Nationale, Paris. It is reproduced in Edgar Wind, *Pagan Mysteries in the Renaissance*, 2nd edn (London: Faber & Faber, 1968), fig. 80.
60 Philippe Desportes, *Les Amours de Diane*, ed Victor E. Graham, 2 vols (Geneva: Droz, 1959), I, p. 31, ll. 9–11.
61 ibid., II, 'Plainte', pp. 201–5, l. 52.
62 ibid., I, p. 111, ll. 1–2.

63 ibid., I. p. 119, ll. 1–4.
64 Yates, 'Religious processions in Paris 1583–1584', in *Astraea*, pp. 173–207.
65 Desportes, *Les Amours de Diane*, II, p. 266, ll. 12–14.

3 Three-personed queen

1 Ernst Kantorowicz, *The King's Two Bodies* (Princeton: Princeton University Press, 1957), p. 221.
2 Louis Adrian Montrose, ' "Shaping Fantasies": figurations of gender and power in Elizabethan culture', *Representations*, 44, 2 (Spring 1983), pp. 61–94.
3 See *Men in Feminism*, ed Alice Jardine and Paul Smith (London: Methuen, 1987).
4 E.C. Wilson, *England's Eliza*, 2nd edn (London: Frank Cass & Co. Ltd, 1966); Frances Yates, *Astraea* (London: Routledge & Kegan Paul, 1975).
5 Roy Strong, *The Cult of Elizabeth* (London: Thames & Hudson, 1977).
6 Wilson, *England's Eliza*, p. vii.
7 The self-consciousness of the late Renaissance poet has been explored in Daniel Javitch, *Poetry and Courtliness in Renaissance England* (Princeton: Princeton University Press, 1976), especially chapter 6; Richard Helgerson, *Self-crowned Laureates: Spenser, Jonson, Milton and the Literary System* (Berkeley: University of California Press, 1983); and John Guillory, *Poetic Authority: Spenser, Milton, and Literary History* (New York: Columbia University Press, 1983).
8 Yates, *Astraea*, p. 76.
9 Leonard Tennenhouse, *Power on Display: the Politics of Shakespeare's Genres* (London: Methuen, 1986), p. 103.
10 Claire Cross, *The Royal Supremacy in the Elizabethan Church* (London: Allen & Unwin, 1969), p. 23.
11 *The Public Speaking of Elizabeth I: Selections from her Official Addresses*, ed George P. Rice Jr (New York: Columbia University Press, 1951), p. 117.
12 See Chilton Latham Powell, *English Domestic Relations 1487–1653* (New York: Columbia University Press, 1917); C. and K. George, *The Protestant Mind of the English Reformation* (Princeton: Princeton University Press, 1961); Louis B. Wright, *Middle Class Culture in Elizabethan England* (Chapel Hill: University of North Carolina Press, 1935); Juliet Dusinberre, *Shakespeare and the Nature of Woman* (London: Macmillan, 1975).
13 Cited in 'The Puritan art of love', William and Malleville Haller, *Huntingdon Library Quarterly*, V (1942), pp. 235–72.
14 Pierre de la Primaudaye, *The French Academye, Wherein is Discoursed the Institution of Maners*, trans. B.T. (London: 1586), p. 480. The courtly conduct book is discussed in Violet Jeffery, *John Lyly and the Italian Renaissance* (Paris: Bibliothèque de la révue comparée, 1938), pp. 23–5, and Wright, *Middle Class Culture*, pp. 122–6.
15 Kantorowicz, *The King's Two Bodies*, p. 19.
16 Marie Axton, *The Queen's Two Bodies: Drama and the Elizabethan Succession* (London: Royal Historical Society, 1977).
17 Edgar Wind, *Pagan Mysteries in the Renaissance*, 2nd edn (London: Faber & Faber, 1968), pp. 204–5.
18 John Knox, *The First Blast of the Trumpet against the Monstrous Regiment of Women*, ed Edward Arber (London: English Scholars Library, 1880), pp. 12–13, 20.

19 See Celeste Turner Wright, 'The Amazons in Elizabethan literature'. *Studies in Philology*, XXXVII, iii (July 1940), pp. 433–56.
20 Linda Woodbridge, *Woman and the English Renaissance: Literature and the Nature of Womankind* (Brighton: Harvester, 1984), pp. 139–51.
21 Philip Stubbes, *The Anatomy of Abuses* (London: 1583), sig. 38r.
22 Cited in Arber's introduction to his edition of Knox, *The First Blast*, pp. 1–2.
23 John Aylmer, *An Harborowe for Faithfull and Trewe Subiectes* (London: 1559), sig. I i v.
24 Cross, *The Royal Supremacy*, p. 21.
25 John Foxe, *The Acts and Monuments* (London: 1563), pp. 1710v–1711r.
26 ibid., p. 526.
27 Maria Dowling, 'Anne Boleyn and reform', *Journal of Ecclesiastical History*, 35 (1984), pp. 30–46; E.W. Ives, *Anne Boleyn* (Oxford: Basil Blackwell, 1986), *passim*.
28 Paul Johnson, *Elizabeth I: A Study in Power and Intellect* (London: Weidenfeld & Nicolson, 1974), p. 22.
29 ibid., p. 11.
30 ibid., pp. 7, 72.
31 Violet A. Wilson, *Queen Elizabeth's Maids of Honour and Ladies of the Privy Chamber* (London: Bodley Head, 1922).
32 Dowling, 'Anne Boleyn and reform'.
33 ibid.
34 Ives, *Anne Boleyn*, pp. 282–4.
35 ibid., p. 291; see also Roy Strong. *Gloriana: The Portraits of Queen Elizabeth I* (London: Thames & Hudson, 1987), pp. 138–41.
36 Johnson, *Elizabeth I*, p. 7, thus describes the career of the queen's cousin lord Hunsdon.
37 Norbert Elias, *The Civilizing Process: the History of Manners*, trans. Edmund Jephcott (Oxford: Basil Blackwell, 1982), p. 194.
38 Lawrence Stone, *The Crisis of the Aristocracy, 1559–1641* (Oxford: Clarendon Press, 1965); Brian Manning, 'The nobles, the people and the constitution', in *Crisis in Europe 1560–1660: Essays from Past and Present*, ed Trevor Aston (London: Routledge & Kegan Paul, 1965), pp. 247–70; G.R. Elton, *Studies in Tudor and Stuart Politics* (Cambridge: Cambridge University Press, 1974), p. 282.
39 Alan Sinfield, 'Power and ideology: an outline theory and Sidney's *Arcadia*', *English Literary History*, 52, ii (Summer 1985), pp. 259–77.
40 Hugh Trevor–Roper, 'The gentry 1540–1640', *Economic History Review Supplement*, 1 (Cambridge: Cambridge University Press, 1953); Perry Anderson, *Lineages of the Absolutist State* (London: New Left Books, 1974), pp. 19–20; Manning, 'The nobles, the people and the constitution', p. 253; Penry Williams, *The Tudor Regime* (Oxford: Clarendon Press, 1979), pp. 428–51.
41 Stone, *Crisis of the Aristocracy*, p. 53.
42 Trevor–Roper, 'The gentry', p. 8.
43 ibid., p. 32.
44 W.T. MacCaffrey, 'Elizabethan politics: the first decade 1558–1568', *Past and Present*, 24 (April 1963), pp. 25–41, described the power-wielders at the beginning of Elizabeth's reign as a combination of 'meritocracy' (Elizabeth's personal choice) and aristocrats (usually peers), whose places on the privy council were less dependent on royal favour than on their own power, wealth, and influence. Two years later, in 'England, the Crown, and the new aristocracy', *Past and Present*, 30 (April 1965), pp. 52–64, MacCaffrey called

this group the 'new aristocracy'. Paul N. Siegel used the same term in 'English humanism and the new Tudor aristocracy', *Journal of the History of Ideas*, XII. iv (1952). pp. 450–68, but stressed the continuity between the 'new aristocracy' of Elizabeth's court and the aristocrats who had risen to power under the first Tudors (many of whom had come from the upper levels of the commercial gentry). V.G. Kiernan, 'State and nation in western Europe', *Past and Present*, 31 (July 1965), pp. 20–38, emphasized that the absolute monarchs were themselves often new men (this was certainly true of the Tudor dynasty), and so disposed to sympathize with the aspirations of new aristocrats.

45 MacCaffrey, 'England, the Crown, and the new aristocracy'.
46 See Axton, *The Queen's Two Bodies*, for the criticism of Elizabeth's refusal to marry, in plays performed at the Inns of Court in the first decade of her reign.
47 J.E. Neale, *Queen Elizabeth I*, 2nd edn (London: Jonathan Cape, 1938), pp. 239–40.
48 See for example Tennenhouse, *Power on Display*, pp. 32–6; Sinfield, 'Power and ideology'; Louis Adrian Montrose, 'Celebration and insinuation: Sir Philip Sidney and the motives of Elizabethan courtship', *Renaissance Drama* n.s. VIII (1977), pp. 3–35.
49 For a useful distinction between 'courtiership' and 'courtship', see Ann Jones and Peter Stallybrass, 'The politics of *Astrophel and Stella*', *Studies in English Literature*, 24, i (Winter 1984), pp. 54–68.
50 *The Queen's Majesty's Entertainment at Woodstock*, ed A.W. Pollard (Oxford: H. Daniel & H. Hart, 1910), p. 31.
51 Cited in Yates, *Astraea*, pp. 85–6.
52 Michael Drayton, 'Rowland's Song in Praise of the Fairest Beta', *England's Helicon* (London: 1600), pp. 42–5.
53 Sir Robert Naunton, *Fragmenta Regalia*, ed John Stephen Cerovski (unpublished PhD dissertation: Evanston, Illinois: Northwestern University, 1960), p. 80.
54 Neale, *Queen Elizabeth I*, pp. 322–6.
55 Edmund Spenser, *The Faerie Queene*, *Spenser: Poetical Works*, ed J.C. Smith and E. De Selincourt (Oxford: Oxford University Press, 1970), V. i. 2.
56 Neale, *Queen Elizabeth I*, p. 72.
57 See for example David Kalstone, *Sidney's Poetry: Contexts and Interpretations* (Cambridge, Mass.: Harvard University Press, 1965), p. 46; Roger Howell, *Sir Philip Sidney: the Shepherd Knight* (London: Hutchinson, 1968), p. 155; Montrose, 'Celebration and insinuation'.
58 At this time, in the late 1570s, Spenser was of course closely connected with members of the Leicester–Walsingham faction; indeed, he dedicated *The Shepheardes Calender* to Leicester's nephew Sidney. None the less, in this poem we appear to have an early adumbration of that conflict between the roles of courtier and courtly poet which would be more clearly articulated in book VI of *The Faerie Queene*, and which Javitch analysed in *Poetry and Courtliness*, ch. V.
59 Spenser, *The Shepheardes Calender*, in *Spenser: Poetical Works*, April eclogue, ll. 50–1.
60 ibid., ll. 55–8.
61 ibid., ll. 109–18.
62 Wind, *Pagan Mysteries*, especially chapters 3 and 4.
63 *Shepheardes Calender*, ll. 118–44.
64 Douglas Bush, *Mythology and the Renaissance Tradition in English Poetry* (New York: W.W. Norton & Co., 1963), p. 110.
65 See Wind, *Pagan Mysteries*, p. 130; Thomas Cain, 'Spenser and the

Renaissance Orpheus'. *University of Toronto Quarterly*, 41 (1971), pp. 24–47.
66 Sir Walter Ralegh. *The Poems*, ed Agnes M.C. Latham (London: Routledge
    & Kegan Paul, 1951), pp. 22–3, ll. 1–4. Roy Strong commented on the
    Catholic dimension of Elizabeth's popular cult in *The Cult of Elizabeth*
    (p. 16), and like Yates stressed the links between Elizabeth's iconography and
    that of the Virgin Mary. (Although in fact, her courtly cult more often
    compared the queen to Christ than to the Virgin, a comparison implied in the
    imagery of virgin birth used in Spenser's 'April eclogue'.)
67 'A Nymph's Disdain of Love', *England's Helicon* (London: 1600), pp. 122–34,
    ll. 1–4.

4 Carnival at court

1 Sir John Davies. *Hymnes of Astraea* (London: 1599), I, 'Of Astraea', ll.
   12–15.
2 ibid., III, 'To the Spring', ll. 15–17.
3 See chapter 3, note 57.
4 Eugene F. Rice Jr, *The Renaissance Idea of Wisdom* (Cambridge, Mass.:
   Harvard University Press, 1958), chapter 2.
5 See Michael Walzer, *The Revolution of the Saints* (London: Weidenfeld &
   Nicolson, 1966), and Hans Baron, 'Secularization of wisdom and political
   humanism in the Renaissance', *Journal of the History of Ideas* XXI (1960), i,
   pp. 131–50. The Calvinist emphasis upon activity, upon life as a journey
   through alien country, paralleled to some extent the conception of the 'miles
   Christianus' or Christian knight which had been sponsored by medieval
   monasticism in its support for the Crusades and been promoted in several
   medieval romances: see R.R. Bolgar, 'Hero or anti-hero? The genesis and
   development of the Miles Christianus', in *Concepts of the Hero in the Middle
   Ages and the Renaissance*, eds Norman T. Burns and Christopher Reagan
   (London: Hodder & Stoughton, 1976), pp. 120–46.
6 In *The Court Masque: a Study in the Relationship between Poetry and the
   Revels* (Cambridge: Cambridge University Press, 1927), Enid Welsford
   described the entertainment as 'a genre akin to but not identical with the
   masque, for the main business of the performer is to offer gifts, make
   complimentary speeches, engage in a debate or slight dramatic action, not to
   pave the way for a troup of masquers' (p. 158). Muriel Bradbrook described
   the entertainments as 'welcomes' in 'Drama as offerings: the princely pleasures
   of Kenilworth', *Rice Institute Pamphlet* XLVI, iv (January 1960), pp. 57–70.
   Texts of most Elizabethan entertainments are collected in *The Progresses and
   Public Processions of Queen Elizabeth*, ed John Nichols, 4 vols (London: John
   Nichols, 1788–1821). A very useful discussion of the entertainment, together
   with editions of three entertainments and a tilt, can be found in *Entertainments
   for Elizabeth I*, ed Jean Wilson (Woodbridge: D.S. Brewer, 1980).
7 The Elizabethan tilt has been discussed in Frances Yates, *Astraea* (London:
   Routledge & Kegan Paul, 1975), pp. 88–111, and Roy Strong, *The Cult of
   Elizabeth* (London: Thames & Hudson, 1977), pp. 129–63.
8 David M. Bergeron, *English Civic Pageantry 1558–1642* (London: Edward
   Arnold, 1971), p. 21.
9 ibid., pp. 28–9.
10 ibid., p. 40.
11 For the connection of Artemis, the Greek goddess from whom Diana derived

most of her traits, with the Amazons, see Callimachus, 'Hymn to Artemis', *Hymns* III, ll. 237–50; Pliny, *Natural History*, XXXI, v.

12 The surprising yet usually ambiguous prominence accorded to Amazons within Renaissance literature has been discussed by Abby Wettan Kleinbaum in *The War against the Amazons* (New York: McGraw–Hill, 1983), ch. 3; Celeste Turner Wright, 'The Amazons in Elizabethan literature', *Studies in Philology*, XXXVII, iii (July 1940), pp. 433–56; Simon Shepherd, *Amazons and Warrior Women: Varieties of Feminism in Seventeenth-century Drama* (Brighton: Harvester, 1981).

13 For Leicester's position as the most influential secular leader of radical Protestants (or Calvinists) in England at this time, see Derek Wilson, *Sweet Robin: a Biography of Robert Dudley, Earl of Leicester 1533–1588* (London: Hamish Hamilton, 1981).

14 The attitude of this faction to the Netherlands situation has been analysed in detail by Jan Albert Dop, *Eliza's Knights: Soldiers, Poets and Puritans in the Netherlands, 1572–1586* (Alblasserdam: Remak, 1981). An additional factor influencing their belief in the importance of swift and militant action on behalf of the Protestant cause was Elizabeth's excommunication by the Pope in 1570, which signalled the beginning of a long series of Catholic plots against her. Critical interest in a pro-Calvinist court circle has often seen Sidney, rather than Leicester, as the group's leading protagonist (mistakenly, in my view); see for example Roger Howell Jr, 'The Sidney circle and the Protestant cause in Elizabethan foreign policy', *Renaissance and Modern Studies*, xix (1975), pp. 31–46. It is interesting to note, however, that one of his earliest involvements in courtly revelry had identified Leicester with religious reform: in *The Queen's Two Bodies* (London: Royal Historical Society, 1977), Marie Axton shows how his role as Prince Pallaphilos in the 1561/2 masque at the Inner Temple entrusted him with the *defence* of Elizabeth's religious settlement (p. 44).

15 Lawrence Humphrey, *The Nobles: or of Nobilitye* (London: 1563), sig. A 4v–A 5v.

16 See Raymond Williams, *The Country and the City* (London: Chatto & Windus, 1973), for the relationship of pastoral to divisions of class.

17 See J.B. Black, *The Reign of Elizabeth 1558–1603* (Oxford: Clarendon Press, 1936), p. 251; W.G. Hoskins, *The Making of the English Landscape* (London: Hodder & Stoughton, 1955); Mark Girouard, *Life in the English Country House* (New Haven: Yale University Press, 1978), p. 112.

18 A letter from sir Christopher Hatton to sir Thomas Heneage, as he was preparing to visit one of his smaller houses, stated that he was leaving that 'other shrine, I mean Holdenby, still unseen until that holy saint may sit in it, to whom it is dedicated'. Cited in John Buxton, *Elizabethan Taste* (London: Macmillan, 1963), p. 49.

19 Cited in E. St John Brooks, *Sir Christopher Hatton: Queen Elizabeth's Favourite* (London: Jonathan Cape, 1946), p. 158.

20 ibid., pp. 161–2.

21 R.H. Tawney, *The Agrarian Problem in the Sixteenth Century* (London: Longmans & Co., 1912), p. 154.

22 Besides the seminal discussions of the many and complex associations of this figure in medieval culture by Richard Bernheimer, in *Wild Men in the Middle Ages* (Cambridge, Mass.: Harvard University Press, 1952), and Frank Kermode, in the introduction to his edition of *The Tempest* for the Arden Shakespeare (London: Methuen, 1954; 6th edn 1962), there have recently been several critical discussions of the subsequent prominence of this figure

within an emergent colonialist discourse. See especially Paul Brown, ' "This thing of darkness␣I acknowledge mine": *The Tempest* and the discourse of colonialism', in *Political Shakespeare: New Essays in Cultural Materialism*, ed Jonathan Dollimore and Alan Sinfield (Manchester: Manchester University Press, 1985), pp. 48–71.

23 Paul Brown, in ' "This thing of darkness" ', suggests that as well as the inhabitants of the New World, the vagrants or 'masterless men' who wandered the Elizabethan countryside are sometimes identified with the wild man in late Renaissance representations.

24 See C.L. Barber, *Shakespeare's Festive Comedy: a Study of Dramatic Form and its Relation to Social Custom* (Princeton: Princeton University Press, 1959), ch. 2.

25 Chrétien de Troyes, *Yvain*, trans. Ruth Harwood Kline (Athens: University of Georgia Press, 1975), ll. 2637–57.

26 See for example *The Wild Man: Medieval Myth and Symbolism*, ed Timothy Husband, exhibition catalogue (New York: Metropolitan Museum of Art, 1980), fig. 17, pp. 89–91.

27 ibid., p. 9.

28 Bernheimer, *Wild Men*, pp. 97–8.

29 Eugene M. Waith, *The Herculean Hero in Marlowe, Chapman, Shakespeare and Dryden* (London: Chatto & Windus, 1962), p. 46.

30 See Harry Levin, *The Myth of the Golden Age in the Renaissance* (London: Faber & Faber, 1970), chapter 3.

31 Brown, ' "This thing of darkness" '. See also Peter Hulme, 'Hurricanes in the Caribbees: the constitution of the discourse of English colonialism', in *1642: Literature and Power in the Seventeenth Century*, ed Francis Barker *et al.* (Colchester: University of Essex, 1981), pp. 55–83.

32 Spenser, *The Faerie Queene*, II. iii. 40.

33 *The Wild Man*, ed Husband, *passim*.

34 Yates, *Astraea*, pp. 106–8. For the hermit's role in medieval romance see also Richard Cavendish, *King Arthur and the Grail* (London: Weidenfeld & Nicolson, 1978).

35 Thomas Merton discussed the roots of monasticism in eremitical solitude, and the consequent close relationship of Western eremitism to the Catholic monastic orders, in *The Monastic Journey*, ed Brother Patrick Hart (London: Sheldon Press, 1977), and in *Contemplation in a World of Action* (London: Allen & Unwin, 1980), pp. 260–8.

36 Charles VI of France had participated in a masque of wild men in 1392: see *The Wild Man*, ed Husband, pp. 147, 149. I noted in chapter 2 above that the persona of a figure related to the wild man, that of Hercules, was frequently related to French Renaissance kings.

37 Marie Axton, 'The Tudor mask and Elizabethan court drama', in Marie Axton and Raymond Williams (eds), *English Drama: Forms and Development. Essays in Honour of Muriel Bradbrook* (Cambridge: Cambridge University Press, 1977), pp. 24–47.

38 Another similarity between the personae of queen and courtier in these entertainments was that like Diana, the wild man was associated with leadership of the Wild Hunt or Wild Horde of European folk tradition: see Bernheimer, *Wild Men*, p. 59; *The Wild Man*, ed Husband, pp. 152–3. Diana is depicted with Pan and an assembly of nymphs and satyrs in a medieval manuscript in Ghent Cathedral library reproduced in Jean Seznec, *The Survival of the Pagan Gods: the Mythological Tradition and its Place in Renaissance Humanism and Art* (Princeton: Princeton University Press, 1972),

fig. 88. See also the connection of Elizabeth's developing pastoral persona as
spring queen with Pan in the April eclogue of Spenser's *The Shepheardes
Calender.*

39 C.L. Barber, *Shakespeare's Festive Comedy*, p. 21.
40 Axton, *The Queen's Two Bodies*, pp. 40–6; 'The Tudor mask', p. 39.
41 Axton, *The Queen's Two Bodies*, pp. 48–53.
42 George Gascoigne, *The Princelye Pleasures at the Court at Kenewoorth*,
(London: 1576), p. 1.
43 In *Entertainments for Elizabeth I*, Jean Wilson points out that this questing
persona was probably indebted in part to the quest-like structure of the
queen's summer progresses (p. 42).
44 Gascoigne, *The Princelye Pleasures*, p. 3.
45 Marie Axton points out in *The Queen's Two Bodies* that Leicester had had his
family tree 'traced back' to Arthur (p. 62).
46 Robert Laneham, *A Letter: Whearin, part of the entertainment untoo the
Queenz Maiesty, at Killingworth Castl, In Warwik Sheer in this Soomerz
Progress 1575. iz signified* (London: 1575), p. 4.
47 ibid., pp. 18–19.
48 ibid., p. 20.
49 ibid., p. 33.
50 Gascoigne, *The Princelye Pleasures*, p. 8.
51 *The Wild Man*, ed Husband, passim.
52 ibid., p. 8.
53 Laneham, *A Letter*, pp. 44–5. For the significance accorded this act
within both medieval and Renaissance conceptions of monarchy, see
Marc Bloch, *Les Rois thaumaturges* (Strasbourg: Publications de la
faculté des lettres de l'Université de Strasbourg, 1924).
54 Axton, *The Queen's Two Bodies*, pp. 61–6.
55 ibid., p. 66.
56 *The Progresses and Public Processions of Queen Elizabeth*, ed John
Nichols, I, p. 85.
57 Axton, *The Queen's Two Bodies*, pp. 63–6.
58 It was one of the accusations levelled against Leicester in the
anonymous pamphlet, *Leycesters Commonwealth*, ed Frank J. Burgoyne
(London: Longmans, Green & Co. 1904), that it was through the earl's
influence with the queen that sir Henry Lee obtained the manor of
Woodstock in 1571, and dispossessed its rightful owners (pp. 110–11).
59 *The Queen's Majesty's Entertainment at Woodstock*, ed A.W. Pollard
(Oxford: H. Daniel & H. Hart, 1910), p. xxiii.
60 ibid., pp. 11–12.
61 ibid., p. 32.
62 See for example A.C. Hamilton, *Sir Philip Sidney: a Study of his Life
and Works* (Cambridge: Cambridge University Press, 1977), p. 24;
Robert Kimborough, 'The Helmington Hall Manuscript of Sidney's *The
Lady of May*', *Renaissance Drama*, n.s. I (1968), pp. 67–8; Stephen
Orgel, *The Jonsonian Masque* (Cambridge, Mass.: Harvard University
Press, 1965), p. 55.
63 Sir Philip Sidney, *The Lady of May*, *The Countesse of Pembrokes
Arcadia*, 3rd edn (London: 1598), p. 570.
64 This interpretation has been proposed by David Kalstone, *Sidney's
Poetry: Contexts and Interpretations* (Cambridge, Mass.: Harvard University
Press, 1965), p. 46; Roger Howell, *Sir Philip Sidney: the Shepherd Knight*
(London: Hutchinson, 1968), p. 155; and Louis Adrian Montrose,

'Celebration and insinuation: Sir Philip Sidney and the motives of Elizabethan courtship'. *Renaissance Drama*, n.s. VIII (1977).
65 Kalstone, *Sidney's Poetry*, p. 62.
66 *The Progresses . . . of Queen Elizabeth*, I, p. 51.
67 Sir William Segar, *Honour, Military and Civill* (London: 1602), p. 200; *Correspondance Diplomatique de Bertrand de Salignac de la Mothe Fenelon*, 3 vols (London and Paris: n.p., 1838–40), II, pp. 203–4.
68 Gerard Legh, *Accedens of Armory* (London: 1562). The masque is discussed in Axton, *The Queen's Two Bodies*, pp. 42–5.
69 'The Four Foster Children'. *Entertainments for Elizabeth I*, pp. 75–6.
70 Montrose, 'Celebration and insinuation', p. 28.
71 *The Wild Man*, ed Husband.
72 'The Four Foster Children', pp. 78–9.
73 For a discussion of this pattern, see Edgar Wind, *Pagan Mysteries in the Renaissance*, 2nd edn (London: Faber & Faber, 1968), pp. 37–8.
74 There is a detailed comparison of the green man with the wild man in Larry Benson, *Art and Tradition in Sir Gawain and the Green Knight* (New Brunswick: Rutgers University Press, 1965). St George's association with the green man, together with his role in Elizabethan England, is discussed by David Scott Fox, *Saint George: the Saint with Three Faces* (Windsor: Kensal Press, 1983).
75 Spenser, *The Faerie Queene*, I, x, 46.
76 'The Four Foster Children', p. 84.
77 *Entertainments for Elizabeth I*, p. 62.
78 Yates' and Strong's discussions of the emergence of these spectacular events in the 1580s (in *Astraea* and *The Cult of Elizabeth*) made no reference to privy council politics or the international political scene.
79 See William Segar, *Honour, Military and Civill*, pp. 198–9; *Entertainments for Elizabeth I*, p. 37.
80 *Entertainments for Elizabeth I*, p. 137.
81 'Ditchley 1592', *Entertainments for Elizabeth I*, p. 140.
82 *Entertainments for Elizabeth I*, p. 98.
83 'Elvetham 1591', *Entertainments for Elizabeth I*, pp. 109–10.
84 ibid., p. 112.
85 ibid., p. 112.
86 ibid., p. 104.
87 R. Warwick Bond suggested that this entertainment was written by the dramatist John Lyly. See *The Complete Works of John Lyly*, ed R. Warwick Bond (Oxford: Clarendon Press, 1902), vol. I, pp. 404–16.

5 Chastity and the power of interior spaces

1 Daniel Javitch, *Poetry and Courtliness in Renaissance England* (Princeton: Princeton University Press, 1976), chapter 1.
2 G.K. Hunter, *John Lyly: Humanist as Courtier* (Cambridge, Mass.: Harvard University Press, 1962).
3 George Puttenham, *The Arte of English Poesie*, ed G.D. Willcock and Alice Walker (Cambridge: Cambridge University Press, 1936), p. 186.
4 John Lyly, *Euphues and his England* in *The Complete Works*, ed R.W. Bond, 3 vols (Oxford: Oxford University Press, 1902), II, pp. 208–12. All subsequent citations from Lyly's works are taken from this edition.

5 ibid., II, p. 205.
6 Patrick Collinson, *The Elizabethan Puritan Movement*, 2nd edn (London: Methuen, 1982), p. 198.
7 Hunter, *John Lyly*, pp. 26, 58.
8 ibid., pp. 85–7.
9 For discussions of the complex role played by companies of boy actors in the Elizabethan and Jacobean theatre, see Harold Newcomb Hillebrand, *The Child Actors* (Urbana, Illinois: University of Illinois Press, 1926), and Michael Shapiro, *Children of the Revels: the Boy Companies of Shakespeare's Time and their Plays* (New York: Columbia University Press, 1977).
10 Baldessare Castiglione, *The Book of the Courtier*, trans. sir Thomas Hoby (London: 1561), sig. Kiv–Kiiv.
11 Lyly, *Campaspe*, II. ii. 310–41.
12 ibid., V. iv. 151–5.
13 One of Lyly's sources for *Campaspe* was North's translation of Plutarch's *Lives* (London: 1580). The life of Alexander described his intimate friendship with Hephaestion, but did not speculate about its possible sexual dimension.
14 Castiglione, *The Book of the Courtier*, sig. SS iiir.
15 Lyly, *Campaspe*, I. iii. 59–63.
16 ibid., II. ii. 125–30.
17 ibid., III. iii. 110–13.
18 ibid., court epilogue, 1–14.
19 Lyly, *Sapho and Phao*, I. ii. 38–40; compare Ecclesiasticus 24: 12–17, cited in chapter 1 above.
20 *The Quenes Maiesties Passage through the Citie of London to Westminster the day before her Coronation*, ed James M. Osborn (New Haven: Yale University Press, 1960), pageant 6.
21 Puttenham, *The Arte of English Poesie*, pp. 4–5.
22 Lyly, *Sapho and Phao*, IV. iii. 6–10.
23 ibid., IV. iii. 11–15.
24 ibid., V. ii. 94–6.
25 For knowledge of lesbianism in classical, early Christian, and medieval texts, see John Boswell, *Christianity, Social Tolerance and Homosexuality* (Chicago: University of Chicago Press, 1980). Some Renaissance treatments of this topic are discussed by Lilian Faderman, *Surpassing the Love of Men: Romantic Friendship and Love between Women from the Renaissance to the Present* (London: Women's Press, 1985). See also the introduction to Judith C. Brown's *Immodest Acts: the Life of a Lesbian Nun in Renaissance Italy* (Oxford: Oxford University Press, 1986).
26 George Turberville, *The heroycall epistles of Pub. Ovidius Naso, in Englishe verse* (London: 1567), p. 109v.
27 Pierre de Bourdeilles, Seigneur de Brantôme, *Lives of Fair and Gallant Ladies*, trans. A.R. Allinson (New York: Liversight Publ. Corp., 1933), p. 131.
28 Lyly, *Gallathea*, V. ii. 128–30.
29 ibid., V. ii. 132–3.
30 See for example Peter Saccio, *John Lyly's Court Comedies: a Study in Allegorical Dramaturgy* (Princeton: Princeton University Press, 1979), p. 147.
31 See Ovid *Metamorphoses* X, and *Il Galateo* of G. della Casa, trans. Robert Peterson (London: 1576).
32 The Renaissance interpretation seems most indebted to Fulgentius; see *Fulgentius the Mythographer*, trans. Leslie George Whitbread (Columbus: Ohio State University Press, 1971), p. 81.

33 Bruno's two works which complimented Elizabeth in these terms, *Cena de le ceneri* and *De Gli Eroici Furori*, were published in 1584 and 1585 respectively, but probably circulated in manuscript form before their publication. They are discussed in Frances A. Yates, *Giordano Bruno and the Hermetic Tradition* (London: Routledge & Kegan Paul, 1964).

34 There is some doubt about the exact date of *Endimion*'s first court performance: G.K. Hunter suggested 2 February 1588; Lyly's editor R.W. Bond, 2 February 1586.

35 In *The Feminine in Fairy Tales* (Dallas, Texas: Spring Publications, 1976), Marie Louise von Franz points out that Italian and French versions of this fairy tale existed as early as the fourteenth century (p. 8). It is interesting to note that they were antedated by the Endimion myth, with its apparent reversal of gender roles.

36 Lyly, *Endimion*. II. i. 39–43. See also V. ii. 166–78.

37 ibid., V. iii. 285–91.

38 Leone Ebreo, *Dialoghi d'Amore*, ed S. Caramella (Bari: Laterza & Figli, 1929), p. 179.

39 Lyly, *Endimion*. I. i. 30–65.

40 A year later, at the end of 1585, the queen did reluctantly yield to Leicester's entreaties and allowed him to lead an expedition to the Netherlands. But although he himself was much acclaimed, and even, to Elizabeth's fury, offered the title of governor-general (which appears simply to have confirmed her anxieties about the dangers of granting too much military power to her courtiers), the expedition accomplished very little.

41 Natale Conti, *Mythologiae* (Venice: 1567), cap. xviii, p. 82.

42 Lord Burghley asserted as late as 1579 that the queen was still capable of childbearing, having 'no lack of natural functions in those things that properly belong to the procreation of children'. See Conyers Read, *Lord Burghley and Queen Elizabeth* (London: Jonathan Cape, 1960), p. 210. Barbara Walker, in *The Crone: Woman of Age, Wisdom, and Power* (New York: Harper & Row, 1985), has presented a detailed and convincing account of the deep-seated fear of the aged or ageing woman in Western society.

43 See for example *Witchcraft in Old and New England*, George Lyman Kittredge (Cambridge, Mass.: Harvard University Press, 1929); K.M. Briggs, *Pale Hecate's Team: an Examination of the Beliefs on Witchcraft and Magic among Shakespeare's Contemporaries and his Immediate Successors* (London: Routledge & Kegan Paul, 1962).

44 Reginald Scot, *The Discoverie of Witchcraft* (London: W. Browne, 1584), III, p. 66.

45 ibid., I, iii, p. 7.

46 Lyly, *Endimion*. III. iii. 52–60.

47 Hunter, *John Lyly*, pp. 77–8.

48 Lyly, *Midas*, IV. i. 133–8.

49 ibid., V. iii. 119–28.

50 Lyly, *The Woman in the Moone*, V. i. 307–10.

51 John Donne, *The First Anniversary*, in *Donne: Poetical Works*, ed Herbert J.C. Grierson (Oxford: Oxford University Press, 1929).

52 The astrological significance of the different planets formed the framework for Dante's *Paradiso*, for example, where the moon is the lowest of the seven heavenly spheres and is connected with inconstancy.

53 Lyly, *Sapho and Phao*, court prologue, 14–17.

54 Lyly, *The Woman in the Moone*, prologue, 12–19.

6 Rewriting chastity

1 See E.C. Wilson, *England's Eliza*, 2nd edn (London: Frank Cass & Co. Ltd., 1966), for a general survey of many of these representations.

2 Robert Greene, *Montanus his madrigal* in *England's Helicon* (London: 1600). This must antedate Greene's death in 1592. Note the way in which he makes himself the 'ground' of this pastoral idyll by punning on his name.

3 Frances A. Yates, *Astraea* (London: Routledge & Kegan Paul, 1975), plate 12c.

4 Sir John Davies, *Nosce Teipsum, Hymnes of Astraea, and Orchestra* (London: 1622), dedicatory poem, ll. 1–2.

5 Abraham Fraunce, *The Third Part of the Countesse of Pembroke's Yvychurch, Entitled Amintas Dale* (London: 1592), p. 107.

6 Natalie Zemon Davis, *Society and Culture in Early Modern France* (London: Duckworth, 1975), p. 124.

7 See G.R. Elton, *England under the Tudors* (London: Methuen, 1955; rpt 1957), p. 456; and J.B. Black, *The Reign of Elizabeth 1558–1603*, 2nd edn (Oxford: Clarendon Press, 1959), pp. 408–10.

8 See chapter 3 note 7.

9 Stefano Guazzo, *The Civile Conversation*, trans. G. Pettie and B. Young (London: 1586); Pierre de la Primaudaye, *The French Academye*, trans. B.T. (London: 1586).

10 See chapter 3 note 14.

11 There is a detailed discussion of the stylistic features of the Elizabethan epyllion in William Keach, *Elizabethan Erotic Narratives: Irony and Pathos in the Ovidian Poetry of Shakespeare, Marlowe and their Contemporaries* (New Brunswick: Rutgers University Press, 1977).

12 For changing attitudes to Ovid in the late Renaissance, see Ann Moss, *Ovid in Renaissance France* (London: Warburg Institute, 1982); Davis P. Harding, *Milton and the Renaissance Ovid* (Urbana: University of Illinois Press, 1946).

13 The importance of sight in the Neoplatonic hierarchy of the senses is discussed by Frank Kermode, *Renaissance Essays: Shakespeare, Spenser, Donne*, 2nd edn (London: Fontana, 1973), pp. 94–5.

14 See for example Leonard Tennenhouse, *Power on Display* (London: Methuen, 1986), p. 94.

15 Shakespeare, *Venus and Adonis* in *The Poems*, ed F.T. Prince, 3rd edn (London: Methuen, 1960), ll. 241–4.

16 Christopher Marlowe, *Hero and Leander* in *Longer Elizabethan Poems*, ed Martin Seymour–Smith (London: Heinemann, 1972). Keach, in *Elizabethan Erotic Narratives*, emphasizes what he terms the homoerotic perspective of many epyllia.

17 Michael Drayton's *Endimion and Phoebe* (1595) is the exception to this pattern, for its comic treatment of sexual role-reversal is followed by a Platonic rather than physical consummation of relationship.

18 In an article written with Christine Berg, I explored a religious rather than a specifically cultural version of this dilemma which occurred in the next century, during the English revolution. The 'prophetic' discourse adopted by certain women at this time implicitly claimed that woman too had access to the *logos*, or a spiritual/philosophical source of meaning. See Christine Berg and Philippa Berry: 'Spiritual whoredom: an essay on female prophets in the seventeenth century', *1642: Literature and Power in the Seventeenth Century*, eds F. Barker *et al.* (Colchester: University of Essex, 1981), pp. 37–55.

19 Chapman would have found Orphic elements in the Greek texts of Homer and

Hesiod, as well as in Ovid's *Metamorphoses*. For the survival of Orphism in certain aspects of both Platonism and Neoplatonism see D.P. Walker, *Spiritual and Demonic Magic: from Ficino to Campanella* (London: Warburg Institute, 1958), *passim*.

20 *The Poems of George Chapman*, ed Phyllis Brooks Bartlett (New York: Modern Language Association of America, 1941), *The Shadow of Night:* 'Hymnus in Cynthiam', ll. 1–3.

21 Chapman, *The Shadow of Night:* 'Hymnus in Noctem', ll. 29–49.

22 ibid., ll. 395–9.

23 ibid., l. 153.

24 D.P. Walker, *The Ancient Theology: Studies in Christian Platonism from the Fifteenth to the Eighteenth Century* (London: Duckworth, 1972), *passim*.

25 Chapman, 'Hymnus in Cynthiam', ll. 269–82.

26 See Hesiod, *Theogony*, 408–52.

27 See chapter 1 note 59.

28 Chapman, 'Hymnus in Cynthiam', ll. 515–28.

29 This was the view put forward by Arthur Acheson, and later by Frances Yates and Muriel Bradbrook. They asserted the existence of an elite cadre of the Elizabethan cult, entitled the 'School of Night', which included Chapman and Ralegh as well as courtiers such as the 'wizard' earl of Northumberland. See Arthur Acheson, *Shakespeare and the Rival Poet* (London: John Lane, 1903); M.C. Bradbrook, *The School of Night: a Study in the Literary Relationships of Sir Walter Ralegh* (Cambridge: Cambridge University Press, 1936); and F.A. Yates, *A Study of Love's Labour's Lost*, (Cambridge: Cambridge University Press, 1936).

30 Chapman, 'Hymnus in Noctem', ll. 81–7. The original myth can be found in Ovid, *Metamorphoses* VIII.

31 ibid., 'Hymnus in Cynthiam', ll. 58–9.

32 For the likely date of the play's composition, see *A Midsummer Night's Dream*, ed Harold F. Brooks (London: Methuen, 1979), pp. xxxiv–lvii.

33 ibid., p. lix.

34 ibid., V. i. 369–72.

35 ibid., II. i. 103–6.

36 George Puttenham, *The Arte of English Poesie*, ed G.D. Willcock and Alice Walker (Cambridge: Cambridge University Press, 1936), p. 89.

37 Shakespeare, *A Midsummer Night's Dream*, V. i. 393–6.

38 ibid., V. i. 12–17.

39 *Spenser: Poetical Works*, ed J.C. Smith and E. de Selincourt (Oxford: Oxford University Press, 1970), p. 409.

40 Stephen Greenblatt, in *Sir Walter Ralegh: the Renaissance Man and his Roles* (New Haven: Yale University Press, 1973), first emphasized Ralegh's 'role-playing', and discussed his attempt to define himself with reference to various external symbols of authority (the queen, God, the state). See also Leonard Tennenhouse, 'Sir Walter Ralegh and the literature of clientage', *Patronage in the Renaissance*, ed Guy Fitch–Lytle and Stephen Orgel (Princeton: Princeton University Press, 1981), pp. 235–60.

41 Sir Walter Ralegh, *The 11th: and last booke of the Ocean to Scinthia*, in *The Poems of Sir Walter Ralegh*, ll. 269–70.

42 ibid., ll. 271–2.

43 Sir Robert Naunton, *Fragmenta Regalia*, ed John Stephen Cerovski (unpublished PhD dissertation; Evanston, Illinois: Northwestern University, 1960), p. 103.

44 Pierio Valeriano, *Hieroglyphica* (Basle: 1556), p. 115.

45 The details can be found in any one of the many biographies of Ralegh. See for example Robert Lacey, *Sir Walter Ralegh* (London: Weidenfeld & Nicolson, 1973); J.H. Adamson and H.F. Folland, *The Shepherd of the Ocean* (London: Bodley Head, 1969).

46 Walter Oakeshott, *The Queen and the Poet* (London: Faber & Faber, 1960), p. 205.

47 Ralegh, *The Ocean to Scinthia*, ll. 21–4.

48 ibid., ll. 450–4.

49 ibid., l. 3.

50 ibid., ll. 25–6.

51 ibid., ll. 478–9.

52 ibid., l. 138.

53 ibid., ll. 221–31.

54 ibid., l. 14. According to the *Oxford English Dictionary*, 'erection' was being used as a sexual metaphor by 1594.

55 ibid., ll. 71–2.

56 ibid., ll. 73–4.

57 ibid., ll. 327–30.

58 ibid., ll. 482–4.

59 ibid., ll. 201–11.

60 ibid., l. 220.

61 *Spenser: Poetical Works, The Faerie Queene*, IV. x. 41.

62 Jonathan Goldberg, in *Endlesse Worke: Spenser and the Structures of Discourse* (Baltimore: Johns Hopkins University Press, 1981), pp. 123–4, has commented upon the absence of the queen from Spenser's text, but has drawn different conclusions about its significance.

63 See John Guillory, *Poetic Authority: Spenser, Milton, and Literary History* (New York: Columbia University Press, 1983); Richard Helgerson, *Self-crowned Laureates: Spenser, Jonson, Milton and the Literary System* (Berkeley: University of California Press, 1983).

64 For an influential reading of this passage as articulating Spenser's rejection of a courtly poetic style see David Javitch, *Poetry and Courtliness in Renaissance England* (Princeton: Princeton University Press, 1976).

65 Spenser, *The Faerie Queene*, Proem II. 4.

66 ibid., Proem I. 4.

67 In fact, Spenser's choice of virtues was highly idiosyncratic. He did not follow the distinction made in Aristotle's *Ethics* between moral and political virtues.

68 Spenser, *The Faerie Queene*, Proem I. 4. Marina Warner, in *Monuments and Maidens: the Allegory of the Female Form* (London: Weidenfeld & Nicolson, 1985), *passim*, points out that virtues were usually gendered feminine in the middle ages and the Renaissance.

69 Spenser, *The Faerie Queene*, Proem III. 2.

70 Alastair Fowler has discussed the poet's use of this pattern as a structuring device in 'Emanations of glory: Neoplatonic order in Spenser's *Faerie Queen*', in *A Theatre for Spenserians*, ed Judith M. Kennedy and James A. Reither (Toronto: University of Toronto Press, 1973), pp. 53–82.

71 Spenser, *The Faerie Queene*, I. ix. 13–14.

72 ibid., Proem III. 5.

73 ibid., II. iii. 22.

74 A similarly ambiguous combination of attraction and reserve characterizes Belphoebe's twin sister Amoret, although in this case attraction eventually conquers reserve. She marries the original knight of chastity, sir Scudamour, whose quest was in fact fulfilled by the woman warrior Britomart.

75 ibid., II. iii. 26–8.
76 In 'The Elizabethan subject and the Spenserian text', *Literary Theory/Renaissance Texts*, ed Patricia Parker and David Quint (Baltimore: Johns Hopkins University Press, 1986), pp. 303–40, Louis Adrian Montrose has stressed the function of these knots as boundaries to the inviolable virgin body of the monarch which have a crucial political dimension, and has commented upon a notable parallel in George Gower's 'Armada portrait' of the queen. My argument is rather that they emblematize the links between a specifically female eroticism and chastity which are always implied in Elizabethan iconography: a female body in touch with itself. See Luce Irigaray, *This Sex Which Is Not One*, trans. Catherine Porter (Ithaca: Cornell University Press, 1985), chapter 11, 'When our lips speak together'.
77 Spenser, *The Faerie Queene*, II. iii. 31.
78 ibid., IV. vii. 43–4.
79 ibid., III. iii.
80 ibid., V. v. 3.
81 Gregory of Tours, *The History of the Franks*, trans. O.M. Dalton, 2 vols (Oxford: Clarendon Press, 1927), I. pp. 62–7, 82–5, 102.
82 Spenser, *The Faerie Queene*, III. vi. 46. C.S. Lewis first pointed out the matriarchal character of Spenser's mythic dimension, in his review of Robert Ellrodt's *Neoplatonism in the Poetry of Spenser*, in *Etudes Anglaises*, 14 (1961), pp. 111f.
83 Spenser, *The Faerie Queene*, V. vii. 22.
84 There is an interesting discussion of the ties between Athene and the father in Karl Kerényi, *Athene: Virgin and Mother in Greek Religion*, trans. Murray Stein (Zurich: Spring Publications, 1978).
85 Spenser, *The Faerie Queene*, V. vii. 42.
86 For the links between Athene/Minerva and the Gorgon mythos in Renaissance mythography, see Vincenzo Cartari *Le imagini colla spozione degli dei antichi* (Venice: 1556) sig. lxxvi r. For a modern interpretation, see Kerényi, *Athene*. pp. 60–9.
87 Arthegall's 'salvage' attributes are discussed by Donald Cheney in *Spenser's Image of Nature: Wild Man and Shepherd in 'The Faerie Queene'* (New Haven: Yale University Press, 1966).
88 *Faerie Queene*, V. ix. 21–30.
89 Davies, 'Of her Justice', *Hymnes of Astraea*.
90 Spenser, *The Faerie Queene*, VI. x. 27.
91 Spenser, *Cantos of Mutability*, vi. 52.
92 ibid., vi. 55.
93 ibid., vii. 5.
94 ibid., vii. 58.
95 ibid., vii. 59.

Index